Macromedia®
Flash™ 5

from scratch

Cheryl Brumbaugh-Duncan

201 West 103rd Street,
Indianapolis, Indiana 46290

Macromedia Flash 5 from Scratch

Copyright © 2001 by Que Publishing

International Standard Book Number: 0-7897-2461-8

Library of Congress Catalog Card Number: 00-108775

Printed in the United States of America

First Printing: December 2000

02 01 00   4   3   2   1

Trademarks

Warning and Disclaimer

Executive Editor
Beth Millett

Acquisitions Editor
Heather Banner Kane

Development Editor
Laura Norman

Managing Editor
Thomas F. Hayes

Project Editor
Andy Beaster

Copy Editors
Kay Hoskin
Chuck Hutchinson
Mary Ellen Stephenson

Indexer
Aamir Burki

Proofreader
Jeanne Clark

Technical Editor
Doug Scamahorn

Team Coordinator
Julie Otto

Media Developer
Michael Hunter

Interior Designer
Gary Adair

Cover Designer
Aren Howell

Production
Darin Crone

Overview

Contents

About the Author

Cheryl Brumbaugh-Duncan is committed to education and learning. She has been teaching individuals and companies through creative techniques, courses, books, and programs for the past 15 years. This includes a combination of education techniques, communication technologies, and various delivery methods such as books, curriculums, Intranet/Internet communications, CD-ROM, and lectures. With many years of teaching and course development behind her, in 1992 her writing career began when she co-authored the Que book, *Look Your Best with Excel 4 for Windows*. Using educational theories and concepts, she helped integrate learning techniques that made this book very easy to understand and use. Since then she has been involved with the writing and technical editing process for more than 10 computer software–related books. She currently runs her own company that specializes in Web site development and online learning courses. Visit her company's Web site at www.virtuallyglobal.com. She currently teaches Flash courses to people in the Denver, Colorado, area at the Rocky Mountain Digital Arts Center. Her commitment to the combination of education, technology, and various delivery methods for communicating information keeps her very busy in this ever-changing world of communications and technology.

Dedication

This book is dedicated to the people who have made it possible: my husband, David; my parents, Barb and Phil; my parents-in-law, Jack and Doris; all the people at Macromedia who developed this great product; Allen Ellison for his help with the final two chapters and knowledge of Flash 5; and the very talented people at Que! I'd also like to add a special dedication of this book to my new baby girl, Tasmin Nicole. During these past months I have been developing two babies, this book and my little one who came into our lives in October.

Acknowledgments

First of all I would like to acknowledge Que and the many talented people that have helped with the development of this book. In particular, Laura Norman and Heather Kane for all their support, fantastic insight, and helpful suggestions that have made this book much better than what I had originally submitted. They have truly helped shape the flow and content of this book. I would also like to thank the numerous editors that provided constructive criticism and have checked, and double-checked, the accuracy of this book's content and information: Doug Scamahorn, my Technical Editor; Andy Beaster, my Project Editor; Kay Hoskin, the Copy Editor; and everyone else who had a hand in this project. Without these talented people, this book would not be half the book that it is today.

I would also like to acknowledge the people and programmers at Macromedia. Flash is a wonderful product with much to offer Web developers and graphic designers. It was fun to write this book on such a great product as Flash!

And finally, I would like to thank my husband for his daily support of my efforts to create this book. As with many books, there are long hours and stressful deadlines that have influenced our relationship these past months. His love and support have been constant and I cannot thank him enough!

Tell Us What You Think!

As the reader of this book, *you* are our most important critic and commentator. We value your opinion and want to know what we're doing right, what we could do better, what areas you'd like to see us publish in, and any other words of wisdom you're willing to pass our way.

As an Executive Editor for Que, I welcome your comments. You can fax, email, or write me directly to let me know what you did or didn't like about this book—as well as what we can do to make our books stronger.

Please note that I cannot help you with technical problems related to the topic of this book, and that due to the high volume of mail I receive, I might not be able to reply to every message.

When you write, please be sure to include this book's title and author as well as your name and phone or fax number. I will carefully review your comments and share them with the author and editors who worked on the book.

Fax: 317-581-4666

Email: quefeedback@macmillanusa.com

Mail: Beth Millett
         Executive Editor
         Que
         201 West 103rd Street
         Indianapolis, IN 46290 USA

Introduction

Learning Flash Can Be Fun!

Flash is often perceived as a high-end, Web-authoring software package, and therefore, as difficult and complicated to learn. In reality, it is a very straightforward approach for developing Web content and sites. It offers many advantages over traditional Web development tools. This book attempts to take the mystery out of Flash, as well as to present the features and techniques of Flash 5.

This book assists you in learning the skills required to use Flash by developing a complete project—from planning to publishing. If I were to help you learn Flash, I would not just give you a book and say, "Work through it!" I would actually sit down with you and walk you through many of the skills and techniques required to build something relevant to your work or area of expertise. This book is written in this fashion. Since Flash is growing in popularity as a Web development tool, you will create a fictional Web site using Flash.

Project-Based Learning

This book presents Flash 5 skills and concepts in the format of a project-based learning experience. Unlike other Flash books on the market that teach Flash by starting with simple skills and then presenting others that might, or might not, build upon each other, this book provides a context for learning the skills presented. For the project presented in this book, you build a Web site for a travel company from scratch. First, you plan the Web site and develop the planning documents that guide you through the site's development. Then you begin to create the site architecture, graphics, animations, and special effects. You learn and use many of the skills and techniques of Flash to complete this project. Project-based learning is a number one way to learn, and many educators feel it is the best way to learn a skill or technique.

This book is very hands-on in its presentation of skills and concepts of Flash. If you do not have a copy of the software yet, you will benefit fully from the book and the information presented by attaining a copy of the software to use as you work through the book. Macromedia offers a 30-day demo version of the Flash software on its Web site, `http://macromedia.com/software/flash/trial/`. You can download it and begin to test and learn the product through this book's instruction.

Parts and Chapters in This Book

This book is divided into four distinct parts: Part 1, "Getting Started with Flash"; Part 2, "Building Blocks of Flash: Creating Graphics for the Travel Company Web Site"; Part 3, "Experience the Power of Flash: Create the Movie"; and finally, Part 4, "Putting It All Together: Creating the Fully Flashed Travel Company Web Site." The following chapters make up these sections.

Part 1, "Getting Started with Flash"

- **Chapter 1: "Why Use Flash?"**—This chapter covers the advantages that Flash offers over typical Web design and graphic design techniques. You learn why people are using Flash and examples of how they are using Flash are provided.

- **Chapter 2: "What's New with Flash 5"**—This chapter introduces many of the new features and functionality of Flash 5.

- **Chapter 3: "Introduction to the Flash Workspace"**—In this chapter, you explore the Timeline, toolbox, panels, Stage, work area, and Launcher Bar.

- **Chapter 4: "Planning Your Travel Company Web Site"**—Throughout this chapter, you will develop the preliminary document that you need for planning your Web site. This includes identifying the delivery method, planning your Web site flow through storyboards, developing the layout architecture and branching diagram of your Web site, identifying the site graphics, and planning the movie's scenes.

Part 2: "Building Blocks of Flash: Creating Graphics for the Travel Company Web Site"

- **Chapter 5: "Creating and Editing Graphics for the Travel Company Web Site"**—This chapter tells how to create the graphics that you will need for your Web site. You will learn how to use many of the tools in the toolbox by creating these graphics.

- **Chapter 6: "Importing Graphics for the Travel Company Web Site"**—You will import and optimize graphics that you need for your site throughout this chapter. You will learn about Flash's new Freehand import technique as well as how to import GIF and JPEG files. After importing the files, you will convert the files to vector format and optimize them to be as small in file size as possible.

- **Chapter 7: "Using Text in Flash"**—This chapter instructs you on how to create and use text in your Web site. You will learn how to add text to buttons and make sure that all elements of a button are aligned with the button as well as with other buttons.

Part 3: "Experience the Power of Flash: Create the Movie"

- **Chapter 8: "Using Symbols, Libraries, and Instances to Recycle and Organize Graphic Elements"**—Here you begin to use the power of Flash by creating symbols and using instances of these symbols throughout your Web site. You will use your Library and many of the features of the Library for organizing your graphics. Flash's new feature of a Shared Library is explained.

- **Chapter 9: "Using Layers to Organize the Movie"**—This chapter provides information on creating and manipulating layers. You also learn how to edit a layer's content and objects.

- **Chapter 10: "Animating the Movie"**—You will learn how to work with the Timeline to create animation in this chapter. You will create motion tweens and size and rotation tweens, as well as color and shape tweens.

- **Chapter 11: "Creating the Movie's Scenes and Buttons"**—This chapter instructs you on creating your scenes for each page of the Web site. You will also create buttons that begin to add interactivity to your site. You will attach actions to both frames and buttons in this chapter.

- **Chapter 12: "Attaching Actions and Sounds to the Buttons and Frames"**—Flash is ideal for creating interfaces, and that is just what this chapter explains. You begin to create the interactivity for moving around in your site by using ActionScripting. Then you will add some flare and begin to attach sounds to your movie.

- **Chapter 13: "Publishing the Movie for the Travel Company Web Site"**—This chapter instructs you on how to set your publishing settings and then how to publish your movie.

Part 4: "Putting It All Together: Creating the Fully Flashed Travel Company Web Site"

- **Chapter 14: "Advanced Animation Techniques"**—Teaches you how to create a movie clip symbol and use it in an animation. You will also learn how to create a gate page that will not allow the end-user to advance into the site until all features of the site have loaded or streamed down. You will also create a mask and apply it to your movie.

- **Chapter 15: "Creating the Contact Us Form for the Web Site"**—This chapter covers how to create a form and editable text fields for your Web site. You will begin to use variables in the form. Troubleshooting techniques are implemented.

- **Chapter 16: "Creating the Accommodations Page"**—Learn how to create a pop-up menu and to use the new Flash 5 feature of smart clips. This chapter also covers drag-and-drop functionality. You will begin to use more advanced ActionScripting commands and troubleshooting techniques throughout this chapter.

- **Chapter 17: "Next Steps with Flash"**—This chapter instructs you on creating a Flash screen saver. You will also create a panoramic 360° movie and use it in your Web site.

Conventions Used in This Book

Some of the unique features in this series include

Geek Speak—An icon in the margin indicating the use of a new term. New terms will appear in the paragraph in *italics*.

An icon in the margin indicates that you need to play, publish, or test your movie or animation. You can play a movie in the Flash development mode or you can test the movie in the Flash Player. You can leave the Flash Player open or close it after you test your movie. You can also publish your movie to preview it in a browser. These are the three techniques referred to when the Try It icon is presented.

Excursions are short diversions from the main topic being discussed, and they offer an opportunity to flesh out your understanding of a topic.

In the front of this book, you will find a Concept Web. A Concept Web is a graphical representation of how all the topics in the book relate to one another. In this Flash book it represents the planning and development process for creating a Web site with Flash.

Notes offer comments and asides about the topic at hand, as well as full explanations of certain concepts.

Tips provide great shortcuts and hints on additional techniques and skills for developing in Flash.

Warnings help you avoid the pitfalls of development mistakes that will make your Flash experience much more difficult.

In addition, you'll find various typographic conventions used throughout the book:

- Menu commands appear in **bold**.
- Text that you should type appears in `monospaced font`.
- Folders and filenames that are called out appear in `monospaced font`.

System Requirements for Flash 5

The following are the system requirements that Macromedia recommends for using the Flash 5 product:

Windows	*Macintosh*
133MHz Intel Pentium processor	Power Macintosh
Windows 95, 98, NT 4, 2000, or later	Mac OS 8.5 or later
32MB of RAM	32MB of free Application RAM
40MB of available disk space	40MB of available disk space
256-color monitor capable of 800×600 resolution	256-color monitor capable of 800×600 resolution
CD-ROM drive	CD-ROM drive

Graphics and Animations Are Simple

Because of the various levels of users who will be working through the book, the project, graphics, and animations are very simple in design and structure. This enables all readers to working through the instruction successfully. However, the skills and techniques taught can be transferred easily into your work and development style. Therefore, you can begin to apply Flash immediately to your work and projects in the style and complexity with which you are used to developing.

Relax and have some fun with the book. You will find that Flash is a wonderful tool for Web development as well as for other graphic design and development areas. Flash has a lot to offer all users of any skill level!

Part I

Getting Started with Flash

Chapter 1

Why Use Flash?

The World Wide Web is growing in leaps and bounds. Traditional *Web sites* with static informational pages no longer capture the end-user's attention like they used to. People are becoming more Internet savvy and want a richer, more interactive experience when they surf the Web. Static pages are quickly becoming boring for the average end-user. So, Web designers and developers try to make their pages more compelling by adding graphics and animated GIF files. Using the traditional compression formats GIF, JPEG, and PNG, graphics add some splash to a site, but downloading these pages can be very time consuming due to the file sizes of these graphics. End-users tend to lose interest waiting on pages to download and move on to the next site in the hope of a better experience. Today, Web sites with animation and interactivity are catching people's attention—and their money. This is what the Internet world is coming to. If you want to compete and profit in this world, you will need to expand your skills and knowledge of how to develop interactive Web sites. But, never fear, there is a product available that will help you reach your Web development goals—Macromedia Flash.

How Flash Developed

Flash is, and has been, the Web animation solution for the Internet. Flash's roots come from an early vector animation program named FutureSplash. Macromedia bought FutureSplash in 1997 and changed the name to Flash. Since then, with each new release, Flash becomes stronger and more versatile for design and development both on and off the Internet. Now Flash 5 is here and adds new features and controls for Internet designers and developers.

Flash combines all the tools and features needed to create eye-catching Web sites and graphics. It can also apply interactivity to the graphics and animations, as well as create the interactive interface components required for a richer Web site navigation experience. And to add the final touch, Flash creates the *HTML code* for displaying the graphics, animations, and interface components, making it a must-have for every Web designer.

Flash can be used to create an entire Web site or just the individual components that make up a Web page. You can create an exciting banner ad to liven up a page or striking interactive buttons. You can create cartoons or an animation that helps drive home a concept or feature of your Web site. Animations can contain controls or navigational features that allow users to have control over their experience with your Web site. This sense of control can help drive home your point or message to the end-users, allowing you to sell or influence them.

Advantages of Using Flash for Animation

Flash offers many advantages over other Web and graphic file applications. The Flash tools for creating graphics are simple to use when compared with those in other graphic applications. New with Flash 5 is the Pen tool (see Figure 1.1). The Pen tool allows you to create a shape using point-to-point drawing similar to the *Bézier* tool of other design programs. Prior to this release, this tool was missing from the palette and many designers lamented its absence. But Macromedia listened to its users and implemented this tool in the new 5 release. You will find that using the Flash tool palette is easy for both nonartists and highly accomplished artists alike.

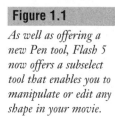

Figure 1.1

As well as offering a new Pen tool, Flash 5 now offers a subselect tool that enables you to manipulate or edit any shape in your movie.

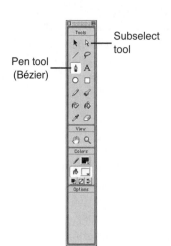

Pen tool
(Bézier)

Subselect
tool

Low File Size

The big advantage of Flash is its use of *vector* graphics. This type of graphic is really a mathematical set of instructions describing the size, color, and location of a shape. A vector graphic is composed of lines and curves, whereas a *bitmapped* graphic is composed of little dots or *pixels*. Each dot tells the computer its color and its location on the screen. Because a bitmapped graphic is composed of dots, when the image is enlarged, you see *jaggies*. The image edges are not smooth but composed of a stair-case effect of dots (see Figure 1.2). The larger you make the image, the worse the jaggies get. Notice that the vector image in Figure 1.2 is smooth. When you enlarge a vector graphic, the figure maintains its smooth curves and lines. Therefore, any Web browser, no matter what size, can display a Flash file in the format it was designed—clean and jaggie free. The vector graphic is described by a series of lines and curves. The formula also includes the coordinates for the graphic's position on the screen. Using a mathematical formula is a major advantage for displaying graphics and keeping the file size low, especially when being displayed on the Web.

Bitmap graphic

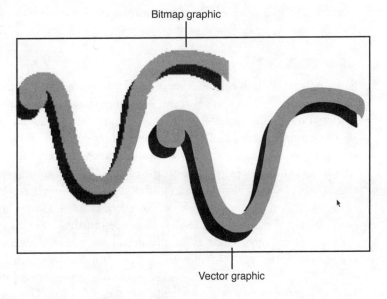

Figure 1.2

A vector graphic displays images clean and jaggie free, no matter what size the image is made.

Vector graphic

As I mentioned previously, one of the biggest benefits of Flash is its capability to create low file size graphics. When these graphics are used in an animation, the file size for the animation is also very small. This is a great reason to use Flash rather than traditional HTML animation techniques. Prior to Flash, animation was created through animated *GIF* files. Although these animations worked, they were composed of numerous GIF files that rotated in succession to create the animation effect. This form of animation, though compressed through GIF compression, can be large in file size and is limited in what can be shown. A Flash animation offers new flexibility for Web developers and designers for creating exciting Web pages.

Improved Download Speed for Web Pages and Graphics

Another benefit of Flash is its use of compression for animation, graphics, and sound. Because graphics are vector based, files created in Flash are already low in file size. To further reduce the size of files, Flash also applies a compression format to the file. Within this file compression is a *streaming* feature that allows your site to be displayed in a Web browser prior to all the content being downloaded. This means that some of the vector graphics on your site are displayed while other graphics, sound, and animations are still downloading. As a result, an end-user can access your site quickly without noticing the behind-the-scenes downloading of other features necessary for your site to operate and display properly. Flash even allows you to set controls that do not allow the user to advance to a new page until all features required for your site to function correctly have been downloaded. Streaming is very powerful for Web development. It allows you to create a very large site with lots of features and enhancements that is quickly accessible to any user, no matter what connection speed she is logged in at.

Interactivity

Interactivity in Flash can be composed of many different features. You are not limited to simple graphics, animations, or banners but have the power to add full navigational features to any object or area of your site. You can add buttons and menus, or animations that control where the end-users go or what they see. You create interactive movies by setting up *actions*. Flash comes with a scripting language for creating interactive controls. In releases prior to Flash 5, this scripting language was easy for beginners to use and learn but robust enough for programmers to have a very dynamic scripting experience. The Flash 5 release brings new actions and commands and expands the *ActionScripting* language even further by incorporating JavaScript-like syntax and other features for advanced programmers and developers. You can create very intricate commands and controls for your interfaces. Flash also links beautifully with database back-end engines so that you can create a full-featured Web site. This book does not cover database interactivity, but you should be aware that this feature is part of Flash's functionality.

1

EXCURSION

Database Interactivity and Flash

Communicating with host applications such as JavaScript and CGI scripts has never been easier than with the new Flash 5 version. By using an editable text field and setting the properties of each of these fields, you can create a variable that can be posted to a Web server. The data from each variable is posted or transferred to a database on the Web server, with user-entered information for each of the variables plugged into a database field of the same name. You can also use a text field to load variables and then send them to a text file.

You connect with a database and your Web site through other applications, such as Microsoft Active Server Pages and Allaire Cold Fusion. No matter what method you use, you need to provide the scripts to complete the variable transfer or posting process.

New with Flash 5 functionality is its increased compatibility and integration with Macromedia Generator. Macromedia Generator 2 Developer Edition can be used to automatically update Flash Web sites. Dynamic content needed for a Flash Web site can be stored in a Generator database and then automatically updated in the site. This capability allows for easy maintenance and updating of a complex Web site.

Flash Versus HTML

HTML is the fundamental language for Web development, but Flash is becoming more integrated into this language. It is fast becoming the preferred tool by many developers who need to create exciting, stimulating Web sites that download quickly. Prior to Flash, Web developers used many techniques to keep graphics low in file size and to create visually stimulating sites, but they always fought the size versus download time war to achieve their results. Now Flash makes this war almost fun and very winnable.

Automatically Size Movies to Web Browser Window

Another challenge for Web developers is the fact that Web browser window size varies from user to user. Therefore, when designing a page, the developer must guess the size so that desired elements of the page fit in the window. This means that the developer must guess the size Web browser window the majority of viewers will be using. Many times, the page does not appear for the site visitor as the developer intended due to a small Web browser window. Flash helps take the guesswork out of window size. Because Flash uses vector graphics, which are communicated to the computer using a mathematical formula, window size is not an issue. A Flashed Web site or page automatically fits within any window. All components of the Web page size themselves to the correct proportions so that the page can be displayed as the developer created it—no matter what size the window. It is the mathematical formula for vector art that allows this to occur.

Images and Text Are Perfect Every Time

Images and text are always clear and crisp when designed in Flash. Again, they're clear because they're vector graphics. Flash images look great on everyone's computer display because the images are communicated to a user's computer mathematically, not pixel by pixel as with bitmapped images. In the past, graphics created for HTML pages could contain a stray pixel or two that caused the image to be slightly fuzzy or not quite precise. This never happens with Flash.

Another neat feature of Flash is that it can help you draw. Flash can recognize basic geometric shapes as you create them. It then reforms your scribbled shape into the geometric shape that it thinks you are trying to create. For example, if you quickly draw an oval or circle by creating a round shape, Flash smoothes and rounds your shape to a perfect oval or circle. Flash also helps you create straight or smooth lines, too. So, you don't need to be a professional artist to get professional results. Flash will help you.

Text is always created as antialiased. This is part of the compression process that Flash performs on all movies, graphics, and text that it exports or publishes. Text on a Flashed page is clean, clear, and sized to the proportion that the developer intended (see Figure 1.3). HTML developers fight the battle of text being displayed according to the predefined text preference size that the user set for his Web browser. An HTML page is not always displayed as the developer intended, no matter how the page is designed (see Figure 1.4). A Flash page appears exactly as designed, with text displayed in the exact size and proportion; it is always clean and clear.

Figure 1.3

This page is Flashed—text and graphics always remain in proportion to each other, no matter what the browser settings.

Figure 1.4

On this HTML page, text and graphics reflect the size of the end-user's browser settings; therefore, text and graphics are out of proportion with each other.

Flash Plug-in Available in Most Web Browsers

Independent studies have shown that 92% of Web users can view Flash content without downloading a plug-in (statistic compiled by Macromedia in July 2000). With the release of Netscape 4.0, AOL 5.0, Excite@Home, WebTV, RealNetworks, and Microsoft Internet Explorer 4.0 and all versions from this point forward, the Flash plug-in is included in the browser or application functionality. Macromedia estimates that approximately 195 million people on the Internet can view sites with Flash content without downloading and installing a plug-in. Flash is becoming more and more a standard for Web animation.

This increase in capability for viewing Flash content is due to Macromedia's policy of distributing the source code for Flash freely to any parties interested in incorporating it into their products. This source code is now being incorporated into many of the palm-held Internet devices available on the market today.

If a user has an older Web browser that does not support Flash content, he can download the plug-in directly from Macromedia's Web site. This plug-in is under 200KB in size and can be installed in five minutes or less, depending on connection time. Flash also has made it easy to detect whether a Web browser is Flash enabled. As of the Flash 4.0 release, the publishing feature is capable of automatically creating the HMTL code that can interpret whether the user's Web browser is Flash enabled. If the Web browser is not, a link to the plug-in is provided for downloading. This is a neat and timesaving feature for all.

Another point of interest is that QuickTime 4.0, RealAudio, and Macromedia's Shockwave plug-ins are also capable of reading Flash content. These plug-ins have been around longer than the Flash plug-in, and many users have already installed them in their Web browsers. Viewing Flash content is a reality for almost all end-users on the Internet today.

Easy to Learn

Flash 5 now offers a wonderful feature called the Macromedia Dashboard. The Dashboard is a one-stop resource for information, support, training, and feedback on Flash. You can quickly locate information or get questions answered through the various help and support avenues that this feature offers (see Figure 1.5). You can access the Macromedia Dashboard by choosing **Help**, **Macromedia Dashboard**.

Figure 1.5

You can access many Web sites that are devoted to Flash help and training through the Macromedia Dashboard.

Macromedia has also added a new feature to its Web site for learning Flash. Now you can find a link to Macromedia University, which offers lists of Authorized Training Providers on all Macromedia courses as well as online training courses. You can take the online training courses no matter where you live. These training avenues allow beginner or intermediate Flash users the opportunity to learn Flash in as much detail as they need.

You'll also find the Macromedia Web site very useful. It includes many helpful tips and techniques as well as examples of Flashed Web sites at www.macromedia.com/flash. You can also find other Web sites devoted to teaching Flash. Many discussion groups have been formed for people to collaborate and share information on Flash. The Flash electronic community is very strong and growing. You can find many of these resources by performing a search on any of the major search engines using the keyword Flash.

Flash also ships with sample files that you can use as a reference on how to create or use an interface or design that you might want to implement in your own work. You can find these sample files by choosing **Help**, **Samples** (see Figure 1.6). It's always nice to be able to look at an example of a feature similar to what you're trying to create. You can learn a lot about correct programming and design from studying examples of other work. Macromedia provides many samples for you to preview. Take some time and explore these sample files. You can test them on the Flash Player to explore their content.

Figure 1.6

The many sample files provided with Flash illustrate programming techniques and design interfaces that you can copy and implement in your own movies.

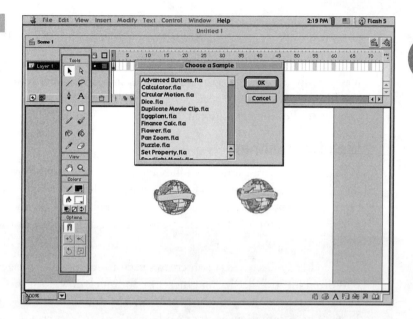

Macromedia has made it easy for you to try out Flash before you decide to buy it. Macromedia offers a 30-day demonstration version on its Web site at `http://macromedia.com/software/flash/trial`. This demonstration version is fully functional, identical to the resale version of Flash. The only difference is that this demonstration version is functional for only 30 days. It includes all the tutorials and sample files that come with the resale version of Flash. You can begin to learn Flash before you even own the product!

Who's Flashing and Why

Flash is quickly growing in popularity. The Flash 5 release further extends the capabilities of Flash for the Web development and graphic design communities. More and more, people are converting to Flash for their daily work. This work ranges from Web development to graphic design to storyboarding.

Graphic Design

Graphic designers in many areas are using Flash. Because of its capability to convert artwork into vector format, designers are using it to improve their bitmapped images. They are converting their images to lower file sizes as well as taking advantage of the other features of vector artwork. This includes smoothing their images' edges to get rid of the jaggies, as well as making their images scalable to whatever size they might need for integration in other work. Flash also has a great gradient feature that allows designers flexibility in colors used in the gradient as well as control of the direction of the gradient pattern.

Flash's tools are easy to use and are similar in functionality to tools used in other design programs. Experienced designers will find many advantages to using these tools instead of their traditional design program's tools.

Web Development

Web developers are using Flash files and movies more and more. They are realizing that the Internet viewing audience requires much more from its Internet surfing experiences, and Web sites need to be spruced up. Flash fits the bill for meeting this requirement. Although Flash can be used to create graphics, it truly shines as a Web development tool.

As I've already discussed, Flash creates vector graphics and images. These files are optimized for low file size and therefore for quick download time on the Web. Many of the limitations that previously affected a Web design are now eliminated through Flash. These limitations include Web browser size, text size, page proportions, and clean, clear images. Web developers are seeing the advantage of using Flash and converting sites and site content to Flash format.

Storyboarding

Many artists are using Flash as a storyboarding tool to communicate ideas and concepts. Because of its easy-to-use tools, many designers are using it to quickly sketch out ideas and concepts.

Quickly Arranging Ideas

Storyboards can be created through Flash and then presented for approval to the required third party. Using Flash's frames, you can rearrange a sequence of storyboards in a different order or flow. By choosing **File, Print Margins** for Macintosh or **File, Page Setup** for PC, you can set options to print each frame of a movie. Therefore, you can create each frame of a movie as a separate storyboard to convey a concept. You can also set the movie to print all frames with borders around the storyboards or in a grid of thumbnails on a page (see Figure 1.7). Using these features and the easy-to-use tools of Flash, artists and nonartists alike can quickly create clean storyboards that convey an idea or concept.

Figure 1.7

Communicating ideas through Flash is easy with storyboards.

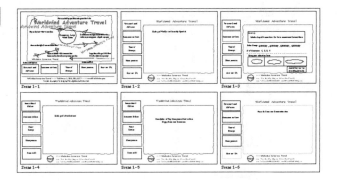

Managers Using Flash for Doodling Ideas and Concepts

Flash's forgiving drawing feature automatically cleans up a quick sketch created by a nongraphics person. Lines are straightened, and geometric shapes are cleaned up and displayed as perfect circles, squares, or ovals. Text is automatically anti-aliased. Ideas and concepts can quickly be created in a quick sketch.

Presentations

The creation of presentations is another area in which Flash excels. Flash can be used to present movies both on and off the Web. Experienced designers and non-graphics business types can use Flash to create presentations. This chapter discusses the advantages of using Flash for Web development, but you also can create a Flash movie to be presented on CD-ROM, a standalone projector, or even a floppy disk. You need to have the licensed Flash Player included with these other formats, but the Player ships with the Flash software. The Flash Player is small enough that it can fit on a floppy disk. Therefore, you have many mediums for showing off your work both online and offline.

Easy for Nongraphics People

With Flash's easy-to-use tools, many nongraphics people can quickly begin to use the program to create their presentations. Flash provides an intuitive starting point by providing the Sample files, the Macromedia Dashboard, and many Flash Web sites. These users can begin to create a presentation with confidence.

Importing and Exporting for File Exchange

Flash can import graphics in the GIF, JPEG, EPS, and PNG formats. Any bitmapped image can also be imported or simply copied and pasted into Flash. This capability allows you to generate professional, multifaceted presentations. Any chart or graph created in another program, such as Microsoft Office, can be copied and pasted into Flash. Most presentations are created to be presented offline, and this is easily accomplished through Flash's Export Movie or Publish feature.

Flash also has a very powerful Publish feature that allows designers to quickly convert their artwork to many different file formats. You can access the Publish feature by choosing **File**, **Publish** (see Figure 1.8).

Figure 1.8

*Flash's **Publish** command also allows you to create the HTML code required to display a Flash movie on the Internet.*

Flash also provides a dialog box in which you can select the exact settings you need to convert a file (see Figure 1.9). You can access this dialog box by choosing **File**, **Publish Settings**. You can turn these settings on or off and then publish the file, and Flash does the rest by converting the file to the formats you have chosen.

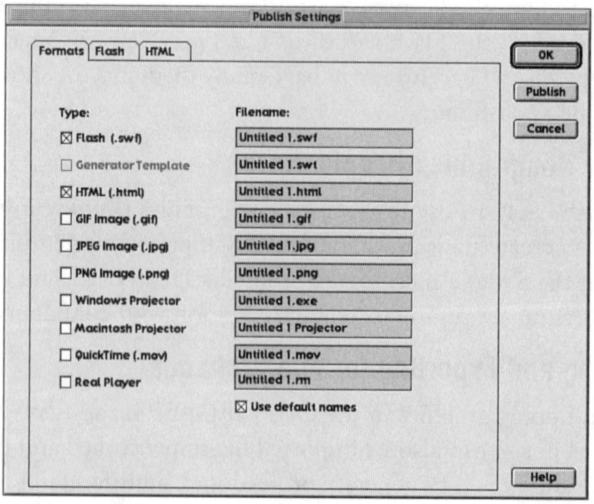

Figure 1.9

The multiple formats available allow you to quickly convert graphics and movies. This capability can be a huge time-saver.

The following file formats are available in the Publish Settings dialog box:

- **Flash (.swf)**—Flash Player format. The file extension *.swf* stands for *Small Web Format*.

- **Generator Template**—A Web server application for combining templates with specific content of a data source.

- **HTML (.html)**—Standard Web page code and programming. When this option is chosen, Flash automatically converts the file to both HTML and Flash format.

- **GIF Image (.gif)**—Bitmap *lossless* compression format commonly used in Web pages. Images that have large areas of exact colors convert best in this format.

- **JPEG Image (.jpg)**—Bitmap compression format commonly used in Web pages. Images that are photo quality are commonly converted best in this format. This compression format is *lossy*.

- **PNG Image (.png)**—New Web graphic format. Files saved in this format use compression similar to JPEGs but also use lossless compression typical of GIF files.

- **Windows Projector**—Projector file created to play on the Windows platform.

- **Macintosh Projector**—Projector file created to play on the Macintosh platform.

- **QuickTime (.mov)**—Movie file created to run through Apple's QuickTime player.

→ For more detailed instruction on how to publish movies in other graphic formats, **see** Chapter 13, "Publishing the Movie for the Travel Company Web Site," **p. 287**.

Flash also offers great Export features that can be used to export a movie or an image. You can access the export movie feature by choosing **File, Export Movie** and access the export image feature by choosing **File, Export Image**. If you're familiar with placing a Flash movie into an HTML page, you can just use the Export feature instead of the Publish command. You can export a movie or graphic created in Flash to a specific graphic format and then place the file in your HTML document yourself. Figure 1.10 shows the various export formats of Flash. The Export command works by taking the Flash graphic or movie and exporting it as a single image. If it is a movie, Flash takes the first frame and exports that image to the specified graphic format. So, converting images in Flash is easy, and you can convert an image to multiple graphic formats.

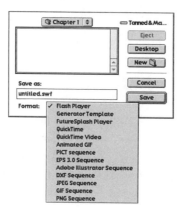

Easy-to-Enhance Imported Graphics

Flash also is great for cleaning up and enhancing imported graphics. When these files are in Flash, you can begin to optimize them by converting them into vector format. This book presents various techniques for converting and optimizing imported graphics in Chapter 6, "Importing Graphics for the Travel Company Web Site."

You will find that the best visual quality for images and the lowest file sizes come from images that you create in Flash, not those that you import. But often you might want to have a certain graphic effect for an image that cannot be created with Flash, such as a soft edge. For instance, if a company logo has a soft edge, you cannot re-create this image in Flash. To be consistent with the company's other marketing material, you need to import the logo, not re-create it.

Great Auto Tracing Feature

Flash's Trace Bitmap feature is excellent for converting an image to vector format. You can access this feature by choosing **Modify**, **Trace Bitmap**. This form of conversion takes the image's colors and, based on input settings, transforms the image into a vector composed of colored shapes. It creates a watercolor effect (see Figure 1.11).

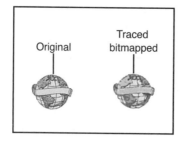

→ For more detailed instruction on how to import and optimize images in Flash, **see** Chapter 6, "Importing Graphics for the Travel Company Web Site," **p. 127**.

Flash Integration with Other Web Tools

Macromedia designed Flash to play well with others. As you've learned already, Flash can import and export many graphic file formats, and Macromedia has provided the Flash code to any parties who want it so that they can integrate it into their products. Aside from these features, Flash movies and images are also easily integrated into other Web development and graphic design applications available on the market today.

Flash with the Macromedia Suite of Software

As you would expect, Flash works seamlessly with other Macromedia products, in particular with the Macromedia suite of Web development software. This suite is composed of Macromedia's Dreamweaver and Fireworks software. Flash graphics and movies are imported into these packages with a simple menu command. Very few properties need to be reset. The Flash file is imported with many of the preset settings intact. You can also import Fireworks graphics directly into Flash as well as use the typical import or copy and paste methods. A Fireworks graphic file is imported into Flash in vector format with its layers intact.

New with the Flash 5 release is a common user interface that is represented throughout the Macromedia suite of Web design products. This makes learning the products very easy because the interface and menu commands are identical or similar in structure and functionality. This suite for Web development is very popular and used by beginners and professionals alike.

Flash with Other HTML Editors

When publishing a Flash file, Flash publishes the movie as an .swf file and includes the HTML file with all the coding needed to integrate it within any HTML file. As a result, Flash can be freely used and integrated in any HTML editor. You can just copy the code from one document to another to add a Flash file to your HTML page or use the Flash-generated HTML page for your Web site.

Flash with Generator

Another powerful application that extends the power of Flash is *Macromedia Generator*. Flash can read information from external data sources through an intermediary text file or a script and then connect this information to a Flash movie. Generator takes this interconnectivity one step further by allowing direct access to the data source, bypassing the text file or script. Generator provides all the necessary commands and features to allow this access. You do not need to provide any additional scripting. Using Generator with Flash, you can create a dynamic Web page with all the fun and interactivity of Flash!

Where You've Been!

This chapter provided an introduction to Flash. You learned some of the advantages that Flash offers Web developers and graphic designers, why people use Flash, some of the powerful features of Flash, and how to integrate Flash with other applications and HTML editors. This book will cover many of these points in greater detail as you move along through the project.

What's Next?

Next, you will learn what is new with Flash 5, the latest release from Macromedia, and how to use these features in the Web site project that you'll be building. This version of Flash takes some of the already powerful features of Flash 4.0 and extends them with a new look or feel, as well as adds new functionality that will only improve your productivity with Flash!

Chapter 2

In this chapter

- *Flash 5 New Interface*
- *Overview of Movie Explorer*
- *Overview of New ActionScript Programming Language*
- *Overview of Integration with Macromedia Generator*
- *New Import and Export Formats*

What's New with Flash 5

Macromedia continues to guide the world of Web development with its latest release of Flash—Flash 5. Features that were missing in the earlier releases of Flash are now present in the new 5 release. This chapter introduces you to the new features of this dynamic animation product.

Redesigned Interface

The first thing you will notice about the 5 version of Flash is the redesigned interface. Macromedia devoted a lot of development time to make the new release closely resemble the appearance and functionality of other graphic design applications, in particular the Macromedia Web development suite made up of Dreamweaver 3 and Fireworks 3. The new layout is more intuitive and consistent and, therefore, easier to work with and to learn.

The Panels

You now will find most of your commonly used commands in floating, tabbed panels displayed directly on your desktop (see Figure 2.1). Each panel has various tabs for accessing commands and features of Flash. You can access individual panels by choosing the **Window, Panels** menu command and then choosing the appropriate panel, or by using the Launcher Bar (covered in the next section).

Figure 2.1

Click a tab to switch to another panel.

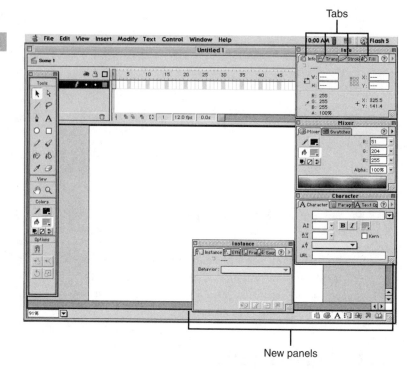

Table 2.1 describes the new panels in Flash 5.

Table 2.1   New Flash 5 Panels

Panel Name	Panel Description
Info	Precisely position and size objects, symbols, and graphics.
Transform	Scale, resize, and rotate objects, symbols, and graphics.
Stroke	Set the line size, color, and style for a shape.
Fill	Choose a solid fill color, gradient fill, or bitmapped fill for a shape.
Mixer	Choose colors in RGB, HSB, or Hex as well as set alpha transparencies for shapes. You can switch between stroke and fill colors, too.
Swatches	Manage colors and gradient fills for a movie. This panel also allows you to import, save, and sort color sets.
Scene	Manage a movie's scenes. This panel allows you to create, rename, delete, reorder, and edit all scenes in a movie.
Character	Choose and edit fonts, font sizes, font attributes, kerning, leading, and baseline shift. You can also set links for text.
Paragraph	Set paragraph margins and indents as well as line spacing and paragraph alignment.

Table 2.1 continued

Panel Name	Panel Description
Text Options	Set parameters for dynamic or text form fields.
Align	Align, distribute, and match objects relative to each other or the Stage.
Clip Parameters	Set parameters for movie clip instances.
Instance	Set or change the behavior for an instance or a symbol used in a movie. You also can swap, edit, and duplicate symbols.
Effect	Set the color, transparency, and brightness effect for an instance.
Frame	Set motion and shape tweens for a frame. You also can add or edit labels for a frame.
Sound	Edit sounds and special effects used in a movie. You also can set a sound to loop in a movie.

You can quickly hide all displayed panels by pressing the Tab key. Press the Tab key again to redisplay the panels.

You can now choose multiple objects on your Stage and apply new attributes to them by using panels. For instance, you can select both an oval shape and a rectangle shape and apply a common fill or line stroke to both shapes at the same time.

The Launcher Bar

Flash 5 offers a quick way to access the most commonly used panels. The Launcher Bar is located in the lower-right corner of the Flash window (see Figure 2.2). To quickly display a panel, click its associated button from the Launcher Bar. To hide the displayed panel, click the button again.

The Toolbox Layout

The toolbox has been redesigned to be more consistent in choices for all tools. Notice that this toolbox now has four distinct areas: Tools, View, Colors, and Options (see Figure 2.3).

Figure 2.2

You can toggle between showing and hiding panels by clicking the associated button from the Launcher Bar.

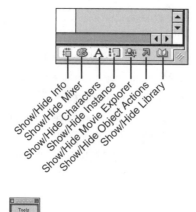

Show/Hide Info
Show/Hide Mixer
Show/Hide Characters
Show/Hide Instance
Show/Hide Movie Explorer
Show/Hide Object Actions
Show/Hide Library

Figure 2.3

Click the tool you want and then choose from the other areas for the various attributes to be applied to the tool.

 Note

The toolbox now has two new tools: the Subselect tool and the Pen tool. You will learn more about these tools later in this chapter and throughout the rest of the book.

 Tip

On the Windows platform, the toolbox can be docked or snapped to a window edge using the same process as with other toolbars. Click and drag the toolbox to the edge of your window, and it docks to the window's edge.

 Tip

If you have docked the toolbox on the Windows platform, causing it to join and become one with another toolbar, you can separate them by Ctrl+clicking the toolbox to separate it and dragging it apart from the toolbar.

Panel Management

Another nice feature that Macromedia has added to the Flash 5 product is the capability to manage your displayed panels. You can move a panel by clicking its title bar and dragging the panel to a new location on your screen. This way, you can arrange your Flash window and displayed panels to suit your workflow. When you have a layout that you like, you can then save the layout by choosing the **Window, Save Panel Layout** menu command. Choosing this menu command displays the Save Panel Layout dialog box.

You can switch between layouts by choosing the **Window, Select Panel Set** menu command and selecting the layout you want from the submenu.

 Tip   Any panel can be ungrouped from a panel group by clicking the panel tab and dragging it out of the panel group. You can also rearrange panels by clicking and dragging the panel tab from one panel group to another.

New Menu Structure

Now Flash 5 has better menu organization. You will find that many menus now have submenus. This new organization allows you to choose from menu commands with a common theme (see Figure 2.4).

Figure 2.4

*You can display panels by selecting them from the **Panels** submenu list of the **Window**, **Panels** menu command.*

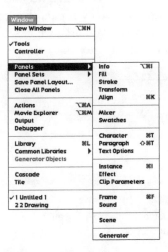

New Guides for Precision Alignment

Another new feature of Flash 5 is the addition of horizontal and vertical guides that allow you to align objects on your Stage. Now you can pull guides from the rulers and position them on your Stage. Under the **View** menu, you will now find a **Guides** menu and submenu that give you all the commands you need to access guides for positioning graphics and objects on the Stage with precision.

New Pen Tool

Many graphic designers familiar with other graphics applications found the toolbox of previous versions of Flash missing their favorite drawing tool, the Bézier tool. This tool is now present in the Flash 5 release and is called the Pen tool. The Pen tool is similar to the Bézier tool used in other graphics applications (see Figure 2.5). It allows you to create and edit paths of straight-line segments and curved-line segments with precision previously not found in the Flash drawing tools.

Figure 2.5

The keyboard equivalent for accessing the Pen tool is P.

Pen tool —

You can create paths composed of straight-line segments and curved-line segments by using the point-to-point drawing of the Pen tool. This means you can click to set a point and then move to the location that you want another curve or extension of a line and click again to set a second point. If you drag while setting a point, you can adjust the flow of the curve, as shown in Figure 2.6.

Figure 2.6

You can use the Pen tool to create straight-line segments and curved-line segments with precision.

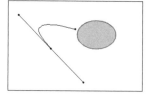

Tip   To constrain the Pen tool to 45° multiples, use the Shift key as you drag the line segments or click the anchor points.

Tip   To complete an open path, double-click the last point. This allows you to leave the shape open.

New Subselect Tool

Along with the Pen tool, Macromedia has added another tool, the Subselect tool (see Figure 2.7). This tool allows you to edit and reshape any graphic, regardless of the tool that created it.

Figure 2.7

The keyboard equivalent for the Subselect tool is A.

Subselect tool

When you select a graphic with the Subselect tool, you see a series of points that make up the path of the shape. You can then click and drag an anchor point to reshape the line segment. Or you can click the anchor point to access the tangent handles to reshape the curve (see Figure 2.8).

Figure 2.8

This shape was originally created with the Oval tool but can be altered with the Subselect tool.

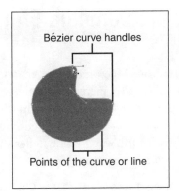

Bézier curve handles

Points of the curve or line

Customizable Keyboard Shortcuts

Customizing keyboard shortcuts is now a feature of Flash with the 5 version. You can change an existing keyboard shortcut to a new keystroke that might be easier for you to remember or use by choosing the **Edit, Keyboard Shortcuts** menu command.

When you select this menu command, you open the Customize Shortcuts dialog box (see Figure 2.9).

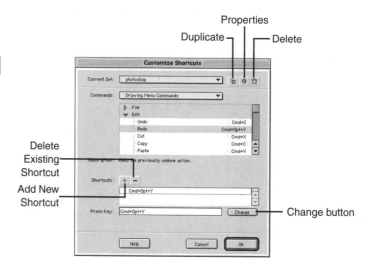

Figure 2.9

*You can choose a set of commands by selecting a menu choice from the **Commands** drop-down menu.*

Through this dialog box, you can add a new keyboard shortcut for any drawing menu command, drawing tool, or test movie menu command of Flash. After you select a command to change, you need to delete the shortcut, press the keystrokes for the new keyboard shortcut, and then click the Change button. Click OK to close the dialog box.

Seamlessly Importing Macromedia Freehand Images

Flash now supports direct imports from Macromedia Freehand, including versions 7, 8, and 9. After you choose the **File**, **Import** menu command, select a Freehand file to import. When you begin the import process, the Freehand Import dialog box opens (see Figure 2.10). After the Freehand file is imported into Flash, you can manipulate the image easily because of the way Flash handles the various features that you might have applied or used to create your Freehand document.

→ For more detailed instruction on importing images into Flash, **see** Chapter 6, "Importing Graphics for the Travel Company Web Site," **p. 127**.

Figure 2.10

If you used layers when creating your Freehand image, you can keep these layers in the imported image in Flash by selecting the Layers option.

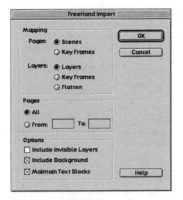

2

This new Freehand import feature of Flash allows you to map a multi-paged Freehand document to Flash scenes or individual keyframes. You can also map Freehand layers to Flash layers, keyframes, or a flattened, imported image. Flash also precisely color-maps the colors used in the Freehand image to the Flash image. Any Lens fills used in your Freehand image are converted to the Flash equivalent. If you use any symbols in the Freehand Library, they are imported into the Flash movie's Library. Macromedia made it easy to move between Flash and Freehand with this new feature.

→ For more detailed instruction on the Flash movie's Library, **see** Chapter 8, "Using Symbols, Libraries, and Instances to Recycle and Organize Graphic Elements," **p. 177**.

New and Improved Selection Features

Macromedia has revised the appearance of the selection marquees. It is now easier to view your selected object when using these marquees.

Colored Selection Marquees

Flash 5 now includes selection marquees that can be colorized by layers for text blocks. If you choose the **Edit**, **Preferences** menu command, the Preferences dialog box is displayed (see Figure 2.11). Select the Use Layer Color option from Highlight Color on the General tab. This option makes your selection marquees match the color of the layer.

Figure 2.11

You can choose a color for all text block marquees by selecting the Use This Color option and then clicking the down arrow to display the color palette and selecting a new color.

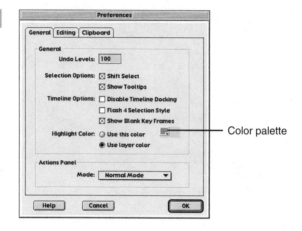

Color palette

Semitransparent Fill Selections

Another improvement Macromedia has made to the 5 release is in the selection fill that appears when you activate an object. Now the selection fill is made up of smaller dots that allow the color of the fill to show through (see Figure 2.12). In previous versions of Flash, this selection fill was a black-and-white dotted fill no matter what color the shape's fill was.

Figure 2.12

The new selection fill makes it easier to see what you are doing as you manipulate and edit a shape.

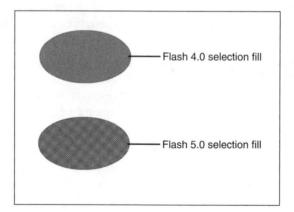

Flash 4.0 selection fill

Flash 5.0 selection fill

New Movie Explorer

A brand new feature of Flash 5 is the Movie Explorer (see Figure 2.13). Flash movies have matured from simple animation to complex Web applications that involve groups of individuals working as a team. The Movie Explorer was created to help manage and analyze complex projects. It displays your movie's nested objects in a hierarchical structure as well as shows this structure with relation to each object's location over time. The Movie Explorer helps with movie organization and structure navigation of authoring documents.

2

Figure 2.13

Using the Movie Explorer, you can analyze a movie by scene or by the movie's individual assets and objects.

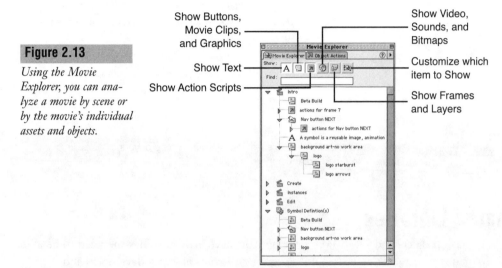

Show Buttons, Movie Clips, and Graphics

Show Text

Show Action Scripts

Show Video, Sounds, and Bitmaps

Customize which item to Show

Show Frames and Layers

You can display the Movie Explorer by choosing the **Window, Movie Explorer** menu command or by clicking the Show Movie Explorer button from the Launcher Bar.

Table 2.2 describes what each button under the Show option enables you to do with the Movie Explorer.

Table 2.2   Movie Explorer Functionality

Show Button	*Button Name*	*Button Functionality*
A	Show Text	When clicked, shows all text used in a movie, scene by scene. You can search for text through the Movie Explorer.
▢	Show Buttons, Movie Clips, and Graphics	When clicked, shows all buttons, movie clips, and graphics used in a movie. It allows for easy identification of your movie's assets, scene by scene, so you can edit and manipulate the assets.
▢	Show ActionScripts	When clicked, shows all ActionScripts used in a movie, scene by scene, frame by frame. You can search for ActionScripts through the Movie Explorer.
▢	Show Video, Sounds, and Bitmaps	When clicked, shows all videos, sounds, and bitmaps used in a movie. It allows for easy identification of your movie's assets, scene by scene, so you can edit and manipulate the assets.

Table 2.2   continued

Show Button	Button Name	Button Functionality
	Show Frames and Layers	When clicked, shows all frames and layers used in a movie. It allows for easy analysis of your movie's frames and layers, scene by scene, so you can edit and manipulate the frame and layer contents.
	Customize Which Item to Show	You can save a view to display any of the other button features. This way, you can create your favorite view and save it for later use with the movie as well as other movies.

Tip

The Movie Explorer is printable, so you can print a map of your movie's structure to share with other team members or clients.

Shared Libraries

As Flash projects and Flash Web development have grown, so has the need to be able to manage a project's assets or objects among a group of many developers and designers. Now Flash 5 offers a solution to this management problem by creating the Shared Library (see Figure 2.14). This new Library allows multiple people to access assets from a Library stored outside the project they are working on.

Movie Library   Shared Symbol Library

Figure 2.14

A Shared Library is slightly different in display from a movie's Library. When you view the Shared Library, you'll notice the dark gray background of both the preview window and the actual symbol listing area.

The Shared Library allows for symbols and instances to be used across many movies. In previous releases of Flash, this duplication of assets had to be downloaded per usage, which caused longer download times for each item being used. Now, shared symbols can be downloaded once and used across many projects that refer to the shared symbol. Therefore, download time is greatly reduced, improving productivity by the development team as well as viewing of the movie.

Tip

If a change is made to a symbol in the Shared Library, the change is reflected in all instances of the symbol for any movie that uses it. This feature is a huge time-saver for development teams.

→ For more detailed instruction on the Flash movie's Library, **see** Chapter 8, "Using Symbols, Libraries, and Instances to Recycle and Organize Graphic Elements," **p. 177**.

2

Improved ActionScript Development Tools

Flash 5 also has beefed up the ActionScript programming language that is part of Flash. The ActionScript programming language includes new commands that will thrill advanced programmers as well as new tools for creating and editing ActionScript commands and programs.

ActionScript Syntax Matches JavaScript

Flash 5 now offers ActionScript that very closely matches the syntax and structure of JavaScript (see Figure 2.15). Advanced programmers familiar with JavaScript will find the new ActionScript more to their liking and more powerful for their programming.

New ActionScript syntax

Figure 2.15

The new ActionScript syntax is similar to JavaScript syntax.

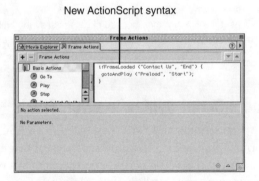

Expert and Novice Modes

Another new tool provided with the Flash 5 version is the Frame/Object Actions feature of the Movie Explorer (see Figure 2.16). Because you can access actions for both a frame and an object, the dialog box is named appropriately. In other words, if you access an action, the dialog box is named Frame Actions, and if you access an object, it is named Object Actions.

Figure 2.16

You can create and edit ActionScripts through the Frame Actions tab of the Movie Explorer.

This feature offers two ActionScript modes: Normal and Expert. By choosing the Normal Mode, beginning ActionScript programmers can use the intuitive, user-friendly preset actions to build and create their ActionScripts. The Expert mode enables advanced programmers to create their powerful scripts and actions by typing the code, using the preset actions, or using a combination of both. This versatility allows beginners to the most advanced programmers the tools they need to develop in Flash.

> **Tip**
>
> You can set the Flash preferences to always display the Normal Mode actions, which are the Basic ActionScript commands (the default setting), or to display the Expert Mode. You do so by using the Preferences dialog box.

Exportable ActionScript Syntax to ASCII File

With Flash 5, all ActionScript syntax can be exported to an ASCII file. When the syntax is in this format, programmers can use any external text editor to edit the ActionScript. After editing the ActionScript, programmers can re-import it into Flash. This way, programmers have all the flexibility they need to create and edit ActionScript programs and commands.

New Debugger

Flash 5 has added another new feature called the Debugger that will help in programming and troubleshooting ActionScript programs. You can use it to isolate problems with your movie's variables and properties used in ActionScript (see Figure 2.17).

2

Debugger window

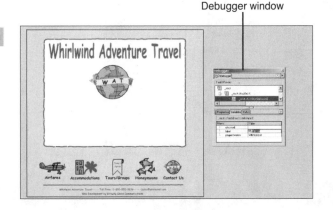

Figure 2.17

You can set a Watch in the Debugger to help examine your ActionScript code as you develop your movie.

Reusable Smart Clips

Smart clips have been added to Flash 5. *Smart clips* provide a way to isolate and encapsulate complex interactivity into a special movie clip symbol. Using this feature, you can take ActionScript programs and functions that perform complex interactivity, such as a menuing system, and save them as a parameterized movie clip—a smart clip. Smart clips are stored in the movie's Library as movie clip symbols, but the representative icon looks different from the typical movie clip icon (see Figure 2.18).

Figure 2.18

Because the smart clip is stored in your Library, you can reuse and share it across projects and with other people.

Smart clips—

To customize a smart clip for your movie, you need to use the Clip Parameters feature of Flash 5. After you add a smart clip to your movie, you then must open the Clip Parameters dialog box by choosing the **Window**, **Panels**, **Clip Parameters** menu command. Through this feature, you can customize the features of the smart clip (see Figure 2.19).

Figure 2.19

Smart clips allow you to create reusable user interface elements and functionality, including check boxes, option buttons, navigational menus, and pull-down menus.

Many third-party sites on the Internet distribute examples for creating navigation systems, preloaders, and other techniques for complex interactivity within Flash. You can use smart clips to begin to develop a Library of this type of interactivity so that you can use them in many of your movies.

XML Transfer Supported

As I discussed in Chapter 1, "Why Use Flash?" Web sites are changing because end users want a richer viewing experience. These changes require a Web site that presents data-rich pages with interactive interfaces—hence, the new feature of XML (Extensible Markup Language) integration that is included in Flash 5. Developers can now integrate XML-structured data within a Flash movie. This allows for a Web site with a broad range of e-commerce services. You can now create an invoice form with virtual shopping carts, communication surveys, and real-time availability of products displayed.

Integration with Macromedia Generator

Macromedia has further integrated the use of the Generator 2 Developer Edition within the new Flash 5 product. Generator allows for automatic updates of Flash content, which improves productivity of the development team (see Figure 2.20). No longer do developers need to spend numerous hours updating a content-rich Web site as new products are released or old ones terminated. Now they can use the Macromedia Generator 2 Developer Edition to automatically update a Flash Web site. As Macromedia states in its *Flash 5 Review Guide*, "The Macromedia Generator 2 Developer Edition is the data-driven solution for automatically updating Macromedia Flash Web sites and for developers creating Web prototypes for customers."

Figure 2.20

*You can access the Generator panel by choosing the **Window**, **Panels**, **Generator** menu command.*

RealPlayer and QuickTime Support

The importing and exporting capabilities for Flash have been extended to include some new formats. In Flash 5, you can now import and export QuickTime movies. You can also export Flash movies to RealPlayer format. RealPlayer G2 and RealPlayer 7 and 8 can play published RealFlash movies. These two new formats broaden the already wide arena of viewers that can play Flash-generated movies.

Import MP3 Audio

Another nice feature that has been missing from earlier versions of Flash is the capability to import MP3 audio. Flash 5 now allows for this compression format of music to be imported into Flash for use in a movie. This feature further extends the type of data that can be imported into Flash.

New Macromedia Dashboard

Another new feature of the Flash 5 release is the Macromedia Dashboard (see Figure 2.21). This feature is a direct link to many resources and communities devoted to Flash and accessible on the Internet. You can access the Macromedia Dashboard by choosing the **Help**, **Macromedia Dashboard** menu command.

Figure 2.21

You can access Flash news, communities, support, and training through the Dashboard. You can also link to Flash resources and feedback as well as access the latest Flash player.

Tip

When you first open Flash 5 and the Dashboard feature, you need to follow the instructions for updating the panel. You can click the Update button in the lower-right corner to update the panel. You might need to close the Dashboard and then reopen it to see the newly updated dialog box. But when you are linked in, you can click the Auto-Updated option so that the Dashboard will automatically update itself each time it is accessed.

Where You've Been!

This chapter covered the many new features of Flash 5, including the redesigned interface, new features of smart clips, Movie Explorer, and Shared Libraries. New import and export technologies were covered as well. The Flash 5 product is capable now, more than ever, of being the Web design, animation, and interface development tool of choice for beginning and advanced developers of Internet communications.

What's Next?

The next chapter will introduce you to the Flash workspace. You also will learn about the Timeline and its features. You will examine the Stage and the toolbox, and you will learn how to set up and manipulate the workspace area of Flash.

Chapter 3

Introduction to the Flash Workspace

Before you can begin to use any application, you need to understand the application's workspace area. Flash is no different. If you are familiar with the Flash 4 or any earlier version of Flash, the Flash 5 version has a new look and feel to the workspace. It now is very similar in its interface to other Macromedia products, such as Dreamweaver and Fireworks. If you haven't yet, launch Flash 5 so you can begin to explore this new workspace.

Components of the Flash Workspace

Before you can begin to use Flash to create graphics and animation, you need to understand your workspace in Flash. When you first launch Flash, it opens into a new blank document. The Flash workspace is divided into various features with their own functionality. The workspace is comprised of these six major areas: *Timeline*, *Stage*, work area, layers, panels, and the toolbox (see Figure 3.1).

Toolbox   Timeline   Default layout panels

Figure 3.1

The Flash workspace might look familiar to you in some aspects and dauntingly different in others. As you progress through this chapter, you will become comfortable with this workspace.

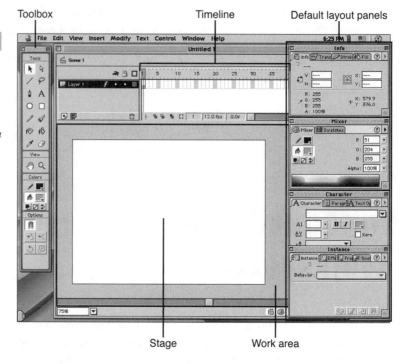

Stage   Work area

The Stage is the area on which you position all the content of your movie. The work area allows you extra space for organizing graphics and images that you want to include in a movie but might not be ready for yet on the Stage. The panels are a new feature of Flash 5 and allow you easy access to the customization and editing features of the Flash tools and menu commands. The Timeline controls your animation and helps organize your Stage content. All the tools you need to create graphics are located on the toolbox. These features comprise the Flash workspace.

Exploring the Features of the Timeline

The Flash Timeline controls the flow, interactivity, and organization of the movie. The Timeline contains all the layers that are used in the movie, as well as all the frames and scenes used in the movie (see Figure 3.2). You can compare the Timeline to a calendar. A scene can be compared to a month and a frame or *keyframe* can be compared to a day. With a calendar, if you want to see what is happening on a certain day in a certain month, locate that day within the month. Same with the Timeline, if you want to see what is happening in a certain frame or keyframe in a certain scene of the movie, you would click that frame within the scene. The playback head advances to that frame and the contents of the frame display on the Stage. You will use this technique a lot as you develop your movie.

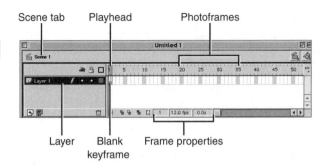

Figure 3.2

Each frame or keyframe presents a movie's content in the order that they need to be to create the effect of animation.

 Note

When a new Flash document is opened, the Timeline appears with only one frame occupied and it contains a blank keyframe. The remainder of the frames in the Timeline are actually photoframes, segmented in groups of five. A *photoframe* is a blank holding space for you to create your frames and keyframes.

➔ For more detailed instruction on the Timeline and animation, **see** Chapter 10, "Animating the Movie," **p. 211**.

Timeline Features

This analogy of comparing the Timeline to a calendar is very simple when truly compared to the functionality of the Timeline. A closer look at the Timeline reveals many other features and the functionality of the Timeline, such as layers (see Figure 3.3).

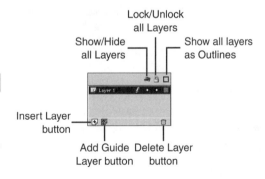

Figure 3.3

Layers offer you the flexibility that you need to work on a complex animation or image. You can use the Show/Hide feature to display only the layer that you want to work on, as well as lock other layers so they cannot be worked on.

Layers

Layers are a fundamental building block for your movie. They help you organize your images as well as organize your animation. You can create as many layers as you want to help you keep track of your images and the animation. Click the Insert Layer button to add a new layer and click the Delete Layer button to delete a layer. Similar to Adobe Photoshop, you can also hide and lock layers, which enables you to focus on one layer's contents and not disturb any other layer's content. You can also show a layer and its contents in outline format, which can be useful for troubleshooting animation.

Editing Features

There are other features and buttons available on the Timeline (see Figure 3.4). These are the Onion Skin buttons, the Edit Scene button, and the Edit Symbols button. The onion-skinning feature is comprised of three buttons located on the bottom of the Timeline window. These features allow for the Stage contents to be converted into an outline view or dimmed view. You will find this feature excellent for fine-tuning animation or for tracing images. As you can see, the Timeline is essential for animation and has many features and the functionality for creating and troubleshooting animation.

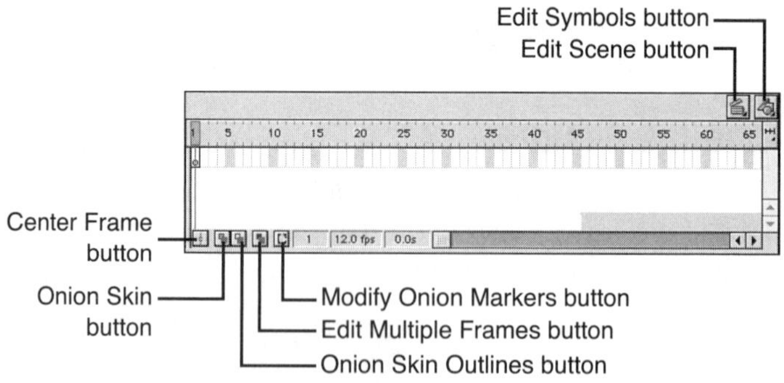

Figure 3.4

Additional buttons are available on the Timeline that can help you design and troubleshoot your images and animations. Use the Edit Symbols to quickly locate and edit a symbol or the Edit Scene button to quickly switch to another scene in your movie.

→ For more detailed instruction on how to use layers in Flash, **see** Chapter 9, "Using Layers to Organize the Movie," **p. 197**.

Resizing the Timeline

You can resize the Timeline to allow for more or less viewing area of your Stage or to view all layers in your Timeline. The default size is spaced to show four layers, but you will find that your movies will consist of many more layers than just four. So, you need to be able to resize your Timeline to view these features. To do this, just grab the lower Timeline window border and drag up or down to resize the window (see Figure 3.5).

Figure 3.5

Your cursor changes to a double arrow resize tool when you position it on the Timeline window's lower border.

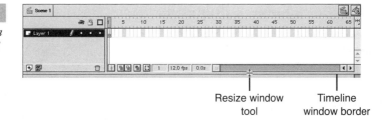

Resize window tool

Timeline window border

3

Hiding the Timeline

There might be times when you want to hide the Timeline so you can see your Stage in a full view. This can be accomplished through the menu command **View**, **Timeline**. After you hide the Timeline, you can display it again by choosing the menu command again. This command is a *toggle* switch that will toggle the Timeline between hidden and displayed.

Examining the Stage

Thinking back to the calendar analogy of the Timeline, you can think of the Stage as a day-timer schedule for a selected date. A day-timer schedule contains all activities for a date just as the Stage presents all content for the active frame.

Stage Area

Anything that you place on the Stage appears in your movie. If you position something half on the Stage and half in the work area, only the part of the image that is on the Stage appears in your movie. This allows for many special effects with animation. If you want something to appear to fly into a movie, position the image in the work area first and then create the animation to carry it onto the Stage. This creates the illusion of the image flying into the movie.

Work Area

The Flash work area is similar to the work area of other graphic packages. It can be compared to your desktop area. When you are working on a particular document, you have all this extra desktop space surrounding the document. This extra space allows you to keep on hand any additional tools, papers, or notes that you might need to complete your main document. The Flash work area can be compared to extra desktop space. You can use this to store other images or graphics that you might want to use in a movie but do not need yet on the Stage.

  Tip

You can turn the work area on and off through the **View**, **Work Area** menu command.

Examining Movie Properties

Every movie has its own set of properties that determine the size and appearance of the Stage, as well as many parameters of the movie. Choose **Modify, Movie** to display the Movie Properties dialog box (see Figure 3.6).

Tip

You can double-click the Timeline's Frame Properties setting of fps (frames per second) at the bottom of the Timeline to display the Movie Properties dialog box.

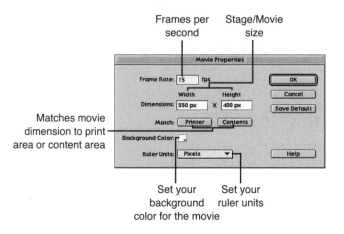

Figure 3.6

You can set the Frame Rate in the Movie Properties dialog box by inputting a number for the fps (frame per second) setting. Twelve–fifteen fps is a good setting for Web delivery of animation, but you might want to set this higher for offline delivery of a movie.

Note

Clicking the Match Printer button sets the movie size to the maximum print area based on your settings in the Page Setup dialog box. Clicking the Match Content button sets the movie size to the minimum Stage area required to display your movie's contents.

Sizing Your Stage

You will create a travel company Web site as you progress through this book. This Web site represents a fictitious company called Whirlwind Adventure Travel. To begin this project, you need to set your Stage dimensions for displaying the home page in the user's browser. A common size for Web pages that can be viewed easily on an 800×600 resolution screen display is 650×500 pixels. This size allows most visitors to easily view your Web site pages within their browser's window without having to scroll to see any of the contents on the page. In the Dimensions setting area, set the screen dimensions of 650×500px by clicking in the Width box and entering

650px. Then click in the Height box and enter 500px. This will set your movie's dimensions. Do not close the Movie Properties dialog box yet because we need to set the background color, which will be covered next.

 Note

> The default unit setting for the Dimensions Width and Height input box is *px*, which is short for pixel. You can type in a number without px following the number and Flash will automatically assume you mean pixel and add this unit to your number entry.

Background Color

You can use the Movie Properties dialog box to set your background color for the Whirlwind Adventure Travel movie to be displayed throughout this Web site. To display the color palette from which you can choose a new background color, follow these steps:

1. Display the Movie Properties dialog box by double-clicking the fps button on the Timeline.

2. Click the Background Color icon and move your mouse into the palette. Notice that it is now a dropper tool.

3. Click the third yellow color from the bottom on the far right column, Hexidecimal number FFFF99 (see Figure 3.7). Your Background Color icon will change to the light yellow color that you selected in the Background Color palette.

4. Click OK to close the Movie Properties dialog box. Your Stage background is now the light yellow color that you selected.

Figure 3.7

The background color palette contains the 216 Web-safe colors.

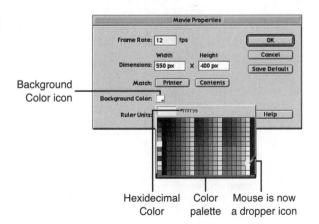

Background Color icon

Hexidecimal Color   Color palette   Mouse is now a dropper icon

Setting Frame Rate

You can also set the frame rate for your Whirlwind Adventure Travel movie in the Movie Properties dialog box. The Flash default setting is 12 fps (frames per second). This is the standard rate for viewing a movie on the Web by the average browser and average connection speed. You can go up to higher frame rates, but you are counting on your viewing audience having fast-processing computers and fast connections to the Internet. Typically 12 to 15 fps is common for Web delivery of movies. Increase this setting to 12 by clicking the fps box and typing 12. Click OK to close the Movie Properties dialog box.

Saving Your Movie

Before you go any further, you need to save your movie. It is recommended that you set up a special folder to save all the files that you create for the Web site. Set up this folder on your local drive in the location that you feel is appropriate. Click the **File**, **Save** menu command and name your movie `whirlwind`. Click OK when you are ready to save the movie.

Overview of the Toolbox

The toolbox is where you will find all the tools you need to create images and graphics, as well as manipulate your Stage view. It has been redesigned in the Flash 5 version. The toolbox is now more consistent in its presentation of tools and tool *options* (see Figure 3.8). This new layout of tools, views, and options of the toolbox is consistent with other Macromedia products and their toolbox features.

Figure 3.8

When Flash is launched, the toolbox displays floating in the application window. You can quickly access any of the tools by clicking them.

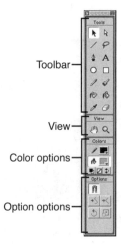

The toolbox contains the toolbar, which is very similar to other graphic package's toolbars. You will find that many of the tools in the toolbar function like many of the tools that you have used in other graphics packages. New with Flash 5 is the Pen tool, which is a *Bézier* drawing tool. You also have a new Subselect tool. Each tool has its own set of option settings that allow you to change or alter a feature of the tool. When you select a tool, the option area displays option settings under Colors or Options for that tool. You can also alter the view of the Stage through the View settings.

View the Toolbox

By default, the toolbox displays when Flash is launched. But this toolbox can be closed and opened through a menu command. You would close the toolbox so that you have a full view of your Stage. Use the menu command of **Window**, **Tools** to display or hide the toolbox.

You can also close the toolbox by clicking the close button on the Toolbox title bar.

You can dock and undock the toolbox on a PC machine. Typical of docking any toolbar, if the toolbox is floating, select it by clicking on any part of the toolbox that is not a tool and drag it to the right or left edge of the Flash application window. The toolbox will dock itself in that location, becoming a toolbar. You cannot dock the toolbox on the top or bottom of the Flash application window. If you want to undock the Flash toolbar, again click any part of the toolbar that is not a tool and drag it away from the edge of the Flash application window. It will become a floating toolbox.

A toolbox on the Macintosh is always floating. It can be moved to any location in the Flash application window by clicking on the title bar or the very edge of the toolbox, and dragging it to a new location.

Tools and Options

As discussed, the toolbox is comprised of a toolbar and various options. See Figure 3.9 for a listing of all tools available in the toolbox. You can select a tool from the toolbar or view area of the toolbox by clicking it. Click each tool and notice that the

Colors and Options areas change to reflect specific features that are available for the active tool.

Figure 3.9

The toolbar contains all the tools you will need to create vector images and graphics. You will also use these tools, in conjunction with menu commands and panels, and other options when you convert bitmapped images into vector graphics.

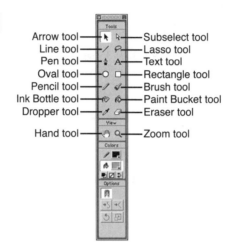

Arrow tool —— Subselect tool
Line tool —— Lasso tool
Pen tool —— Text tool
Oval tool —— Rectangle tool
Pencil tool —— Brush tool
Ink Bottle tool —— Paint Bucket tool
Dropper tool —— Eraser tool
Hand tool —— Zoom tool

Note

Another very nice feature that Flash offers (especially to people new to Flash) is *ToolTips* for all tools and options of each tool. Position your mouse over the Text tool but do not click. A ToolTip displays with the tool name (see Figure 3.10).

ToolTip

Figure 3.10

ToolTips quickly identify a tool or option feature. This is a wonderful feature for those new to Flash.

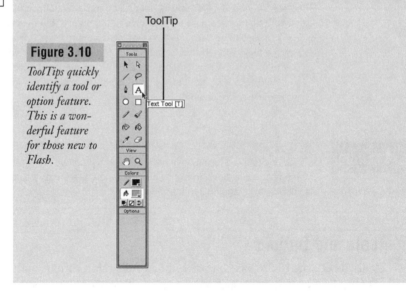

Accessing Tools Through Keyboard Commands

Flash provides a keyboard shortcut for quickly selecting tools from the toolbox. You might have noticed that when you display a ToolTip, at the end of the ToolTip label is a letter in parentheses. This is the keyboard shortcut or *hotkey* for quickly accessing a tool. Press the assigned hotkey and you will activate the tool in the toolbox. This way your hands do not need to leave the keyboard. The following table lists all tools and their assigned hotkeys.

Table 3.1   Hotkeys

Tool	Hotkey
Arrow tool	V
Subselect tool	A
Lasso tool	L
Line tool	N
Pen tool	P
Text tool	T
Oval tool	O
Rectangle tool	R
Pencil tool	Y
Brush tool	B
Ink Bottle tool	S
Paint Bucket tool	K
Dropper tool	I
Eraser tool	E
Hand tool	H
Zoom tool	M, Z

 Tip   You can activate the Hand tool at any time, by pressing the spacebar. Your mouse will change to the Hand tool. Let go of the spacebar and the Hand tool disappears.

Using the Zoom Feature

There are various techniques for changing the view of objects on your Stage. You will find that these techniques are very useful when you need to really fine-tune an image or graphic. You can zoom in on the entire shape or just a part of it. With this increased magnification, you can edit the image with precision. You can also zoom out from your Stage to view the entire Stage and all items on it.

Zooming In on the Stage

Use your zoom control in the lower-left corner of the Flash application window to change your magnification view of the Stage. To view your Stage at a 100% magnification, you can click the arrow on the zoom control and click **100%** from the menu list (see Figure 3.11). To have your Stage fit within your monitor display, click the arrow on the zoom control and click **Show Frame** from the menu list. Your Stage will be proportioned to display fully on your monitor screen.

Figure 3.11

The zoom control option allows you to zoom in or out on your Stage.

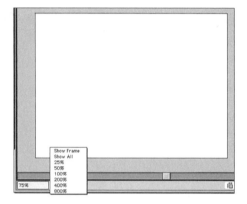

 Tip   You can change views by using menu commands. Choose **View**, **Magnification**, **100%** menu command to change to a 100% magnification view of your Stage or choose **View**, **Magnification**, **Show Frame** to display your Stage fully on your screen.

 **Tip**   You can also enter a number in the zoom control box to access any magnification at which you want your Stage to display. This provides the flexibility you need to attain any magnification view.

 Tip   Use (Cmd-3) on a Mac or [Ctrl+3] on a PC to quickly display your movie so it fits to your monitor size.

Tip If you select your Hand tool, you can click and drag on your Stage area to move to a new location or view of the Stage.

Zooming In and Out on an Object

By using your Zoom tool, you can zoom in on an object on your Stage or work area. Select the Zoom tool and, when you move your mouse within the Stage area, notice that your mouse cursor has changed to a magnifying glass icon with a plus sign in the middle of it. Move your cursor over the object on your Stage where you want to zoom in and click your mouse button. You will double your magnification view of the object. If you want to zoom in more, click your mouse again on the object. Repeat this process until you have the magnification you want.

Just as you learn how to zoom in on an object, you can also zoom out in magnification view. Select the Zoom tool and move your mouse onto the Stage. Then hold down your (Option) key on a Mac or your [Alt] key on a PC. Notice that your magnifying glass icon representing the Zoom tool changes to a magnifying glass with a minus sign in the middle of it. Click on the Stage area or on the object that you want to zoom out of and you will decrease your magnification by double its present setting.

 Tip You can designate a certain area that you want to zoom in or out of by selecting the Zoom tool and setting the zoom out or zoom in setting by using the minus or plus sign. Then click and drag a selection rectangle or marquee around the area that you want to view in a different magnification.

Panels

A new feature of Flash 5 is the use of panels for commonly used Flash features. When you first launch Flash 5, you will see four panels that are set as the default layout panels (see Figure 3.12). These panels are free floating and can be rearranged anywhere on your screen. You can also close them by clicking the close button on the panel title bar.

Default layout panels

Figure 3.12

If you click the associated panel icon from the Launch Bar, you will close that default layout panel.

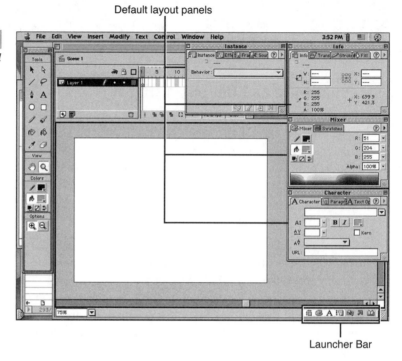

Launcher Bar

Launcher Bar

A new feature of Flash 5 is the Launcher Bar. You will find this bar in the lower-right corner of your Flash application window (see Figure 3.13). This bar allows you to launch panels and features that are frequently used in Flash. This feature also makes Flash as consistent in its operation as that of other Macromedia products that have this same feature.

You can activate any of the Launcher Bar features by clicking the appropriate icon. After the icon is clicked, you will launch a panel. Click the icon again to hide the displayed panel. The Launcher Bar icons are toggle switches.

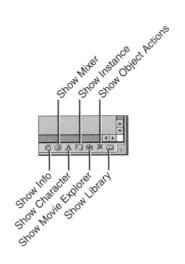

Figure 3.13

You can quickly access commonly used commands and panels with the Launcher Bar.

Where You've Been!

This chapter covered the Flash workspace. You have been introduced to the Timeline, layers, panels, the Stage, your work area, and the toolbox. You've learned how to set your movie's properties for the Whirlwind Adventure Travel Web site. You have also learned how to increase or decrease your view of the Stage and items on the Stage. You should now feel more comfortable with the Flash workspace and have started your project. You should have a Flash file saved on your local hard drive called whirlwind.fla.

What's Next?

In the next chapter, you will begin to plan your Whirlwind Adventure Travel Web site. You will create a storyboard for the flow of the site, as well as identify the architecture and layout of the site. You will locate all graphics and images that will be used. Upon completion of the next chapter, you will have a plan and structure to follow for building the Whirlwind Adventure Travel Web site!

In this chapter

- *Planning for a Web-Delivered Flash Movie*
- *Creating a Storyboard and Branching Diagram of Web Site*
- *Planning Your Scenes*
- *Flash and Other HTML Editors and Graphics Programs*

Chapter 4

Planning Your Travel Company Web Site

Traditional Web project-planning techniques are a must when using Flash to create a Web site. You first need to start by defining the project. Gather your initial information from your clients. What are their goals for the Web site, what do they want to accomplish with the site? Many clients have no experience with the Web and need to be educated about what can and cannot be presented through the Internet. It is your job to help your clients understand the process of creation, implementation, and maintenance of the Web site. The following is a summary of this book's project.

Introduction to the Whirlwind Adventure Travel Company

This book's project is building a Web site for a travel agency. The company's name is Whirlwind Adventure Travel. They specialize in International airfares, group travel, honeymoons, and adventure tours. They also have a unique network of accommodations within many countries. These are the areas that they want to promote in their Web site. As they explain, the travel industry is extremely competitive and they are seeing profits dip because of the competition. They need another avenue for advertising their services. They want a Web site that is user friendly to navigate, very catchy, and that showcases their specialties. The site needs to enable customers to communicate concerns, travel plans, and customer experiences. They want to promote themselves above the traditional travel agencies, airlines, and Internet travel sites. They feel that a Web site with a focus on specialties that go above and beyond the national round-trip flights can accomplish this. What they want to sell is their experience and expertise in other countries throughout the world, as well as the network of accommodations that they also offer in select countries. Their staff is highly traveled and knowledgeable about other countries, cities, and customs. This is their distinction in the industry and they want this communicated to the general public. Your job is to create a Web site for Whirlwind Adventure Travel that will meet their expectations!

This chapter covers the process for planning your project. Even though examples of planning documents are provided on the CD-ROM in the Chapter 4 folder, you will want to follow the instruction and create these documents yourself. These planning steps are a must for all Web sites that you plan to build.

Some of the skills required to create the planning documents are covered in more detail later in this book. If you are re-creating the documents in Flash for planning your Web site, you might want to refer to these chapters as you work through this chapter. You can also use other software applications for creating these documents.

Identifying Your Project Team

Now that you have talked with the client and gathered the initial information that they want to include on their site, you need to identify your project team. This might be just yourself, with you assuming all roles for creation and delivery of the site. Or this might be you working with or overseeing a team of individuals for creation of the site. The team might be made up of a project or account manager to oversee the project, a graphic design department for creation of site design and all graphics, and a Web development department that controls implementing the design into HTML code for browser viewing. Whether you are the team or you are working with a group of talented people, delivery of any site is closely linked with your or the client's Internet service provider (ISP) for the hosting services required for the site. Does your ISP have the server-side applications required to deliver your Web site content to the public? Establishing a relationship with your ISP will help you in many of the areas required for Web development.

Identifying Your Software

You next need to identify the software to use for creation of the Web site. Whirlwind Adventure Travel wants a catchy site and you decide that Flash fits this bill. Now you need to consider the functionality of Flash and how it lends itself to the Whirlwind Adventure Travel site. This includes

- Thinking through the delivery method—Internet-delivered in the Whirlwind Adventure Travel Company case
- Planning your Web site architecture
- Deciding on the scenes that you want to use in the Web site
- Deciding on the design and graphics to be used in the site
- Identifying other applications that you will need to use to help pull the Web site together

All these areas need to be considered before you begin to build your Flash Web site.

Creating the Scope of the Project Plan

After gathering and determining the preceding information, develop a creative brief or scope of the project plan. This document covers the preliminary planning required to begin development of the Web site. Create this document at the beginning of the project. It includes all the milestones or checkpoints from start to finish through the Web site development process. These milestones help guide all parties involved with the creation of the site. The client can see progress both visually as the site develops and on paper as milestones or checkpoints are achieved. The client and all people involved in the project need to sign off on this document. This ensures that everyone is on the same page with the site creation and implementation. You are crossing your *t*'s and dotting the *i*'s with this document. This chapter will guide you through the process of creating this document.

Delivery Method: Browsers or Offline Presentations

Through careful consideration, identify the delivery method for the project. We know that you are developing this Web site for Internet delivery. Now you need to consider the various end-users that will access the site. Identify the average audience that will view your site—will they be more of a corporate audience or home-based user? With what types of connection speeds will the majority of users access your site? Will they have the latest in browsers or will this vary from user to user. In the case of the Whirlwind Adventure Travel Company, most of the audience will be home-based. You cannot assume that they will have the latest browsers but probably will be using many versions of the popular browsers. They probably will connect at an average of a 28.8K modem speed, with some having a faster connection. The more you focus your site on these factors and the more precisely defined your target audience is, the more efficiently and effectively you can present the information. These considerations help you identify the *development goals* of your site.

Because you have identified that your audience is home-based with slower Internet connection speeds, we now know that you need to design and develop the Web site compromising between download speed and special effects. Simpler graphics must be presented in the site. This means limited gradient fills and *shape morphs* of a shape into another shape (if you use them at all), developing the site for a 12fps (frame per second) frame rate, limited use of animated layers, sound, and imported bitmapped graphics. Very detailed drawings or complex images should not be used much in the site either. These design considerations will keep the site size low and allow for quick downloads on a 28.8K modem.

Defining Site Layout

A standard planning technique of traditional Web development is to create a site layout document. This document is a branching diagram that shows all pages of a Web site. It is organized to show the relationship between one page and another. This document resembles a flow chart. You can use Flash to create this document. Think through the client's needs and the specialty areas of their company and let that guide your branching diagram. See Figure 4.1 for an illustration of a possible diagram for the Whirlwind Adventure Travel site.

Figure 4.1

This very simple site layout document focuses on only the first two page levels for this project Web site.

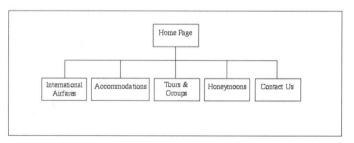

The branching diagram gives you a quick visual reference of the project without having to do any construction of pages in the site. Because you might work on multiple sites at one time, the branching diagram also offers an easy way to refamiliarize yourself with the site after a period of time has elapsed since you last worked on your project.

Working with the Rectangle Tool and Options

To create the branching diagram, you need to begin using some of the Flash tools, in particular the Rectangle, Line, and Text tools. When you set these tools with the desired settings, you will need to work between the toolbox and panels. On the toolbox, click the Rectangle tool. Notice that the Options area of the toolbar has changed to the Rectangle tool options. Then open the Stroke panel by choosing **Window**, **Panels**, **Stroke** (see Figure 4.2).

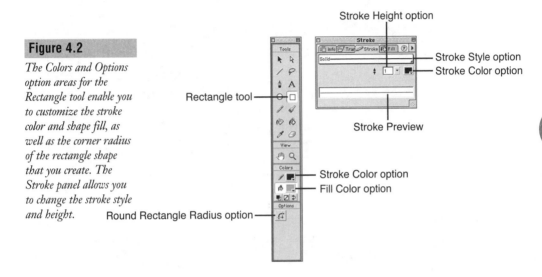

Figure 4.2

The Colors and Options option areas for the Rectangle tool enable you to customize the stroke color and shape fill, as well as the corner radius of the rectangle shape that you create. The Stroke panel allows you to change the stroke style and height.

Stroke Height option
Stroke Style option
Stroke Color option
Rectangle tool
Stroke Preview
Stroke Color option
Fill Color option
Round Rectangle Radius option

To set your rectangle options, follow these steps:

1. Before you start to draw any rectangles, you need to set the Rectangle tool options. To set the fill color, click the Fill Color option on the toolbox to display the color palette and click the black color chip in the upper-left corner (see Figure 4.3).

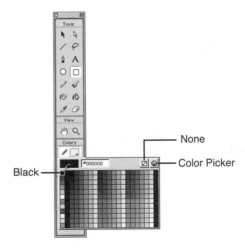

Figure 4.3

You can select None for the fill color by clicking the white outlined chip in the upper-right corner of the color palette.

None
Color Picker
Black

Tip

A new feature of Flash 5 is the Color Picker (see Figure 4.4). This feature is available only on the Macintosh platform. When this icon is clicked it, launches a dialog box that enables you to set any color through the various color options displayed in the left-hand scrolling list of the dialog box.

Figure 4.4

The Color Picker dialog box allows you to select colors through CMYK Picker, HLS Picker, HSV Picker, HTML Picker, and RGB.

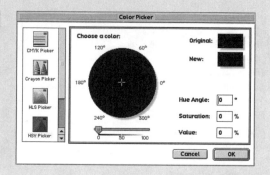

 Tip

If you are using a PC-based machine and click the Color Picker button for the color palette, you will access the standard Color Picker for Windows.

2. Next set your Stroke Thickness option. From the Stroke panel, click the arrow next to the Stroke Thickness option box and drag the disk so that the number option 1 displays in the Stroke Thickness option box (see Figure 4.5). You want to use a solid line for the rectangle. Click the Stroke Style option from the Stroke panel and click the Solid style from the menu list.

Figure 4.5

The Stroke Preview displays your menu choices.

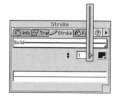

3. Setting the fill color for your rectangle is the same process as setting your line color. Click the Fill Color option on the toolbox to display the color palette and click the None color chip. Your Rectangle option settings should look like Figure 4.6.

Figure 4.6

You can set your rectangle to have rounded corners by clicking the Rounded Rectangle Radius option on the toolbox and selecting the radius setting that you want.

Tip

You can also click the Fill Color option on the toolbox. Then click the None button directly under the Colors area of the toolbox. This also changes the Fill Color option to None (see Figure 4.7).

Figure 4.7

You can return the toolbox Colors area to the default colors of black and white by clicking the Default Stroke and Fill button.

Default Stroke and Fill button
None button
Swap Stroke and Fill button

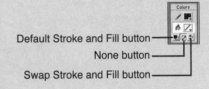

4. Position your mouse on the Stage and notice that it is now a crosshair, not an arrow. Click and drag from left to right at a diagonal direction. You will begin to create a rectangle (see Figure 4.8).

Figure 4.8

You can create a rectangle or square by pulling at a diagonal direction from left to right or right to the left.

5. If you want to create a box to a set dimension, you need to turn on your rulers. Click the **View, Rulers** menu command to display the rulers and then, using the rulers as your guide, create a box that is about 1.5 inches wide by 1 inch tall. If you make a mistake, you can undo your rectangle by choosing **Edit, Undo**.

You can undo a series of actions by activating the Undo command over and over. You can set your number of undo levels through the **Edit, Preferences** menu command. The maximum number you can set is 300 undo levels (see Figure 4.9).

Figure 4.9

The Preferences dialog box General tab allows you to set your Undo levels as well as the selection options. Other highlight and Timeline options are also available.

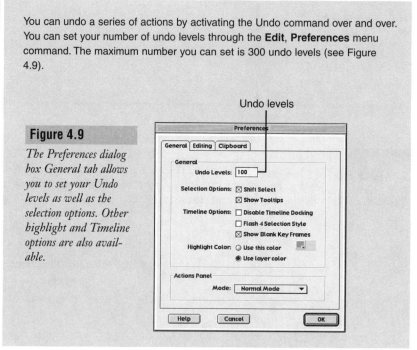

If you set 300 Undo levels, you need to have at least 128MB of RAM installed in your machine. Your computer will use any available RAM for remembering the number of actions that you perform; if you do not have enough RAM, this setting will not work correctly.

→ For more information on the Preferences dialog box, **see** Chapter 5, "Creating and Editing Graphics for the Travel Company Web Site," **p. 93**, and Chapter 9, "Using Layers to Organize the Movie," **p. 197**.

Creating Text

Now that you have a rectangle drawn, you need to add text to label the branching diagram box. This chapter will cover just the basics of creating text. Follow these steps to create your text for the branching diagram:

1. Select the Text tool from the toolbox.

2. Set your Fill Color option to black by clicking the Fill Color option and selecting the black color chip from the color palette (see Figure 4.10).

Figure 4.10

You can set the Text option attributes by clicking the option and selecting an option from the list.

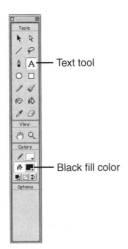

Text tool

Black fill color

4

3. Position your cursor on the Stage and notice that it is now a crosshair with an A in the lower-right corner, indicating the Text tool is the current tool. Click and drag a text block within the rectangle. Don't worry if it is not centered; you will take care of that next.

4. Now that you have a text box started, you can enter text. Type Home Page and Home Page appears in the rectangle (see Figure 4.11).

Figure 4.11

Since you did not designate the font type or size, it appears in the default font settings.

→ For more detailed instruction on how to create and modify text in Flash, **see** Chapter 7, "Using Text in Flash," **p. 153**.

Using the Arrow Tool

After you have created text inside a shape as we just did with the rectangle, you might need to center it within the rectangle. To do this click the Arrow tool in the toolbox and then click the text block. You will see a rectangular outline around the text. This means that the text box is active. Click and drag so that it appears more centered in your rectangle box.

If you wanted to move the rectangle instead of the text box, the process is a little more difficult than selecting and moving text. Because of the way Flash recognizes lines and shapes, you need to double-click the outline of the rectangle to select the shape. If you single-click a line of a rectangle, you will select just that line segment of the rectangle. This is because of the way lines interact with each other when they intersect.

→ For more detailed instruction on how lines and shapes interact with each other in Flash, **see** Chapter 5, "Creating and Editing Graphics for the Travel Company Web Site," **p. 93**.

Using the preceding process for creating rectangles and text, create the other branching diagram boxes representing the Whirlwind Adventure Travel Web site. Use Figure 4.1 as a reference. Remember, if you make a mistake, simply undo it using the **Edit**, **Undo** command; the keyboard shortcut for this command is (Cmd-Z) on a Mac and [Ctrl+Z] on a PC.

 Tip

> You can move any shape a pixel at a time by selecting the shape and then pressing the arrow keys on your keyboard. If you want to move an object eight pixels at a time, hold the Shift key down while pressing an arrow key.

Working with the Line Tool and Options

You should have your branching boxes with text laid out to show two levels for a Web site. Now you need to draw the connecting lines between the boxes to show the flow of the site. You can do this by using your Line tool from the toolbox and opening your Stroke panel. Click the Line tool to select it and then choose **Window**, **Panels, Stroke**. Your toolbox changes to display the option attributes of the Line tool, and the Stroke panel reflects the various line option attributes that you can set for a line (see Figure 4.12).

Keep the default line options as shown earlier in Figure 4.10 and move your cursor onto the Stage. Notice that your mouse is now a crosshair. Position your cursor underneath the Home Page branching box. Click and drag a line so that it connects with the Tours & Groups branching box (see Figure 4.13).

Stroke Height option

Figure 4.12

You can select the Line tool by pressing the N key on your keyboard.

Stroke Style option ——

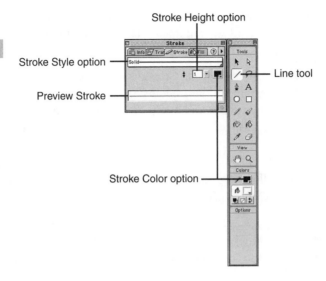

—— Line tool

Preview Stroke ——

Stroke Color option ——

New line

Figure 4.13

You can constrain the line to be perfectly vertical or horizontal by holding down the Shift key as you create the line.

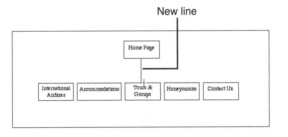

Repeat this process to create the branching diagram by creating the other lines to show the relationship between the Home Page and the second-level pages of the Whirlwind Adventure Travel Web site. Your finished branching diagram should resemble Figure 4.1, which you saw earlier. Save this document as `Branching.fla` in the folder that you created for your Whirlwind Adventure Travel Web site.

➔ For more detailed instruction on how to use the Flash toolbox and tools for creating boxes, text, and lines, and for more instructions on moving items on the Stage, **see** Chapter 5, "Creating and Editing Graphics for the Travel Company Web Site," **p. 93**.

Defining Page Architecture

After you define the site layout, you next need to establish what the page architecture will look like. The page architecture is a design and navigation layout for each page. You're beginning to diagram how each section of the site will look. Using the site layout document that you just created, it is easy to see that you will need to have five buttons for each page: International Airfares, Accommodations, Tours/Groups, Honeymoons, and Contact Us.

Because the client wants a catchy site, using a design on the home page that incorporates a Flash animation will be a good start at adding some flare to the Web site. This page also allows access to all other pages on the site, as well as gives a brief description of the specialty areas of the Whirlwind Adventure Travel Company. The travel company uses the colors of forest green and light yellow for their logo and corporate identity. These colors need to be integrated into the page architecture. You will set a light yellow color for the background color of the movie. Figure 4.14 shows an example of the home page architecture. You will create this page shortly.

Figure 4.14

This figure represents the page architecture of the travel company's home page. The labeled boxes across the bottom represent navigation buttons.

→ For more detailed instruction on how to set the background color of your Stage, **see** Chapter 3, "Introduction to the Flash Workspace," **p. 43**.

The second level of pages representing the specialty areas of the travel company will be similar in design to the home page but different in some aspects. You want to use a color scheme that distinguishes each of the specialty areas. This helps the visitor to visually know that they are in a certain area. Many designers quickly sketch ideas for the page architecture. Because Flash is ideal for doodling and concept presentation, use it to create the page architecture. Figure 4.15 is an example of the page architecture of the second-level pages of the site. The table below details the color scheme that you will use for each of the pages. You will create these pages in the next section.

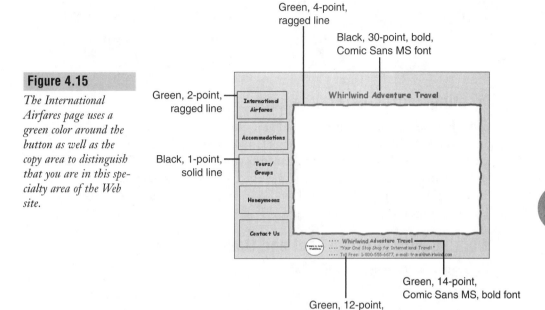

Green, 4-point,
ragged line

Black, 30-point, bold,
Comic Sans MS font

Green, 2-point,
ragged line

Black, 1-point,
solid line

Green, 14-point,
Comic Sans MS, bold font

Green, 12-point,
Comic Sans MS font

Figure 4.15

*The International
Airfares page uses a
green color around the
button as well as the
copy area to distinguish
that you are in this spe-
cialty area of the Web
site.*

Table 4.1 outlines the color scheme to be created for the other second-level pages.
Use Figure 4.15 as a reference on where to apply these formats to the page features.

Table 4.1   Color Scheme for Second-Level Pages

Second-Level Page	Color Scheme
Accommodations	2-point, blue, ragged line around button
	4-point, blue, ragged line around Stage area
	Fonts same as in Figure 4.15
Tours/Groups	2-point, red, ragged line around button
	4-point, red, ragged line around Stage area
	Fonts same as in Figure 4.15
Honeymoons	2-point, purple, ragged line around button
	4-point, purple, ragged line around Stage area
	Fonts same as in Figure 4.15
Contact Us	2-point, aqua, ragged line around button
	4-point, aqua, ragged line around Stage area
	Fonts same as in Figure 4.15

Note

Based on the information in Table 4.1, you must apply attributes to text. This has not been covered in this chapter but you can see Chapter 7, "Using Text in Flash," for more information on setting text attributes if you're having trouble.

Creating Your Page Architecture

Using Figures 4.1, 4.14, and 4.15 as a guide, you now will create your page architecture diagrams. Begin by opening a new Flash document. Open your Movie Properties dialog box by choosing the **Modify** menu and selecting **Movie**. Set the background color to light yellow and the Stage size to 650×500 pixels. Notice that the example home page in Figure 4.14 uses a circle to represent the company logo. The next section covers how to create a circle or an oval.

Working with the Oval Tool and Options

To create a circle, follow these steps:

1. Click the Oval tool in the toolbox to select it. You should have the Stroke panel open; if not, choose the **Window**, **Panels**, **Stroke** menu command to display it. You can work between the toolbox and the Stroke panel for setting the Oval tool options.

2. Change the fill color to None by clicking the None button in the Colors area of the toolbox (see Figure 4.16).

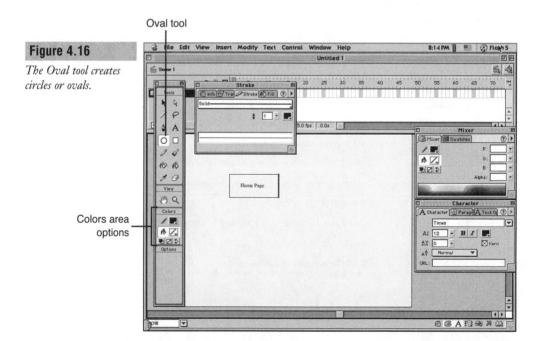

Figure 4.16

The Oval tool creates circles or ovals.

3. Move your mouse onto the Stage and position it in the middle of the Stage. Click and drag a circle about the same size as shown in Figure 4.14. If you need to, reposition the circle by double-clicking the line to select it and move it to the position you want.

Tip

To make a perfect circle, hold the Shift key down before you begin to create the circle. This constrains the oval to a perfect circle.

Next you need to create the company information inside the oval. To create the company logo object, follow these steps:

1. Click the Text tool from the toolbox and create a text block with the words `Company Logo, World Globe` in it. Use a paragraph break between Company Logo and World Globe so that they appear on separate lines.

2. Open your Paragraph panel by choosing **Window**, **Panels**, **Paragraph**. Highlight all text in the text block to select it and then click the center option from the Paragraph panel. This will center all text in the text block.

3. Click the Arrow tool and center the text block in the circle (see Figure 4.17).

Figure 4.17

The Oval tool creates circles or ovals.

Work with the Line, Text, Rectangle, and Oval tools to create the shapes representing the objects for the home page. When your diagram resembles Figure 4.14, save it under the name of `pa_home.fla` in the project folder you've created.

Create a new Flash document for each second-level page, and use Figures 4.1 and 4.15 as a guide to create the page architecture for each page in the Whirlwind Adventure Travel Web site. Save the pages as `pa_airfare.fla`, `pa_accommodations.fla`, `pa_tours.fla`, `pa_honeymoons.fla`, and `pa_contact.fla` in the folder for your Web site files.

→ For more detailed instruction on how to use the Flash toolbar and tools for creating shapes, text, and lines, **see** Chapter 5, "Creating and Editing Graphics for the Travel Company Web Site," **p. 93**.

Storyboarding Your Ideas

After you have a branching diagram, your page layout for the site, and an architecture design, you can begin to *storyboard* your animation and ideas for the Web site. Storyboarding is very beneficial for planning the interactivity and animation flow of your site. Storyboarding is the process of visually detailing the interactivity and action that is to occur on each page. Because the client's company name is Whirlwind Adventure Travel, you might come up with the idea of having the company name fly into the screen and swirl around on the Stage, coming to rest at the top of the page as a header. This type of animation will be low in file size and very visually enticing for the end-user. You also want to have some animation with your buttons that link to the second-level pages. You want to have a short description of each button and to have the linking page content appear on the home page so that the visitor knows the content of each area of the Web site.

Another strategy that you want to use in the site is the *drag-and-drop movie clip* feature of Flash. You plan on using this on the Accommodations page of the site. These drag-and-drop movie clips allow the end-user to drag a continent into a specific location on the Accommodations page to set criteria indicating that they want to select this continent for possible vacation accommodations. You will also create a panoramic 360° movie for the Tours/Groups page. All of these special effects will work well for an Internet-delivered Web site.

➜ To learn more about the drag-and-drop feature, **see** Chapter 16, "Creating the Accommodations Page," **p 339**.

You want to develop your storyboards to relay the flow of the animation and interactivity of the site. This will allow further direction for the development of the site, as well as to visually communicate the animation used in the site to the client. Flash handles storyboarding very well. To use this feature you need to set up *keyframes* for each storyboard that you want to present.

➜ For a description of storyboarding and how it is used in Flash, **see** Chapter 1, "Why Use Flash?," **p. 9**.

Setting Up a Storyboarding Document

To create storyboards, begin by opening a new Flash document using the **File**, **New** menu command. Open the Movie Properties dialog box, set the movie dimensions to 650×500 pixels, and change the background color to a light yellow color. You will use this new document to create your storyboards for each page of the Web site.

The following Figures 4.18–4.23 represent the storyboards for the Whirlwind Adventure Travel Web site that you will create in the next set of instruction. Notice that there are new keyframes in the Timeline. You will learn how to create these keyframes next.

Figure 4.18 illustrates the interactivity for the home page of the Whirlwind Adventure Travel company. This storyboard illustrates the movement of the Whirlwind Adventure Travel text across the screen. The animated buttons are called out as well.

First keyframe

Figure 4.18

Storyboard for the home page for the Whirlwind Adventure Travel animation.

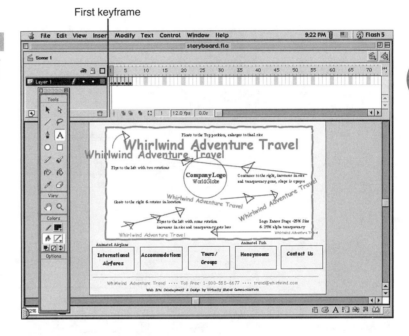

 The storyboard for the International Airfares page shows a *static page*. A static page has no animation or Stage movement on it. You will just develop the architecture and page layout on this page (see Figure 4.19). You can create a list of airfares if you like for this page, but, for the purposes of this book's project, we will not cover more than developing the layout and making sure the page links to the movie and to other second-level pages.

The storyboard for the Accommodations page shows the complex functionality of the drag-and-drop interactivity (see Figure 4.20). Chapter 16 "Creating the Accommodations Page," covers the development of the Accommodations page. This page is complex in its functionality. You will learn how to create the drag-and-drop technology that allows the end-user to interact with the movie, and Chapter 16 also covers general information on how to connect this technology to a back-end database. Again, database connectivity is beyond the scope of this book but you will learn how to create the front-end interface that can be linked into a back-end database.

Second keyframe

Figure 4.19

The storyboard for the International Airfares page shows that the page contains no special effects or animation—it is a static page.

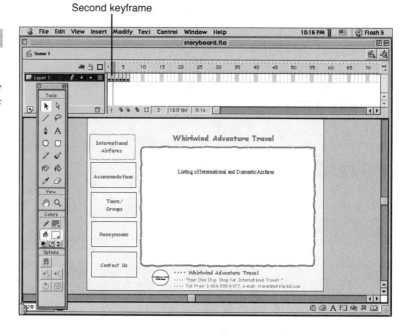

Third keyframe

Figure 4.20

The storyboard for the Accommodations page shows how the drag-and-drop feature of Flash is used for locating an accommodation in a specified country.

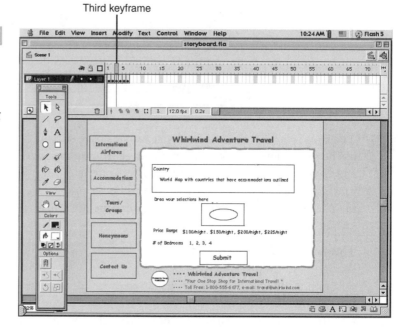

The storyboard for the Tours/Groups page has some interactivity that you will create in Chapter 17, "Next Steps with Flash." You will develop the architecture and page layout on this page, as well as create a panoramic 360° movie for the end-user to explore (see Figure 4.21). You will need to make sure the page links to the movie and to other second-level pages.

Fourth keyframe

Figure 4.21

The storyboard for the Tours/Groups page shows the panoramic 360° movie that you will create for this page.

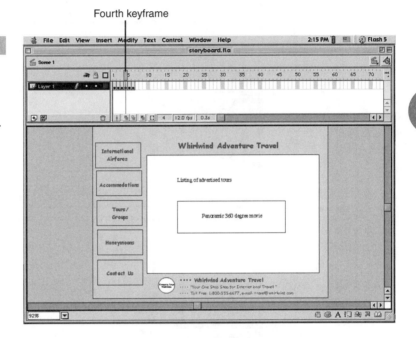

4

The storyboard for the Honeymoons page shows a static page. You will just develop the architecture and page layout on this page (see Figure 4.22). You can create a list of Honeymoon destinations for this page, but as with the other static pages, this book will not cover more than developing the layout and making sure the page links to the movie and to other second-level pages so we can have more time for the fun stuff.

Forms allow for communications to be transferred from the end-user to Webmaster or any other designated personnel of a company. The storyboard for the Contact Us page will illustrate a form used for collecting end-user data (see Figure 4.23). Chapter 15, "Creating the Contact Us Form for the Web Site," covers how to create a form in Flash. You will use editable text blocks to create the front-end interface for this form. Again, the connectivity issues will vary from reader to reader based on the server configuration; therefore, this chapter only covers creating the front-end interface and general steps on how to link it to the server.

Fifth keyframe

Figure 4.22

The storyboard for the Honeymoons page has no special effects or animation.

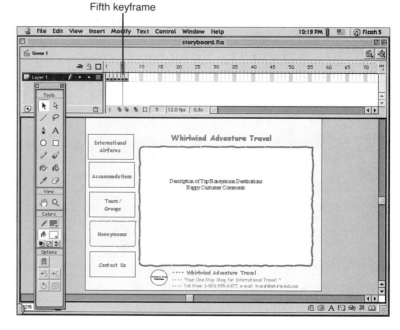

Sixth keyframe

Figure 4.23

The storyboard for the Contact Us page shows no special effects or animation but indicates that a form will be developed.

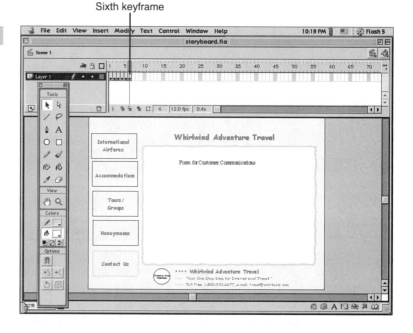

Creating the Home Page Storyboard

Using Figure 4.18 as a guide, add comments, doodles, and references to what the animation or special effects will be for that page using the Line, Text, Rectangle and Oval tools. If you need to move a line, use your Arrow tool. At this point, you might find that it is easier to undo a mistake and re-create the information than to try and fix it.

 Tip

You can select all the contents on your `pa_home.fla` file, and copy and paste the contents on your new storyboard document. To select all objects on your Stage, choose the **Edit**, **Select All** menu command. Notice that all items on the Stage become active. Then select the **Edit**, **Copy** menu command to copy this active object. Switch to your new Flash document and choose **Edit**, **Paste in Place** to paste all selected items from the `pa_home.fla` movie into your new movie in the same location that they were in the `pa_home.fla` movie. The **Paste in Place** command is a very useful command.

→ For a more detailed instruction on creating and editing graphics, **see** Chapter 5, "Creating and Editing Graphics for the Travel Company Web Site," **p. 93**.

Creating the Second-Level Page Storyboards

To create a second storyboard for showing another page of the Web site with the animation and special effects illustrated, you need to insert a blank keyframe into the Timeline of your storyboard document. Click in the second *photoframe* of the Timeline (see Figure 4.24).

Selected photoframe

Figure 4.24

Use your mouse to select a blank photoframe in the Timeline.

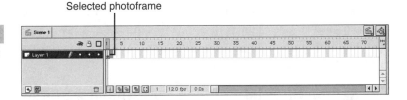

With the second photoframe highlighted, choose the **Insert**, **Blank Keyframe** menu command to insert a blank keyframe in the Timeline (see Figure 4.25).

Blank keyframe

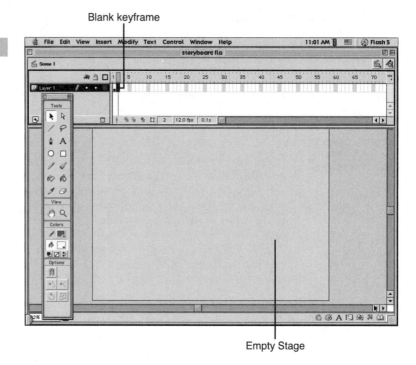

Figure 4.25

Inserting a blank keyframe in the Timeline allows you to create new content for the Stage.

Empty Stage

A new keyframe is added to the Timeline. Notice that your Stage is blank.

Using Figure 4.19 as a guide, create a storyboard for the International Airfares page of the Web site. Create the objects and information for this page on the blank Stage area.

Repeat the "Creating the Second-Level Page Storyboards" process for all additional pages that you want to storyboard your ideas. Insert a blank keyframe for each new storyboard. Use Figures 4.20–4.23 as a guide for these pages. When you have all keyframes with Stage content developed, save this storyboard document as `storyboard.fla`.

Setting Up Print Settings for Printing a Storyboard Document

After you have your storyboarding document set up, you need to set the print options for printing this document. Choose the (**File, Print Margins**)[**File, Page Setup**] menu command and the Print Margins dialog box displays.

Flash offers many different layout options for printing your storyboard document. Change the Frames option by clicking the drop-down menu and selecting **All Frames**. This will print out all the keyframes and their Stage content in the story-board document. You can enter a new number for the number of frames to print across the page in the Frames Across option. Click the drop-down menu for the **Layout** option and select **Storyboard-Boxes** to print a border around all story-boards. This causes other options to display. For the Frames Across option set this setting to 3. Your dialog box should resemble Figure 4.26.

Figure 4.26

You also can set your margins for printing a document in the Print Margins (Macintosh) or Page Setup (Windows) dialog box.

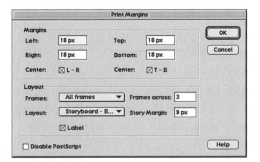

4

 Tip

You can print storyboards in their actual sizes by choosing **Actual Size** from the **Layout** option drop-down menu. You can print storyboards to fit all on one page by choosing **Fit On One Page** from the **Layout** option drop-down menu. You can also print all storyboards with a grid separating them by choosing **Storyboard—Grid** from the **Layout** drop-down menu. If you want to print all storyboards without any boxes or grids separating them, choose **Storyboard—Blank** from the **Layout** option drop-down menu.

Storyboarding your ideas will help guide the Web-site–development process and provide visual guidance to all parties involved in the development process.

Identifying Graphics

Before you begin to develop your Web site, you will need to gather your content material. This means locating your graphics and the copy to be used in the Web site. You can usually count on your client to provide the company logo, font, company information to be used as the copy, and colors. They will also provide graphics or images in some format, either digital or hardcopy. Your job is to convert these files into a Web graphic format. You probably will need to supplement the client graphics with other images or clip art to use in the site. The next stage of planning your Web site involves locating all files that you think you will be using in the site.

 In the case of Whirlwind Adventure Travel, they have a globe logo that has been scanned and will need to be converted to vector format and colorized for the site. You will find a copy of this scanned graphic on the CD-ROM that accompanies this book in the Chapter 4 folder. It is called globe.pic (Macintosh) or globe.bmp (Windows). Their corporate colors are a light yellow and a forest green. This is what you have to begin working with. You also have some *movie clip* images to work with. You will create some of the graphics from scratch. Flash also ships with preset *Libraries* of buttons and sounds that you will use in your Web site.

It is always a good idea to keep a copy of all original files in a separate folder when you develop a Web site. This allows you to keep them in the original format and hopefully in a higher resolution than the file you will be creating of them for the Web site. All Web graphics display at a resolution of 72dpi (dots per inch) no matter what resolution you save them in. If you make any mistakes or need to re-create a graphic, you can do this with ease, because you have the original file. Set up a Source Graphic folder on your hard drive in an appropriate location for holding the source graphics for this project.

Using Libraries for Your Graphics, Movie Clips, Buttons, and Sounds

The Libraries that ship with Flash are useful. They provide many examples of buttons and sounds, which can be used in any of your projects or Web sites. You will use some of the sounds that come in the Sound Library that ships with Flash 5 for the travel company Web site. To open this library, choose **Window**, **Common Libraries**, **Sounds**. This opens the Library of sounds that ships with Flash. We will use three sounds from this library in Chapter 12, "Attaching Actions and Sounds to the Buttons and Frames." You can close this Sounds Library when you are finished exploring it.

→ For more information on Libraries, **see** Chapter 8, "Using Symbols, Libraries, and Instances to Recycle and Organize Graphic Elements," **p. 177**.

You will also use another library that ships with Flash—the Movie Clip library. To open this Library choose **Window, Common Libraries, Movie Clips**. From this library, locate the Biplane movie clip symbol represented by the icon with a tie-dye–like symbol. Click this symbol. The Biplane image displays in the preview window of the Library (see Figure 4.27). Also note that you have a control panel in the preview window. Click the play button and watch the plane animate. This movie clip will work great for our International Airfares button.

Figure 4.27

The Biplane movie clip is a preset animation of a plane with a rotating propeller.

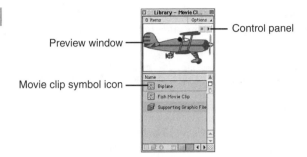

Control panel

Preview window

Movie clip symbol icon

4

Also located in this Library is an item called Supporting Graphic Files. This is a folder that contains all the supporting graphics for each of the movie clips listed above the folder in the Library. Double-click the folder to open it. Locate the Fish Graphic contained in this folder (see Figure 4.28).

Figure 4.28

All the Fish graphics in the Supporting Graphics Files folder are used in the Fish Movie Clip listed above the folder in the Movie Clip Library.

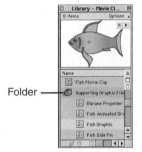

Folder

This movie clip would be nice to use for the Honeymoons button. It represents exotic places that most people go to for their honeymoons.

Graphics to Be Drawn from Scratch

To learn the drawing features of Flash, you will create two button graphics: the Accommodations button and the Tours/Groups button. Because you are creating these files in Flash, they will automatically be vector graphics.

Scanned Photos and Other Graphics

Whirlwind Adventure Travel has a logo of the world that they want to use in the Web site. It is given to you in a bitmapped format. It was a hand drawn image that they had scanned to create a digital format file. You will find this file in two formats: globe.pic for Macintosh and globe.bmp for Windows in the Chapter 4 and Chapter 6 folders on the CD-ROM that accompanies this book. You need to convert this image into a vector graphic through Flash and then colorize it to match the rest of the site's content. Locate this file on the CD-ROM in Chapter 4 and copy it into your Source Graphic folder on your hard drive, which you set up earlier.

Planning Scenes: Travel Company Web Site Components

Scenes are a part of Flash that allow you to organize a movie thematically. You will use scenes to organize the Whirlwind Adventure Travel Web site into the various areas of focus: Home Page, Accommodations, International Airfares, Tours/Groups, Honeymoons, and Contact Us.

Movie Home Page

From the branching diagram, the page architecture and the storyboards that you developed for planning your project, you have a good direction on what will be presented on the home page. This will be the first scene of your movie. It presents the first introduction to the Whirlwind Adventure Travel company. We have already identified that you will be animating the company name in this scene. The buttons presented on this page will link to the other five areas of the site. These five areas are the other scenes used within the Flash movie. Your prior planning has given you the direction needed for developing these scenes.

Five Sublevels: Accommodations, International Airfares, Tours/Groups, Honeymoons, and Contact Us

From the home page, you will create links to the second level of the Web site (see Figure 4.29). As your branching diagram shows, these levels focus on the specialty services that Whirlwind Adventure Travel offers. As you develop the Web site, these areas of focus will be scenes within the movie.

Components of the International Airfares Page

This page or scene presents International airfares on a weekly and monthly basis (see Figure 4.30). It is static in nature and simply lists that week's/month's special. The visitor is encouraged to contact a sales representative at Whirlwind Adventure Travel for more information on a flight. You need to create a simple layout for the information so that it can be updated easily on a weekly or monthly basis.

Figure 4.29

This is an example of the Home Page scene that you will create.

Figure 4.30

This is an example of the Airfares scene that you will create.

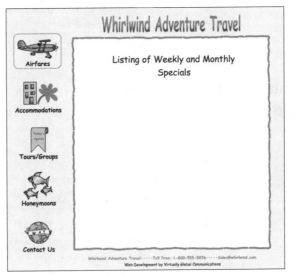

Components of the Accommodations Page

The Accommodations page focuses on the variety of housing and condominium units that the travel company can provide (see Figure 4.31). We have planned on using the drag-and-drop feature of Flash to make this page very interactive. You have already storyboarded this page to show this functionality. Visitors interact with the site by choosing the criteria that they are looking for in their travel accommodations. They select the representing continent and drag it into the search criteria area.

When they activate the search, the matching results will display. This page will be engaging to the visitor while showcasing the variety of accommodations that Whirlwind Adventure Travel has to offer.

Figure 4.31

This is an example of the Accommodations scene that you will create.

Components of the Tours/Groups Page

The Tours/Groups area of the Web site focuses on the current tours that the travel company offers (see Figure 4.32). This page presents a panoramic, 360° movie for the end-user to explore.

Figure 4.32

This is an example of the Tours/Groups scene that you will create.

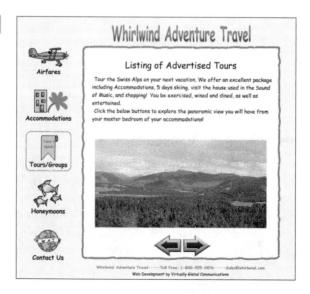

Components of the Honeymoons Page

The Honeymoons page presents the top five honeymoon destinations, focusing on the highlights of each destination and some of the specialty areas that each destination offers to newlyweds (See Figure 4.33). The vast experience of the travel company staff is emphasized. This page or scene is static in nature and encourages the visitor to contact Whirlwind Adventure Travel.

Figure 4.33

This is an example of the Honeymoons scene that you will create.

4

Components of the Contact Us Form

This page presents a form for communicating travel plans, needs, and concerns to Whirlwind Adventure Travel (see Figure 4.34). Using the new form-building capabilities of Flash 5, this form is easy to use and communicates the needed information to the travel company. You will need to investigate the various scripting and data-transfer capabilities of your ISP for this form to function properly.

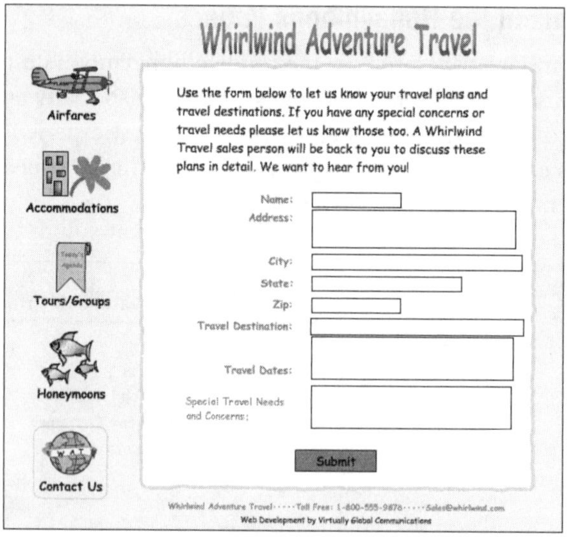

Figure 4.34

This is an example of the Contact Us scene that you will create.

Using Flash with Other Web Development Tools

As presented in Chapter 1, "Why Use Flash?" Flash plays well with other programs. A Flash-published movie must be inserted into HTML code to be visible on the Internet. Flash will create this HTML document when you publish the movie, but you might need to have an HTML editor do more edits to the HTML code after your Flash movie is completed.

HTML Editors

You can use any HTML editor for inserting your movie. Flash makes this very easy for you. When you publish a movie, Flash automatically generates the required HTML code for displaying your movie. If you use Macromedia suite of Web development tools, Flash movies are integrated seamlessly into Dreamweaver. If you prefer another HTML editor, you can simply cut and paste the Flash-generated HTML code into your document or use the HTML page that Flash created as your new document. Pretty neat!

→ For more detailed instruction on how to use the Flash Publish command, **see** Chapter 13, "Publishing the Movie for the Travel Company Web Site," **p. 287**.

Other Graphic Programs

This book presents a project that uses some precreated, bitmapped images that will need to be converted into Flash vector graphics, as well as walking you through the creation of other graphics. You can use any graphic program that you are comfortable with for creating graphics, but they will need to be converted into vector-graphic format to be used within Flash. For the sake of following the project as presented, you will be using Flash for all graphics in this book. But keep in mind that you can use any program that you are accustomed to using for creating graphics and then import them into Flash. Remember, Flash plays well with others!

Where You've Been!

This chapter covers the essential planning phase that you must complete to develop a functional and effective Web site. You learned to create a branching document to show the flow of the site and planned the page architecture as well. You also storyboarded your ideas for each page of the site. You located your graphics to be used, as well as planned your scenes. You now have a good start for the development of your site.

What's Next?

Next you will learn how to create graphics in Flash. You will create from scratch the Accommodations button graphic, as well as the Tours/Groups button graphic. This chapter focuses on drawing skills and features of Flash.

Part II

Building Blocks of Flash: Creating Graphics for the Travel Company Web Site

Chapter 5

Creating and Editing Graphics for the Travel Company Web Site

After you have planned your Web site and created the branching diagram, page architecture, and the storyboards for the special effects and animation, you can begin to create your graphics for the site. In Chapter 3, "Introduction to the Flash Workspace," you set up your movie's size and background color. Now you will begin to add the graphics to that file that you will be using in the site. This chapter will cover how to use the tools of Flash for drawing and how to create and edit graphics. These skills are some of the fundamentals for using Flash.

Drawing Simple Shapes

Learning to use the Flash drawing tools is a must for creating animations. If you do not have any graphics on your Stage, you cannot create any animation. Because the project in this book is presented to many people of various skill levels, the book instructs on creating graphics that are simple in their shape and the creation process. Of course, when you develop other movies, you will want to use your skills and talents to the fullest by creating graphics and illustrations in your own style. The goal of this chapter is to provide you with the Flash skills needed to understand and use the tools to create the graphics for this book's project, and enable you to take what you've learned and use it for your own purpose.

Note You will find that the lowest file size artwork or graphics are those that are created in Flash. Even though you can import graphics and artwork from other graphic applications, you will benefit from knowing how to use the Flash 5 drawing tools to customize and optimize these graphics. It is beneficial to know how to use the Flash drawing tools even though you might be more comfortable with other drawing applications.

Displaying Grids and Rulers

Before you begin this section, you need to have the `whirlwind.fla` movie opened.

➔ For more information on creating the `whirlwind.fla` movie file, **see** Chapter 3, "Introduction to the Flash Workspace," **p 43**.

To open the movie, choose **File**, **Open** and select the movie from the appropriate folder. You should have a movie that is sized to 650×500 px with a light yellow background. If not, you can use the `whirlwind.fla` movie in `Chapter 5` folder on the CD-ROM that accompanies this disk.

First, you need to set up the white area (or copy area) of the movie where information will be presented. (See your Page Architecture document you created in Chapter 4, "Planning Your Travel Company Web Site," for a reference to this area). You already know how to use the Rectangle tool, and will need it to create the white rectangular area on the Stage. So that you can be precise with the rectangle size, you need to turn on your rulers and grid. Choose **View**, **Rulers**.

The default setting for ruler units is pixels. You can set your ruler units to other measurements through the Movies Properties dialog box. As you learned in Chapter 3, to access this dialog box, choose **Modify**, **Movie**, click the **Ruler Units** drop-down menu, and select the unit you want to use from the list (see Figure 5.1).

Figure 5.1

You can set your ruler to the units that you are most comfortable working with in the Movie Properties dialog box.

Movie Properties	
Frame Rate: 15 fps	OK
Width Height	Cancel
Dimensions: 650 px X 600 px	Save Default
Inches	
Match: Inches (decimal) ents	
Points	
Background Color: Centimeters	
Millimeters	
Ruler Units: Pixels	Help

After you have your ruler set, you might want to display the grid to help you draw objects with precision. To turn the grid on select the **View**, **Grid**, **Show Grid** menu command. You can use the grid visually for aligning items on the Stage or if you want objects to automatically align to the grid, turn on the snap feature as explained next.

Using the Snap Feature

If you are used to working with a snap feature, you'll be glad to know that Flash has this feature too. Snap allows for lines and shapes to align or *snap* to the grid. You can turn on the snap feature by choosing **View**, **Grid**, **Snap to Grid**. By turning on this command you will cause all new objects on your Stage to snap to the grid. If you change the size of the grid, you have control over how tight or loose your objects are in their alignment to the grid and, therefore, to each other.

Another nice technique for aligning objects to each other is to use the Snap to Objects feature. This feature allows objects that you move with the Arrow tool to snap to the center and corner points of other objects on the Stage. You turn this feature on through the toolbox or through the menu bar. Click the Arrow tool in the toolbox and then click the Snap to Objects option in the toolbox (see Figure 5.2).

Figure 5.2

The Snap to Objects option is a toggle switch. You can turn the snap feature on or off by clicking the Snap option repeatedly on the toolbox.

Arrow tool —

Snap to Objects option —

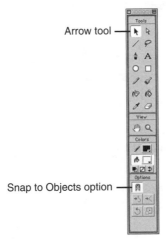

More Uses of the Rectangle Tool and Options

From the menu bar click the Rectangle tool and set your option attributes to a line color of a forest green, and a fill color of white. Then open your Stroke panel by choosing **Window**, **Panels**, **Stroke** and set your option attributes to Stroke Height of 4 points, Stroke Style of a ragged line (see Figure 5.3).

→ For more information on using the Rectangle tool, **see** Chapter 4, "Planning Your Travel Company Web Site," **p. 59**.

Position your cursor on the Stage so that you are at the horizontal ruler setting of 50 and the vertical ruler setting of 10. Click and drag towards the lower-right corner of the Stage. End your drag at the horizontal ruler setting of 600 and the vertical ruler of 420 (see Figure 5.4). This creates the correct sized white area on the Stage for presenting information in this movie.

Ragged line style

Figure 5.3

Set your Rectangle tool option settings to match the illustration's option settings.

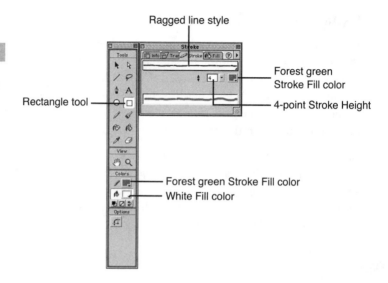

Rectangle tool

Forest green Stroke Fill color

4-point Stroke Height

Forest green Stroke Fill color
White Fill color

Horizontal ruler settings of 50 and 600 px

Figure 5.4

Set your vertical and horizontal ruler settings to match this figure.

Vertical ruler settings of 10 and 420 px

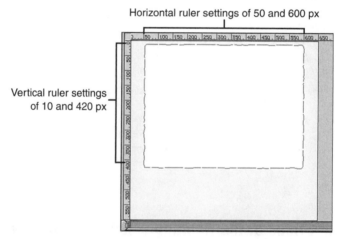

 Tip

Remember, if you make a mistake, you can simply undo it by using the **Undo** command or use the keyboard shortcut for this command (Cmd-Z) [Ctrl+Z]. As you learned in Chapter 4, you have unlimited undo levels up to 300.

EXCURSION

Reverting to Previously Saved File

As you are working on a movie in Flash, you might find that you have gone the wrong direction with the development of graphics or animation. Instead of trying to undo each of the steps that you took to get to the point you are at in the development, you might find that it is quicker to revert to the previously saved document of the file. (This is assuming that you have not saved your new developments yet!) To activate this command, choose **File**, **Revert**. A Revert dialog box displays (see Figure 5.5).

Figure 5.5

Choosing Revert returns you to the last saved version of the document. The previously saved version of the file opens, replacing your present document.

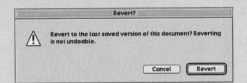

5

Creating the Accommodations Buttons Graphic

From your planning of the Web site, you know that you will need to create two graphics that will be used as buttons for linking to other areas of the site. You need to create an Accommodations button and a Tours/Groups button. First you'll work on the Accommodations button graphic. To create the Accommodations button graphic, you need to understand how to use Flash's drawing tools and how Flash creates lines and shapes. Because you already know how to use the Rectangle tool and the Stroke panel, let's start with that. Click the Rectangle tool and set your options to a Stroke Color of black, and a Fill Color of gold. Then set your Stroke panel to a Stroke Height of 1 point, Stroke Style of **Solid** (see Figure 5.6).

Create a rectangle 2 inches high and 1 inch wide below the white rectangle that you just created. Do not allow the shapes to intersect or touch.

You can also set a line color by clicking the Stroke Color option from the Stroke panel for any line drawn by a tool.

The Mixer panel is another feature of Flash 5 that enables you to set Stroke and Fill colors for your tools. You can access the Mixer panel by choosing **Window**, **Panels**, **Mixer**.

Figure 5.6

Set your Rectangle tool option settings and your Stroke panel to match this Figure's option settings.

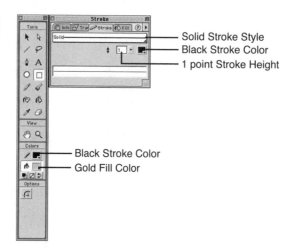

Solid Stroke Style
Black Stroke Color
1 point Stroke Height

Black Stroke Color
Gold Fill Color

Understanding How Lines and Shapes Intersect and Merge

Flash behaves differently than most other graphics programs when it comes to shapes and lines. When a shape intersects another shape, the overlapping fills and lines merge and become one. Anytime a line intersects with another line, it breaks into separate lines at the point of intersection. You may not have noticed it because we haven't discussed this yet, but your two rectangles have intersecting and merging lines and a separate fill shape. Because you will be selecting lines and shapes, click the Arrow tool from the toolbox, then click the center of the rectangle's gold fill. Notice that a solid marquee highlights it. Now drag the fill shape out of the rectangle's line (see Figure 5.7).

Figure 5.7

The rectangle line and the fill are two shapes. You can easily separate any fill color from the surrounding line.

The outline of the rectangle and the gold fill are actually two separate shapes. Undo this move using the **Edit, Undo** menu command. The fill returns to the center of the rectangle shape. Now click one of the rectangle's lines. Notice that instead of selecting the entire outline of the rectangle, you only select one line segment of the rectangle (see Figure 5.8). This is because these lines intersect and each side of the rectangle is now its own line segment.

Figure 5.8

Anytime lines intersect, they become separate lines at the point of intersection.

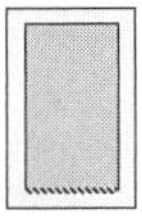

Selecting Graphics

You might be wondering, "If all the lines end at an intersection, how am I going to select all the lines of the rectangle as well as the entire rectangle shape?" Flash allows for techniques to do each of these procedures.

To select the line surrounding the entire rectangle you must double-click the line, not the fill inside the rectangle. This selects the outline around the rectangle (see Figure 5.9).

Figure 5.9

Double-clicking any line of a shape will select all intersecting lines of that shape.

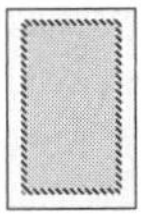

 You can also hold down the Shift key and click each line segment individually to select the line segments of the rectangle.

If you want to select the entire rectangle shape, line, and fill, double-click the fill of the rectangle (see Figure 5.10).

Figure 5.10

Double-clicking a fill of a shape will select the entire shape—all intersecting lines and fills.

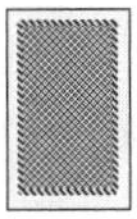

 You can also use the Arrow tool and click and drag a marquee around the rectangle shape to select the entire shape.

EXCURSION

Using the Lasso Tool to Select Shapes

The Lasso tool can be used as another technique for selecting entire shapes or partial shapes. Click the Lasso tool from the toolbox. Move your mouse onto the Stage and notice that it has changed to a lasso. Click and drag a line around the shape that you want to select (see Figure 5.11).

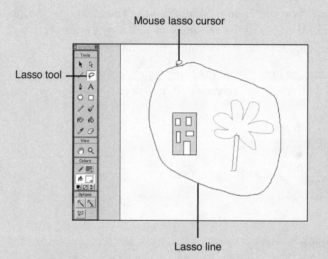

Figure 5.11

You can lasso pieces of shapes so that you can move or edit just part of a shape or image.

Mouse lasso cursor

Lasso tool

Lasso line

When you release the mouse button, any shape, line, fill, or image enclosed in the lasso line will be selected (see Figure 5.12).

Figure 5.12

The lasso line indicates the portions of the shapes that are selected.

You can now edit or move the highlighted shapes. The Lasso tool is a powerful feature for quickly selecting entire shapes or parts of a shape.

Using the Pencil Tool and Options

Next you will create the windows and door for the Accommodations button graphic. You already have the outline of the building. This building will be a tall structure with many windows and one door. Using your Rectangle tool, set your options on the toolbox and the Stroke panel to be a stroke color of black, solid stroke style, 1 point stroke height and a fill color of white. Draw a rectangle to represent a window in the upper-right corner of the building. Make it big enough that you can fit two more layers of windows below it (see Figure 5.13).

Figure 5.13

The Accommodations button will be a simple shape representing a tall building with many windows.

Since you drew this window on top of the gold fill of the building, switch to your Arrow tool and double-click the window to select the entire window shape. Drag it out of the building. Notice that it leaves a hole in the building that shows the light yellow background behind it. Again, this is due to the fact that the two shapes overlap and therefore, they have merged. Undo the move so that the window moves back inside the building.

Finish drawing some more windows and a door so that your building resembles Figure 5.14.

Figure 5.14

All windows and the door of this building have merged with the gold fill of the building.

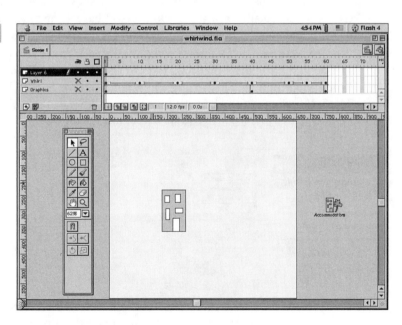

To add a little vacation-destination flare to this Accommodations button graphic, you could add a palm tree to the image. To accomplish this, you need to create it with the Pencil tool and the Stroke panel. Click the Pencil tool on the toolbox. Notice that you get a new set of options for the Pencil tool (see Figure 5.15).

Figure 5.15

The Pencil Mode option of the Pencil tool allows you to draw shapes with various degrees of assistance from Flash.

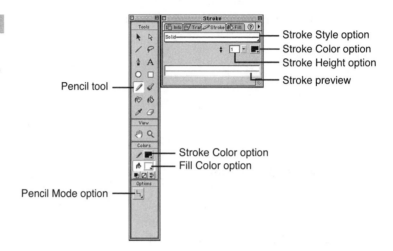

The Pencil Mode option allows you to set the amount of assistance you want Flash to provide while you draw. The default setting is Straighten (see Figure 5.16). This setting straightens the lines of shapes that you draw, regardless of how straight or crooked you actually draw them. Objects will have an angular, modern-art look to them. If you quickly draw a circle, even it if is not perfect, this setting will cause Flash to recognize that you are trying to create a circle. Flash takes over and creates a circle in the size that you drew. You can also choose the Smooth attribute of the Pencil Mode option. This setting will smooth out the lines to be drawn in a shape. The Ink attribute of the Pencil Mode option allows you to draw a shape freehand. Flash will not provide any assistance to your drawing.

Figure 5.16

The Straighten setting of the Pencil Mode option is the default setting, you can quickly switch to another setting by selecting it from the drop-down list.

To create the palm tree, you are going to use both the Straighten and the Smooth settings as well as work between the toolbox and the Stroke panel:

1. Click the Pencil Mode option and select **Straighten** from the list.

2. From the toolbox, select the Stroke Color option and choose a brown color from the color palette.

3. From the Stroke panel, set your Stroke Style option to **Solid** and set your Stroke Height option to 1 point.

4. Position the cursor on the Stage and draw an outline for the trunk of the palm tree. Notice that the Straighten setting automatically straightens your lines. Don't worry if it is not quite the shape you want, you will adjust this in just a moment.

5. Change your Pencil Mode option to **Smooth** and set your Stroke Color option to the same forest green color that you selected for the line color of the white rectangular area you created earlier.

6. Move your mouse onto the Stage and position it above the trunk. Create an outline of about 5 or 6 palm branches.

Your palm tree should look similar to Figure 5.17.

Figure 5.17

Do not worry about drawing the palm tree with precision. You will alter this shape in the following instruction.

Modifying the Button Shapes with the Arrow Tool

A neat feature of Flash is that you have total control over any shape that you create. You can alter a shape using the Arrow tool or the Subselect tool. You will use the Arrow tool for the following edit. Click the Arrow tool from the toolbox and position the cursor over a line in the palm tree trunk. Notice that if you are on a line of the shape your Arrow tool has a curved line under it (see Figure 5.18). This means you will be shaping the line. Click and drag the line to create a slight curve to the trunk.

If you position your Arrow tool over a corner point, the cursor has an angled-line under it (see Figure 5.19). Click and drag the corner point to create a new shape.

Reshape your trunk so that it has a slight curve in its shape (see Figure 5.20). Then reshape the palm leaves to more closely resemble the type of tree that you want for your Accommodations button graphic. Make sure that all end points and corners connect.

Figure 5.18

When using the Arrow tool, the cursor reflects the type of reshaping you are about to perform.

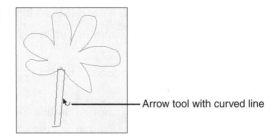

Arrow tool with curved line

Figure 5.19

If you are reshaping a line, the Arrow tool will have an angled line under it.

Arrow tool with angled line

Figure 5.20

Use your Arrow tool to reshape the palm tree trunk.

 Warning

Do not select the line or shape that you want to reshape. If you select the line or shape first and then click and drag, you will move the line or shape.

 Tip

You can create or insert a new corner point to any line with the Pencil tool. Move your Arrow tool to the location that you want to add a new corner point, and (Option-drag) [Ctrl+drag] and drag. This inserts a new corner point while reshaping the line.

Tip

You can also use the Subselect tool to reshape any object you've created in Flash on your Stage (see Figure 5.21). Select this tool and then select the object to be altered. The end points appear as dots or handles on the path that is comprised of the object's lines and curves. Click and drag these dots to reshape the object.

Figure 5.21

The Subselect tool is new with Flash 5.

Subselect tool

5

 Note

If you need to clean up the image by deleting extra lines that overlap the trunk and the palm leaves, click the Arrow tool and then select the line segments and delete them. You might need to zoom in on the area that intersects the trunk with the palm leaves to more easily select these line segments. Use your Magnifier tool and the Enlarge option to zoom in on the area of the shape that you are editing.

EXCURSION

Using the Pen Tool and Subselect Tool to Create Shapes

New with Flash 5 are the Pen and the Subselect tools. The Pen tool uses Bézier point-to-point drawing of artwork to create shapes (see Figure 5.22). You can use this tool instead of the Pencil or Brush tool when creating artwork. To reshape a shape, click the Subselect tool and then select the shape. This causes all the points that make up the drawing to appear. You can then click and drag individual points to reshape the figure. You can adjust any shape with the Subselect tool, regardless of the tool that was used to create the shape.

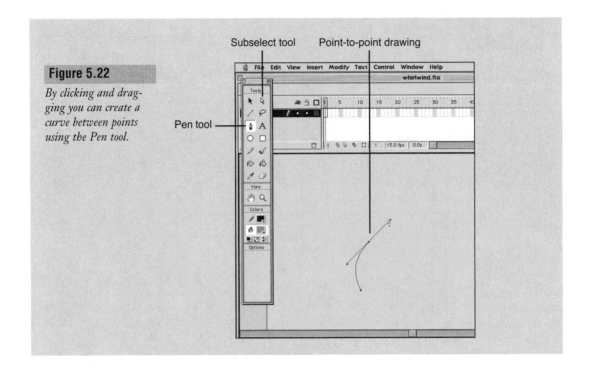

Figure 5.22

By clicking and dragging you can create a curve between points using the Pen tool.

Scaling and Rotating the Shapes

Shapes and graphics can also be scaled or rotated. Flash allows you to perform both a scale or rotate through options and through menu commands. These actions are *transformations* of the shape that allow you to rotate, skew, or resize the shape.

Using the Rotate Option

The first rotation technique you will use is accessed through the Arrow tool options. You might have noticed that you have two option buttons that have not been covered for the Arrow tool (see Figure 5.23).

The palm tree could be rotated slightly to the right so that it is positioned more at an angle next to the building. To rotate it, select the entire shape with the Arrow tool and, with the Arrow tool still selected, click the Rotate option. Notice that after you select the Rotate option, you now have eight round *handles* surrounding the selected shape. Move your mouse over a corner handle. It changes to a semicircle with an arrow (see Figure 5.24).

Figure 5.23

When you use the Arrow tool's Scale or Rotate option, you alter a shape by eye-balling it. You will not alter the shape with much precision using this technique.

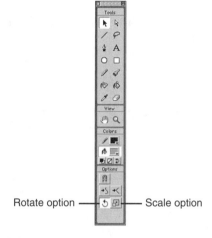

Rotate option ——————— Scale option

Rotate tool

Figure 5.24

If you position the Rotate tool over one of the center handles, you will skew the shape. You can only rotate a shape by using the corner handles.

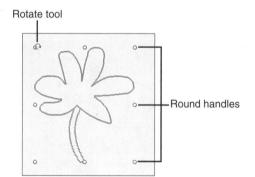

Round handles

Click the handle and drag toward the right at a slight downward diagonal direction. The palm tree rotates to the right as Figure 5.25 illustrates.

Figure 5.25

When you manually rotate a shape, you will see a highlighted outline of the shape indicating its new position.

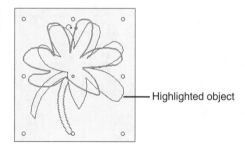

Highlighted object

When you release the mouse, ending the rotation, your palm tree relocates itself to the exact location indicated by the highlighted image.

Tip You can also use the menu command **Modify**, **Transform**, **Rotate** to initiate the Rotate function of Flash.

Using the Scale Option

The palm tree is too large for the Accommodation's button in the movie; it needs to be scaled down to be slightly smaller than the building. Use Flash's Scale function to resize the palm tree. First select the tree with the Arrow tool. With the Arrow tool still selected, click the Scale option. Notice that the palm tree now has eight square handles surrounding it. Position your Arrow tool over the top-left corner handle and notice that it becomes a double-ended arrow tool (see Figure 5.26).

Figure 5.26

If you resize an object from a corner handle, the object will remain in proportion. If you resize from a center handle, you will scale out of proportion in the direction that you drag the handle.

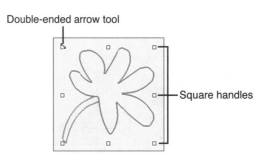

Double-ended arrow tool

Square handles

Click the handle and drag towards the right at a slight downward diagonal direction. The palm tree scales, keeping its proportions to a smaller size, as Figure 5.27 illustrates.

Figure 5.27

Highlighted object indicates the size of the scaled object.

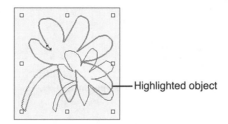

Highlighted object

 Tip You can also use the **Modify**, **Transform**, **Scale** menu command to initiate the Scale function of Flash.

Tip

If you want to scale or rotate an object with precision, use the menu command **Modify**, **Transform**, **Scale and Rotate** (see Figure 5.28).

Figure 5.28

You can enter exact numbers or degrees for scaling or rotating your object.

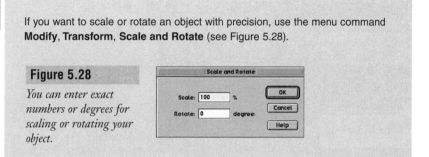

Tip

You can also use the Transform panel to scale or rotate an object with precision (see Figure 5.29). Click the **Window**, **Panels**, **Transform** menu command to display this panel.

5

Click to maintain object's proportions

Figure 5.29

If you click the Constrain option, you will transform your object, maintaining its proportions.

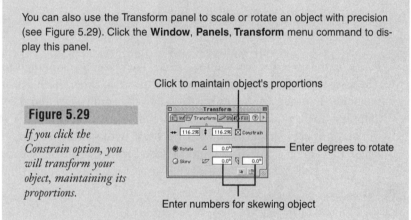

Enter degrees to rotate

Enter numbers for skewing object

Adding Fills and Gradients

The Accommodations button graphic is almost complete. The final touch needed is to fill the shapes with some colors. The fill and gradient features of Flash are very useful and easy to use. You will use the Paint Bucket tool for editing and creating fills for the Accommodations button graphic.

Creating and Modifying a Fill

The palm tree needs to be colorized and the windows and door of the building need a gradient fill. Click the Paint Bucket tool and look at the options associated with it (see Figure 5.30).

To create the fill, you need to choose the fill color. Click the Fill Color option to display the color palette. Select a brown color from the palette. Don't worry if you do not match the brown color you chose for the trunk of the palm tree, you will create an exact match between the fill and the line color later.

Figure 5.30

The Paint Bucket tool and its associated options allow you to easily fill objects and images on your Stage.

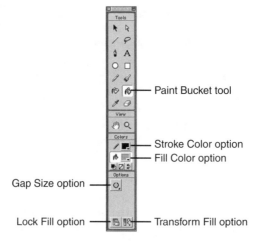

Paint Bucket tool

Stroke Color option
Fill Color option

Gap Size option

Lock Fill option
Transform Fill option

Based on the area that you want to fill, set your Gap Size option (see Figure 5.31). The Gap Size option allows you to fill an area that might have gaps between line segments. In other words, the lines do not fully connect around the shape. In other graphics programs, if there is a gap in the line surrounding a shape you cannot fill the shape. But Flash allows you to fill a shape with small, medium, or large gaps. Click the Gap Size option and select **Close Small Gaps** from the menu list.

Figure 5.31

*You also could have selected **Don't Close Gaps** due to the building shape being created with the Rectangle tool. This selection would still allow for a fill because there are no gaps in the line.*

To fill the trunk of the palm tree, position the Paint Bucket tool so that the tip of the pouring paint is inside the trunk. Click your mouse, and the shape fills with the brown color you selected.

 Tip

You do not need to select the shape that you want to fill. You can fill any shape by positioning the Paint Bucket tool over the shape, selected or not.

If you do not like the fill color, simply select another color from the Fill Color palette and refill the shape. Each time you fill a shape, the new color replaces the old color.

Select a green color from the Fill Color option color palette and fill the palm leaves with a green color. Your Accommodations button graphic should look similar to Figure 5.32.

Figure 5.32

Do not worry about the distance between the palm tree and the building. You will be moving them closer to each other later in this chapter.

5

If the trunk or palm leaves area does not fill, choose another gap size from the Gap Size option list.

If you cannot fill a shape even though you have the **Close Large Gaps** menu command selected from the Gap Size option list, the gaps in the surrounding lines of your shape are too large. Use the Arrow tool or the Subselect tool, and close the gaps or re-create the shape.

Creating and Modifying a Gradient Fill

Next you want to create a gradient fill for the windows of the building that looks similar to reflecting glass. Flash has a powerful gradient fill feature that, like the fill feature, is easy to use. If your Paint Bucket tool is not selected, click it and open your Fill panel by choosing **Window, Panels, Fill**. Before you begin to select a gradient fill be sure that the Lock Fill option on the toolbox is not selected. If it is selected, click it again to deselect it.

If the Lock Fill option on the toolbox is selected, you will not be able to fill a shape with a gradient. This option only allows for one color to fill a shape, not many colors as with a gradient fill.

Then click the Fill Color option on the toolbox to open the color palette. Notice that there are six preset gradient fills at the bottom of the palette. If you wanted to use any of these fills, simply click them and fill the shape as you would with a color (see Figure 5.33).

Figure 5.33

You can choose any of the six preset gradient fills for filling your shape. These are the default gradients of the Flash color palette.

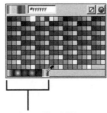

Six preset gradient fills

None of the preset gradients seem to work for the windows of the building, so you need to create your own gradient fill. Open your Fill panel by selecting the menu command **Window**, **Panels**, **Fill**. You can create either a Radial or a Linear Gradient fill from the Fill panel. Click the Fill Style option and select **Linear Gradient** from the list (see Figure 5.34).

Figure 5.34

The Fill panel allows you to also create fills comprised of a bitmap image.

This displays the gradient bar and default markers. The Fill panel now displays all the tools you need to create your own gradients (see Figure 5.35).

Figure 5.35

You can create your own colors and gradient fills through the Fill panel.

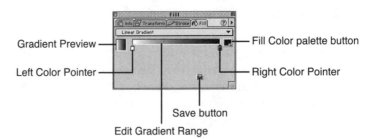

Gradient Preview —   — Fill Color palette button

Left Color Pointer —   — Right Color Pointer

Save button

Edit Gradient Range

You need to create a gradient that resembles glass for the building's windows:

1. Click the Left Color Pointer to select it. This displays the Fill Color button to the right of the Edit Gradient Range Bar. Click the button to display the color palette. Select a light yellow color.

2. Then click the Right Color Pointer. Click the Fill Color button and select a dark gray color from the palette. Notice that the Edit Gradient Range Bar reflects the new colors.

3. You can drag either the Left or the Right Color Pointers toward the middle of the Edit Gradient Range Bar to adjust the flow of the colors in the gradient fill. Drag the Right Color Pointer a little bit toward the middle to cut down on the light color in the gradient fill.

4. You want the windows and door to look like glass reflecting the sun, so you need to make the gradient fill a Radial fill. Click the Fill Style option and select **Radial Gradient** from the list. Your Fill dialog box should look like Figure 5.36.

Figure 5.36

Click the Save button to save your new gradient to the movies color palette.

5

5. From the Fill panel, click the Save button to add this new gradient color chip to the movie's color palette.

 Tip

You can add another Color Pointer to the Edit Gradient Range Bar by clicking between the Left and Right Color Pointers. This adds a new Color Pointer for adding another color to the gradient. You can add up to six additional Color Pointers to the Edit Gradient Range Bar.

EXCURSION

Adding Alpha Transparencies to a Gradient

You could also change the *alpha* of a gradient so that it is slightly transparent. Open your Mixer panel by selecting the **Window**, **Panels**, **Mixer** menu command and open your Fill panel. You will work between the Fill panel and the Mixer panel. From the Fill panel, select the gradient type you want from the Fill Style option and then click the Color Pointer representing the color you want to add the alpha effect to and notice that your Mixer panel reflects this marker. From the Mixer panel, click the arrow by the Alpha box to access the slider and drag the disk to set the amount of alpha you want to add to the color (see Figure 5.37). The ColorProxie option in the Mixer panel displays the color with the alpha effect. Also notice that this new color is also displayed in the Fill panel in the Edit Gradient Range Bar.

ColorProxie

Figure 5.37

You can also create a RGB color for the gradient by inserting the RGB settings in the Mixer panel for the selected Color Pointer.

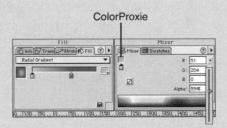

Your Fill Color option on both the Fill panel and the toolbox should display the gradient fill that you just created. Move your mouse onto the Stage and position the Paint Bucket so that the pouring paint is in the middle of a window. Click your mouse button to fill the window. The radial gradient fill expands out from the position of the pouring paint. If you click toward the upper-right corner of the window, the radial gradient fill expands out from the upper-right corner of the window. Click in the upper-right corner of the window to create this effect. Fill the other windows and the door of the building to match (see Figure 3.38).

Figure 5.38

You can create as many gradient fills as you need.

EXCURSION

Adjusting Gradient Fills

You can adjust a gradient fill in a shape. For example, if you want to adjust the radial fill on one of the windows of the building, you would select your Paint Bucket tool and then click the Transform Fill option. Click the gradient filled shape that you want to adjust. You will see a circle with three handles if the fill is a radial gradient fill or you will see two parallel lines with three handles if the fill is a linear gradient fill. Each of the handles adjusts the gradient fill (see Figures 5.39 and 5.40).

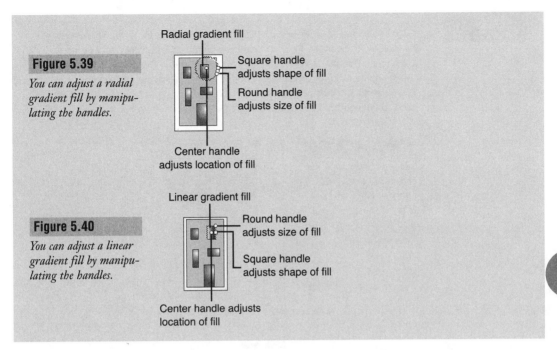

Figure 5.39

You can adjust a radial gradient fill by manipulating the handles.

Radial gradient fill

Square handle adjusts shape of fill

Round handle adjusts size of fill

Center handle adjusts location of fill

Figure 5.40

You can adjust a linear gradient fill by manipulating the handles.

Linear gradient fill

Round handle adjusts size of fill

Square handle adjusts shape of fill

Center handle adjusts location of fill

You are almost finished with the Accommodations button graphic, but first you need to move the palm tree closer to the building. Select the palm tree and then drag it next to the building.

 Tip

Each color palette is associated with the opened movie only. But you can save a color palette with all the new colors or gradients that you have created so you can use it with other movies. To do this you need to open your Swatches panel and then click the **Color Menu** button in the upper-right corner of the panel. Select **Save Colors** from the menu (see Figure 5.41). Then simply save the file with the name and in the location that you want through the Save dialog box.

Figure 5.41

*The **Color Menu** offers many different commands for customizing your color palette. If you want to save the new color swatches you create, you must save them through the color palette menu. After you save the palette, you can then load it into another movie through the **Add Color** command.*

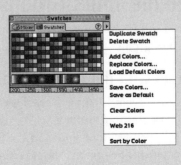

You can also use your Mixer and Swatches panels to set the colors for tools in the toolbox. To open the Mixer or Swatches panel, choose the **Window** menu and choose **Panels**, **Mixer** or choose **Window**, **Panels**, **Swatches**. Each tool has the same Color options present on the toolbox. Click the Fill Color on the toolbox and then choose a new color or color chip from the Mixer or Swatches panel to change the fill or stroke color of the tool (see Figure 5.42).

Figure 5.42

You must select the Color option associated with either a stroke or a fill color before you select a color from the Mixer or Swatches panels.

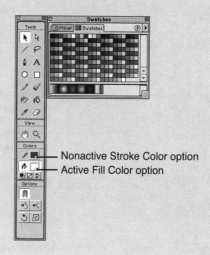

— Nonactive Stroke Color option
— Active Fill Color option

The Flash 5 version has made the toolbox consistent in its layout from one tool to the next. Therefore, some tools will still have the Color options even though these features cannot be applied. An example of this is the Arrow tool. If you select this tool, you will have access to the Color options even though they are not applicable with the Arrow tool's functionality.

Creating the Tours/Groups Button Graphic

Next you will create your Tours/Groups button graphic. This button can be represented by a group of people's faces. You will use the Oval tool to create the faces.

Working with the Oval Tool and Options

As you know from Chapter 4, the Oval tool functions similar to the Rectangle tool. You will use this tool and the Stroke panel to create faces for the Tours/Groups button. Click the Oval tool and open the Stroke panel. Notice the options for each of these features. The options should seem somewhat familiar as they are similar to the Rectangle tool options and Stroke panel options (see Figure 5.43).

Figure 5.43

The Oval tool allows you to create circles and oval shapes.

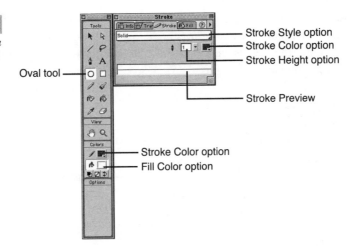

Oval tool

Stroke Style option
Stroke Color option
Stroke Height option

Stroke Preview

Stroke Color option
Fill Color option

5

To begin creating the Tours/Groups graphic, do the following:

1. Select the Stroke Color option on the toolbox and display the color palette. Select a light pink color from the palette.

2. In the Stroke panel, set your Stroke Height option to 1 point and your Stroke Style option to Solid line.

3. In the toolbox, set your Fill Color option to a pink-orange color.

4. Move your mouse onto the Stage. Click and drag an oval to represent the outline of a face.

5. Using the Oval tool, create two eyes. Then use the Pencil tool to create the nose and a mouth. Select your colors appropriately for these shapes. Use the Smooth option for drawing the nose and the Straighten option to create the mouth. Your face should look similar to Figure 5.44.

→ For instruction on using the Oval tool and displaying the color palette, **see** Chapter 4, "Planning Your Travel Company Web Site," **p. 59**.

Figure 5.44

The face needs some hair; you will create that next.

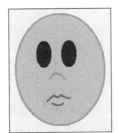

Add some hair to make it a female face. Use your Pencil tool with the Smooth Pencil Mode option and a red color for the Stroke Color option. Create the outline of the hair around the oval as well as into the face to make it look more like the hair is surrounding the face (see Figure 5.45).

Figure 5.45

Just create the outline of the hair for now. You will fill in the hair in just a moment.

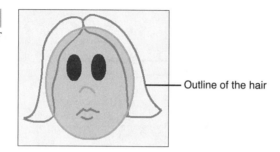

Outline of the hair

Using the Dropper Tool and Options

After you have the outline of the hair drawn, you can now fill the hair in using the same color as the outline. You might have forgotten what color you used for this line but Flash allows you to sample any color using the Dropper tool. Click the Dropper tool (see Figure 4.46).

Figure 5.46

The Dropper tool will sample the color of a line or a fill.

Dropper tool ———

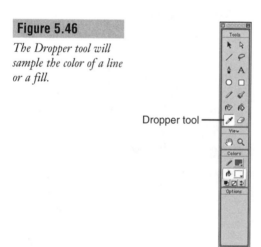

Move your mouse onto the Stage and notice that it is now in the shape of a dropper. Position the dropper so that the tip of it is over one of the lines creating the hair outline. Click once and you'll see that the line color you sampled is now the Stroke Color option of the Ink Bottle tool. The Ink Bottle tool allows you to change the color of a line. This topic is covered next. For now, you want the Paint Bucket tool because you want to fill the hair area. Before you select this tool, click the Stroke Color option of the Ink Bottle tool to display the color palette and note the selected color of red. This is the color of the hair outline. Then click the Paint Bucket tool and click the Fill Color option to display the color palette. Select the same red color from the palette. Move your mouse onto the Stage and fill in the hair (see Figure 5.47).

Figure 5.47

Remember that Flash segments intersecting lines, therefore, you will need to fill in all four areas that make up the hair.

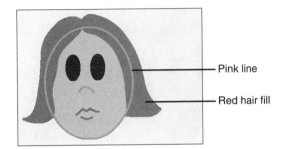

Pink line

Red hair fill

Notice that the oval pink line within the hair shape is still present. You now need to change these line segments to the same color of red as the fill color. You will do this using the Dropper tool and the Ink Bottle tool.

Using the Ink Bottle Tool and Options

The Ink Bottle tool allows for any line to be changed in color. As you saw previously, if you sample a line color with the Dropper tool, as soon as you click to sample the line, Flash switches you to the Ink Bottle tool. Also, if you use the Dropper tool to sample a fill color, Flash will switch you to the Paint Bucket tool. Flash assumes you want to change the line or fill based on whether you sample a line or a fill color. Now we want to use this tool to change the oval line segments. Click the Ink Bottle tool and check out the options (see Figure 5.48).

Figure 5.48

The Ink Bottle tool and the Stroke panel can be used to change the color, size, and style of any line.

Ink Bottle tool

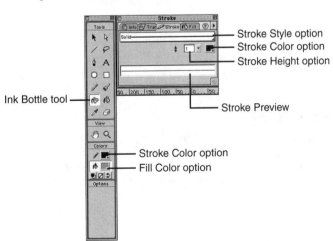

Stroke Style option
Stroke Color option
Stroke Height option

Stroke Preview

Stroke Color option
Fill Color option

The Line Color option retained the Dropper tool's selection of the red color. Move your mouse onto the Stage. Notice that the mouse is now an ink bottle. Position the ink bottle with the tip of the pouring liquid on one of the pink line segments in the hair shape and click to fill the line. Repeat by filling any other line segments in the hair shape. The face you've drawn should look similar to Figure 5.49.

Figure 5.49

If you need to reshape any part of the face, remember you can do this by using your Arrow or Subselect tool and reshaping the area that you want on the face.

Using the previously explained skills and tools for creating the female face, create three other faces. Make them similar to Figure 5.50. Do not have any of the faces touch or intersect.

Figure 5.50

The Tour/Groups button graphic is composed of these four faces.

At this point in your creation of graphics, you now know how to sample the color of a shape or line with the Dropper tool and then refill a line or fill area to change the color. Fix your palm tree so that the trunk and leaves outlines and fills match colors.

EXCURSION

Working with the Brush Tool and Options

The Brush tool is very similar to the Pencil tool in its functionality. This tool allows you to paint with various brush shapes, sizes, and colors. To select this tool, click it and explore the options associated with it (see Figure 5.51).

Figure 5.51

The Brush tool can be used to create interesting lines by choosing a different brush shape.

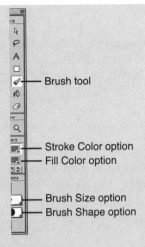

— Brush tool

— Stroke Color option
— Fill Color option

— Brush Size option
— Brush Shape option

The Brush tool also has some special brush painting techniques that are very useful in certain situations. Click the Brush Mode option to display the menu (see Figure 5.52).

Figure 5.52

The default setting for the Brush Mode option is Paint Normal. You can click any of the other menu commands from the list to select them.

Table 5.1 discusses each of the Brush Modes and their functionality.

Table 5.1   Brush Modes

Brush Example	Brush Mode	Mode Description
	Paint Normal	Default setting that allows for any brush stroke to merge and intersect with other shapes.
	Paint Fills	Only paints filled areas, does not cover any lines that might make up a shape.
	Paint Behind	Only paints behind a shape, not touching any of the fills or lines.
	Paint Selection	Only paints within a designated selected shape. You must select the shape you want to paint within before you use this option setting.
	Paint Inside	Only paints inside a shape. Similar to Paint Fills but will not paint outside the shape.

5

 **Tip**

If you select the Paint Inside attribute of the Brush Mode option, you need to start your paint stroke inside the area that you want to paint within. Otherwise, this mode will not work. Flash does not know what image you want to paint in if you do not start the stroke in the image.

Grouping Objects

At this point, you should have your two button graphics created—the Accommodations and the Tours/Groups. You need to do some final touches to these buttons to make it easier to move them, as well as make it harder to edit or change them. First thing you need to do is group them into one shape. Presently, they are each comprised of many lines and fills.

Select the Accommodations button graphic and choose **Modify, Group**.

You should now have one box outline around the Accommodations button graphic (see Figure 5.53).

Figure 5.53

All lines and fills of this graphic have been grouped to one shape.

 **Tip**

You can ungroup any grouped object by choosing **Modify, Ungroup**.

You now want to group each of the faces for your Tours/Groups button graphic. Marquee the first face so that it is selected and click the **Modify, Group** menu command to group it. Repeat this grouping process with the other three faces.

After you have all the faces individually grouped, you will want to position the faces closer together for the button graphic. Because they are grouped, they will not merge with the lines and fills of the other faces. Select each face and move them closer together as Figure 5.54 illustrates.

Figure 5.54

All lines and fills of this graphic have been grouped to one shape.

Tip

The keyboard equivalent for grouping an object is (Cmd-G) [Ctrl+G]. The keyboard equivalent for ungrouping an object is (Cmd-Shift-G) [Ctrl+Shift+G].

Arranging Objects

Depending on the order that you created your faces, they will be arranged out of order in the new layout. Because you have grouped your shapes, you can now arrange them in any order that you need. First select the face that you want to move forward and then choose **Modify**, **Arrange**, **Bring to Front** (see Figure 5.55).

Figure 5.55

*If you only want to move an object one level up or down, select **Bring Forward** or **Send Backward**.*

The selected object moves to the front. Arrange your faces so that they are in the order similar to Figure 5.56.

Figure 5.56

Your Tours/Groups button graphic should look similar to this illustration.

Now that you have your faces arranged, group them as one graphic by selecting all the faces and then choosing **Modify**, **Group** again.

More Use of the Scale Option

The graphics you have for your two buttons are too large. Select the Accommodations button graphic first. Then select the Scale option of the Arrow tool and scale this graphic to be about 75 pixels tall. Scale the image using a corner handle so that it retains its proportions. Do the same scaling to the Tour/Groups button. Arrange your graphics under the rectangular white area (see Figure 5.57).

Figure 5.57

Don't worry about aligning the graphics perfectly under the white area, this will be covered in Chapter 7, "Using Text in Flash."

EXCURSION

Using the Info and Transform Panel

The Info and Transform panels are very useful features. Through them, you can precisely resize and align objects based on Stage coordinates. To access these features choose the **Window**, **Panels**, **Info** or **Window**, **Panels**, **Transform** menu commands. Notice that one panel group contains both the Info and Transform panels (see Figure 5.58). You can switch between the two by simply clicking the associated tab.

Transform panel

Info panel

Figure 5.58

You can change the point on the object that is used to determine the x and y coordinates by clicking the associated dot representing that point.

Object width and height size — Object x and y coordinates — Position of mouse on Stage

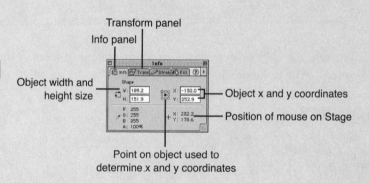

Point on object used to determine x and y coordinates

This panel gives you a lot of information about the selected object. It tells you the exact width and height of the object as well as the precise x- and y- coordinate position of the object on the Stage. Notice that as you move your mouse on the Stage the bottom set of x and y coordinates change to represent the mouse's location. The RGB and Alpha settings also adjust to reflect the current object that the mouse comes in contact with.

Click the Transform tab to display the Transform panel (see Figure 5.59). This dialog box enables you to set resize an object by applying a percentage for increasing or decreasing the object's size. You can also rotate the object a set number of degrees or you can skew an object to create a new shape.

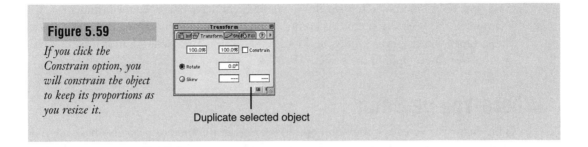

Figure 5.59

If you click the Constrain option, you will constrain the object to keep its proportions as you resize it.

Duplicate selected object

Setting Drawing Preferences

Now that you are familiar with the drawing tools and their options, you might be interested in knowing how to set preferences for each of the tools. To access these preferences select the **Edit**, **Preference** menu command. This displays the Preferences dialog box. Click the Editing tab to display these preferences (see Figure 5.60).

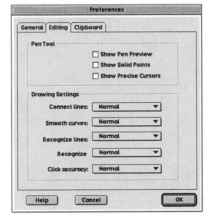

Figure 5.60

The default setting for all tool preferences is Normal. You can choose to increase or decrease the specified assistance.

The following explains the settings and their effects on your movie:

- **Connect lines**—Adjusts how close the end of a line being created must be to any existing lines or line segments before the end points snap together.
- **Smooth curves**—Adjusts the amount of smoothing that Flash applies to curved lines that are being drawn.
- **Recognize lines**—Defines how straight or close to straight a line must be drawn before Flash recognizes it and makes it straight.
- **Recognize shapes**—Controls how close you must draw the shapes of a circle, oval, square, or rectangle for Flash to recognize it as a regular geometric shape.
- **Click accuracy**—Controls how close the pointer must be to an item before Flash recognizes the item.

Save your Web site movie to save all the changes you have made. You will find an example of the Web site up to this point on the CD-ROM that accompanies this book. Open the Chapter 5 folder and locate the file whirlwind05.fla in it if you need to see an example of the project Web site.

Where You've Been!

This chapter covered the tools and option settings in the toolbox. You also have created two buttons that you will use in your travel company Web site. You learned how to group graphics as well as how to arrange them on the Stage. Drawing preferences have been set to your liking for further graphic development. You have learned many of the fundamentals of drawing with Flash.

What's Next?

The next chapter covers importing and optimizing graphics from other graphic programs. You will learn what file formats import into Flash, how to convert them to vector format, and then how to optimize them to bring down file size. You will finish creating all the button graphics that you will use in the travel Web site.

Chapter 6

Importing Graphics for the Travel Company Web Site

As you develop movies in Flash, you will want to use clip art and graphics you created in other programs within your movies. Flash can import clip art in many different file formats. After you import clip art into Flash, you will need to optimize it to lower the file size and convert it to a vector graphic. This chapter covers various techniques for converting clip art into vector format.

Working with Clip Art

You will find that, while Flash has powerful tools for creating graphics, other software programs can create a look that you want for a graphic that you cannot achieve in Flash. For instance, because Flash is a vector program, you might want to use a paint program, such as MetaCreations Painter or Adobe Photoshop, to achieve some of the graphic effects, such as the airbrush effect, that you cannot get with Flash. After you create a graphic in another program, you will need to be able to import it into Flash.

File Types That Can Be Imported into Flash

Flash can import the following file types:

- GIF
- JPEG
- PNG
- Bitmap

- EPS
- Vector—SWF

The process for importing is the same, no matter what file format you want to use in Flash. The following sections will cover these formats and provide additional information on each.

➔ For a description of these file formats, **see** Chapter 1, "Why Use Flash?," **p. 9**.

GIF

GIF format is a popular Web graphic format. It is short for Graphic Interchange Format. CompuServe, which wanted to introduce a file format that could be used on all operating systems, developed the GIF format. GIF format supports indexed, bitmapped images with a color depth of 8 bits or 256 colors. Therefore, GIF format is best suited for images that are composed of large areas of the same colors, not intricate images such as a photograph. To decrease file size, you can set the number of colors used for compressing your image. For instance, if your image uses only 16 colors, you would want to compress it using a color palette with only 16 colors. The fewer colors used, the smaller the resulting GIF file. A browser downloads GIF images in stages. This is called interlacing.

JPEG

JPEG is another popular Web graphic format. It is short for Joint Photographic Experts Group. JPEG is a standard for still images or photographic images and works best on images that are composed of many colors and complex details. It was introduced in 1991 when the Web was just a baby. At that time, Netscape was the only browser that could read this file format, and even at that it required a plug-in. A JPEG file is created by compressing pixel by pixel based on colors. If a series of pixels is close in color and you set a high compression rate, these pixels will all become the same color. Therefore, the format is lossy, meaning you lose information or pixels from the original artwork.

PNG

PNG format is a relatively new Web graphic format. It is short for Portable Network Graphics. The key advantage of PNG format is that it can save in 48-bit colors, as opposed to the 8-bit limit of GIF, and it still can retain a large compression ratio. Images are compressed in a lossless compression, meaning that you are not losing the original quality of the image.

Bitmap

Bitmapped images are created by pixels or dots on the screen. This format can allow you, as the designer, more control over your image because you can edit it down to the individual pixel. When you copy an image to the *Clipboard* you are converting the image into bitmapped format. Bitmap file formats that Flash accepts are

- PICT (Mac) or .pct, .pic (PC)
- .wmf (Metafile)
- .emf (Enhanced Metafile)
- .gif
- .jpg
- .png

Note   If QuickTime 4 is installed on your machine, Flash can import .psd and .tif.

Vector—SWF

Vector graphics are created through an algorithm based on lines and curves. Drawing programs create vector graphics, as opposed to painting programs that create bitmapped images. Vector graphics are sometimes called object-oriented graphics. Flash can import a vector file that is saved in SWF (Flash Player Format). This format imports beautifully into Flash as the image retains all aspects of its shape. If it was created without a background, it will import without a background. Macromedia FreeHand 9.0 exports files in SWF format and so does Adobe Illustrator 9.0. Adobe Illustrator 8.0 requires a plug-in for exporting files in SWF format, which you can download on Adobe's Web site.

Tip   Flash accepts files in Illustrator 88, 3.0, 5.0, and 6.0 format. Flash will also import QuickTime movie files and AutoCAD DXF release 10 files.

Tip   Flash 5 now imports FreeHand files through a import dialog box (see Figure 6.1). Flash 5 supports the mapping of a multi-page FreeHand document into Flash scenes or individual keyframes. FreeHand layers are also imported into Flash layers. There is no loss in the precise color mapping that might have been used in a FreeHand graphic. Lens fills, like magnify or transparency, are converted to a Flash equivalent. Any symbols that might have been used in a FreeHand Library are automatically imported into the Flash Library.

6

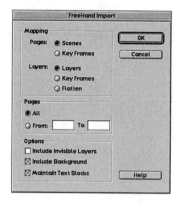

Figure 6.1

The FreeHand Import dialog box allows FreeHand files to be brought into Flash maintaining much of their original design and features.

Importing Images into Flash

You know from your planning of the Web site that you need to import the company logo into your `Whirlwind.fla` file. The globe graphic is a scanned image in bitmap file format.

Whether the file to be imported is a GIF, JPEG, PNG, bitmap, or SWF, the process for importing is the same. You can import these file types through the **File**, **Import** menu command. Follow these steps to add the globe graphic to your site:

1. To get started importing files for the Travel Company Web site, click the menu command **File**, **Import** and import the globe image into the Whirlwind Adventure Travel site.

2. The Import dialog box displays (see Figure 6.2). You want to import the company logo of the globe into Flash. Click the (**Show**) [**Files of Type**] menu and select (**PICT files**) [**Bitmap (*.bmp),(*.dib)**] from the menu list.

Buttons for navigating to
directories or new
file locations

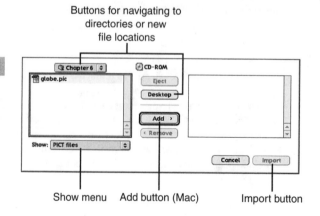

Figure 6.2

You can also choose All Formats from the Show list (Macintosh) or All Image Formats from the Files of Type list (Windows) to view this file.

Show menu   Add button (Mac)   Import button

3. Navigate to the CD-ROM disk. (You must have the book's CD-ROM disk inserted into your machine.) Then double-click the `Chapter 6` folder, and you should see the `globe.pic` (for Macintosh) and `globe.bmp` (for Windows) file.

4. Click the `globe` file to highlight it and then click the Add button (Mac) or the Open button (Windows). On the Mac, the file moves into the right pane of the Import dialog box (see Figure 6.3). Click the Import button (Macintosh) or the Open button (Windows) to import the file into your Flash movie.

Figure 6.3

If you add a file to the right pane of dialog box by mistake, click it in the right pane to select it and then click the Remove button to remove it.

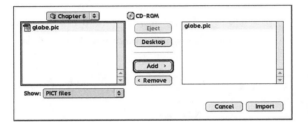

The file is imported into your Flash movie and is placed randomly on the Stage.

6

The globe graphic is a scanned image that needs to be converted to vector format and then optimized. This graphic could have been in a GIF, JPEG, or PNG file format, and the following process would have been the same. You will find the `globe.pic` or the `globe.bmp` file on the CD-ROM that accompanies this book in the `Chapter 6` folder.

You can import more than one file at a time by navigating to the file you want and then clicking the Add button (Macintosh) or the Open button (Windows). On the Mac, you repeat this process to add any number of files to the right pane of the Import dialog box. On the PC, you can hold down the Ctrl key while clicking to select various files, but the catch is they must all be in the same location—you can't browse to other locations to import additional files in the same process as you can on the Mac. When you have all the files identified, click the Import (Macintosh) or Open (Windows) button.

If you want to import images into separate layers, you cannot import them at the same time using the Import dialog box. The Import dialog box imports the designated images to the active layer. You will need to select the layer that you want the image(s) imported into, and then initiate the import process for each layer that you want the images to be located on.

Note

When you import any graphic into Flash, whether it is a GIF, JPEG, bitmap, or PNG image, a bitmap file of the image is automatically added to your Library. You will learn more about Libraries in Chapter 8, "Using Symbols, Libraries, and Instances to Recycle and Organize Graphic Elements."

Converting Graphics to Vector Format

All GIF, JPEG, PNG, or bitmap graphics imported into Flash will appear as a single object. Notice that when you click on the globe graphic, it has a rectangular marquee around it, signifying that it is a single object (see Figure 6.4).

Figure 6.4

Because the globe graphic is its own object, it will not merge with the white area behind it.

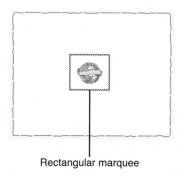

Rectangular marquee

The imported image is still a bitmap at this stage; it is not a vector graphic, and therefore you cannot manipulate it, fill individual areas with color, or add additional lines to it. Next you want to convert the graphic to a format that you can edit in Flash. The globe logo is in a black-and-white state, and it doesn't look very good with the rest of the movie. If you try to click on a black or white area, you select the entire graphic. You need to convert the graphic to vector format so that you can begin to optimize and modify it.

Breaking Apart a Graphic

Before you begin to convert the globe image, you need to move it out of the Stage area into the work area. Click the globe graphic with the Arrow tool and then drag it into a blank area of your work area (outside the Stage area).

One way to convert an imported graphic to a vector graphic is to break it apart. Click the globe graphic to select it and then click the menu command **Modify**, **Break Apart**. You can also use the keyboard equivalent of (Cmd-B) [Ctrl+B] to activate the **Break Apart** command.

The image is broken into discrete areas of colors (see Figure 6.5). You can now select individual areas based on colors and edit or delete them. You can also add lines around these areas by selecting the color area and clicking the Ink Bottle tool.

As individual areas of colors, this image can now be edited.

The **Modify, Break Apart** menu command creates an image that can be compared to a bitmap fill, but it is a special type of object. Macromedia does not have a specific name for it at this stage. The globe image is no longer a collection of individual pixels as a true bitmap is, nor is it a mixture of vector elements. It is in a state somewhere in-between. You need to work a little more with the image to truly convert it to vector format.

The broken-apart graphic is reliant on the Library's bitmap image symbol for the composition and form of its shape. If you delete the bitmap image symbol from the Library, you will also delete the broken-apart instance of this image on your Stage. You will learn more about symbols and instances in Chapter 8.

Modifying and Optimizing

The first optimization that you want to perform is to drop the background out of the shape. Click anywhere in a blank area on your Stage to deselect the globe. Click the Lasso tool and then click the Magic Wand Properties option (see Figure 6.6).

Figure 6.6

The Magic Wand Properties option allows you to set settings for selecting areas of colors.

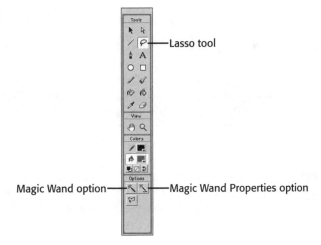

This opens the Magic Wand Settings dialog box (see Figure 6.7).

Figure 6.7

By setting the Threshold to a number, you are determining the color area to select.

The Threshold setting can be compared to the Tolerance setting of the Photoshop Magic Wand tool. The higher the number, the more inclusive the tool is on similar colors, and therefore, it will select a larger area of colors. The lower the number, the more exact the tool becomes when selecting colors and, therefore, it will select a smaller area of colors.

The Smoothing setting is for determining how the edge of the color area will appear. For example, if **Smooth** is selected for the globe, you will get a smooth edge where the white and black pixels meet.

Set the Magic Wand Settings dialog box so that the Threshold is set to 120 and Smoothing is set to **Smooth**. Move your mouse over the white background area of the globe graphic. Notice that the mouse tool is now a magic wand. Click once in the white background area of the globe. All this white area becomes highlighted (see Figure 6.8).

Figure 6.8

The highlight designates the selected background area.

Press the Delete key on your keyboard to delete the background area.

 Note

Take a moment and experiment with this tool by changing the Magic Wand dialog box settings. Use the **Undo** command (Cmd-Z) [Ctrl+Z] to undo your changes and return to the imported graphic.

 Tip

Using your Magnifier tool, zoom in on the edges of the globe to view the effects that different Smoothing settings have on your graphic.

Using this Magic Wand technique for selecting areas of the globe, you can go through and change colors of the various countries and water areas. You can delete other areas too. The more you delete, the smaller in file size your graphic gets. But this is not the visual result that you want for this graphic. It does not match the look and feel of the site, which is more of a cartoon feeling, so let's try another optimization technique. Select the **Undo** command (Cmd-Z) [Ctrl+Z] to undo all your changes to the globe graphic until you get back to the globe graphic in bitmap format. It will appear with the rectangular marquee around it (see Figure 6.9).

Figure 6.9

Undo your optimizations until you get to the globe graphic with the rectangular marquee around it.

You cannot check the file size reduction you have made to a graphic as you optimize it. Unfortunately, this is not a set feature of Flash while you are in the Flash development mode. You must test your movie to generate a Size Report to find out the actual compression you have applied to an imported graphic. To test a movie, choose the **Control**, **Test Movie** menu command. Your movie is launched in the Flash Player for viewing it as it appears in SWF format. This process is similar to publishing your movie. The file compression for the movie, all graphics, and all sound contained in the movie occurs after the movie has been tested in the Flash Player or published. After you test a movie in the Flash Player, you can open the Output dialog box through the **Window**, **Output** menu command. You will get a report on the compression that was applied to your imported graphic and the new file size (see Figure 6.10). You will learn more about publishing a movie in Chapter 13, "Publishing the Movie for the Travel Company Web Site."

Figure 6.10

Notice that the original globe file was 33120KB in size, and the compressed image is 3362KB.

Page	Shape Bytes	Text Bytes	
Scene 1	10893	104	
Embedded Objects	60	0	
Symbol	**Shape Bytes**	**Text Bytes**	
Biplane	2325	0	
Biplane Propeller	180	0	
Fish Graphic	745	0	
Fish Side Fin	144	0	
Fish Top Fin	133	0	
Bitmap	**Compressed**	**Original**	**Compression**
globe.bmp	3362	33120	JPEG Quality=80
Font Name	**Bytes**	**Characters**	
Comic Sans MS Bold	416	ATW	

Compressed graphic

6

Tracing the Graphic

Next you want to try to trace the imported graphic to see if that will generate the look and feel for the globe that fits better into the movie design. By tracing the graphic, you are creating a vector graphic of the imported globe image.

To trace an imported graphic, follow these steps:

1. Click your globe graphic to make it active. Then choose **Modify**, **Trace Bitmap** (see Figure 6.11).

Figure 6.11

*The **Modify**, **Trace Bitmap** menu command is another technique for optimizing imported graphics.*

2. This displays the Trace Bitmap dialog box. Set the settings for each of the boxes to match Figure 6.12 and then click OK.

Figure 6.12

The Trace Bitmap dialog box will convert a bitmapped image into a vector image by tracing the image's color areas based on the setting you input.

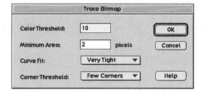

After you have clicked OK to apply the settings, a Tracing Bitmap window displays, showing you the progress of the Tracing command. The more intricate the tracing is, the longer this process takes, and therefore, the larger the file size becomes. Be aware that you can very easily create an image much larger than the original file by being too precise with your settings for tracing the bitmapped image. Your image should look similar to Figure 6.13.

Figure 6.13

The globe now appears very similar to the original scanned image, but it has a slight "watercolor" effect applied to it now.

The settings in the Trace Bitmap dialog box control how closely the traced image will match the bitmap image of the globe. The Color Threshold can be set to any number from 1–500. Again this is similar to the Photoshop Magic Wand tool Tolerance setting. The smaller the number, the tighter the pixel-by-pixel color match becomes. The larger the number, the more inclusive Flash is with colors. For instance, if you have four shades of green in an image, Flash will lump them all together in a selection if you use a large number such as 150. If you use a small number such as 10, Flash would identify each color of green as its own area. Because the globe image comprises tiny areas of black, white, and gray, you want to get pretty precise with your color matching. Therefore, we set the Color Threshold to 10.

The Minimum Area determines how many of the adjacent pixels are included in the color area. A large number value will include more pixels in each color area, whereas a small number will include a smaller number of pixels in a color area, assuming that the surrounding pixels are similar in color. Because the globe is small, with an intricate area of pixels, we enter 2.

The Curve Fit is for setting how smooth the outlines around each area will be. Again, the globe image is very intricate in its areas of detail, so we set this to a **Very Tight** fit.

And finally, the Corner Threshold is for setting how sharp or smooth the corners are for each area. To try to complement the look and feel of the rest of the site, which presents images in a very simple format, we set the Corner Threshold to **Few Corners**.

Take a moment and experiment with the **Trace Bitmap** command by changing the settings in the Trace Bitmap dialog box. Use the **Undo** command (Cmd-Z) [Ctrl+Z] to return to the original bitmap graphic so you can try other settings. Notice that the less precise settings will convert the globe image into a graphic that appears as to be painted with watercolors. The more precise the settings, the more the image appears like the original bitmap. However, you can never truly achieve an exact match to the original bitmap image with the **Modify**, **Trace Bitmap** menu command.

 A traced bitmap graphic is its own graphic. The link between the bitmap symbol in the Library is broken. If you delete the bitmap image symbol from the Library, you will not delete the traced bitmap graphic on the Stage.

Optimizing the Globe

After you have your globe graphic traced, it is now a vector graphic. You can begin to colorize or edit the shape. First, you want to look at what really happened to the globe when it was traced. You can do this by viewing the outline of the vector image. Choose the **View**, **Outlines** menu command (Cmd-Shift-Option-O) [Ctrl+Shift+Alt+O] to see the line segments and curves that make up the image (see Figure 6.14).

Figure 6.14

The globe image is composed of many lines and curves when converted to a vector image.

Notice the intricate curves and lines that make up this image. This is probably too large in file size. However, you can try some optimizing techniques to reduce the number of curves and lines. Remember, the more curves and lines a shape is composed of, the larger in file size the image becomes.

 To view the globe in its normal view, choose **View**, **Fast** (Shift-Option-Cmd-F) [Shift+Alt+Ctrl+F].

You can try three different techniques to optimize this image. Each of the techniques will get rid of some of the curves and lines. The first technique you will try is an automatic optimization technique. With this technique, Flash optimizes the image.

 When you optimize an image you are reducing the file size by reducing the number of lines and curves that make up the shape and the number of colors used. This means deleting curves by smoothing them out and deleting extra lines. You can also reduce the number of colors applied to the shape to optimize it.

Automatic Optimization

Make sure you have the globe image selected. You can marquee it to select it all. Choose the **Modify**, **Optimize** menu command. This displays the Optimize Curves dialog box (see Figure 6.15). You can set the amount of smoothing that you want applied to an image.

Figure 6.15

*You can also use the (Ctrl-Alt-Shift-C) [Ctrl+Alt+Shift+C] keyboard equivalent command to activate the **Optimize** menu command.*

6

Set the options in the Optimize Curves dialog box using the following steps:

1. The globe image has many curves, so set the Smoothing slider to Maximum by dragging the slider to the right.
2. In the Options area, click the Use multiple passes (slower) box and the Show totals message box.
3. Click OK when finished (see Figure 6.16).

Figure 6.16

By setting the Smoothing to maximum, you are telling Flash to reduce the maximum number of lines and curves that make up the shape.

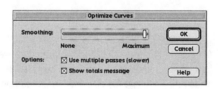

A message window displays telling how many curves the original file had and how many curves the optimized shape now has. Then it gives you the percentage of reduction between these two images (see Figure 6.17). Click OK.

Figure 6.17

The message window telling you the percentage of reduction of curves by which Flash was able to reduce the original figure.

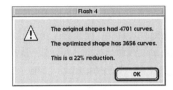

 Tip

You can marquee an area of the image that has many curves using the Arrow tool or the Lasso tool. Then click the **Modify**, **Optimize** menu command to apply this command to the selected area only.

Click anywhere in a blank area of the Stage to deselect the globe image. Now you can view your changes to the globe. You might want to view it in outline mode again (Shift-Option-Cmd-O) [Shift+Alt+Ctrl+O] to see what effect the optimizing command had on the image (see Figure 6.18).

Figure 6.18

The globe has less curves and lines after the automatic optimization command was applied.

 Note

To check the file size of this traced graphic, you must convert it to a symbol (see Chapter 8). Then you can test the movie (see Chapter 13) and view the Output dialog box to check the resulting file size. Because you converted this file to a vector graphic by tracing it, the file size is reflected in the total movie file size, not as an individual bitmapped graphic as you saw earlier in the chapter in the "Breaking Apart a Graphic" section.

After you have completed this form of optimization, your globe graphic has a smaller file size due to the reduction of lines and curves. This is good, but because we're here, let's try a couple of other ways to optimize the graphic to see which one provides us with the best result visually with the smallest file size.

Semiautomatic Optimization

Another technique to optimize involves the Arrow tool. This technique is a semiautomatic optimization. Select the globe image to make it active and click the Smooth option (see Figure 6.19). This will smooth out some of the curves and lines. The more times you click the option, the more curves and lines Flash smooths. View your globe image in outline view as you click the Smooth option. You will see a small number of curves smoothed out each time you click. You will eventually reach a maximum smoothing of the shape, so that when you click the Smooth option you do not see any effect on the image.

Figure 6.19

Using the Smooth option will reduce the number of curves that make up a shape.

Arrow tool —

Smooth option —

6

This option works best for a graphic with few lines and curves whose resulting shape you want to have more control over. But, with the globe graphic, there are a lot of lines and curves, and this technique would be very time consuming.

The following section demonstrates manual optimization, a process that gives you the most control over your optimization of a shape. It would probably not be wise to use this manual optimization for the globe image because of the amount of time it would take to optimize the shape.

Manual Optimization

View the outline of the globe. Select the Arrow tool and position your mouse over a curve. You will see the Arrow tool with an angled line under it signifying that you are on a curve or end point. Click and drag the curve so that it straightens. You can also click a line in the image and then delete it. In this manual process, you control the amount of smoothing or reduction of lines that is performed on the image (see Figure 6.20).

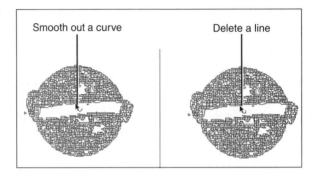

When you are finished optimizing the image with any or all the optimization techniques we just covered, view the globe image in regular mode by choosing **View Fast** (Shift-Option-Cmd-F) [Shift+Alt+Ctrl+F].

→ For more information on using the Arrow tool, **see** Chapter 5, "Creating and Editing Graphics for the Travel Company Web Site," **p. 93**.

After trying all the possible optimizing techniques, you might think that this image still has too many curves and lines, which will make the file size very large. Presently the button graphics have a cartoon look to them, and the globe is too precise. To improve how the image will integrate with the rest of the site, you'll need to re-create the globe image in Flash from scratch.

To prepare for the next section, select the optimized globe image and delete it. Then reimport this graphic. Do not worry about optimizing it. Move the graphic into the work area of the `Whirlwind.fla` file.

Using Onion-Skinning to Re-Create a Graphic

Instead of trying to get a satisfactory result through optimization, we are going to use Flash to re-create the globe image. Drawing an image from scratch in Flash will always create a smaller file than would result when importing the image. You can also control how the image looks in relation to the other images on the Stage. Increase your magnification of the globe image by clicking the Magnifier tool until the globe fills your work area. This will make it easier to work on the image.

To re-create the globe image, do the following:

1. Click Frame 2 of the Timeline so that it is highlighted.

2. Select **Insert**, **Blank Keyframe** (or press F7).

→ For more information on using the Timeline and frames, **see** Chapter 10, "Animating the Movie,"
p. 211.

3. A blank keyframe appears in Frame 2 of the Timeline (see Figure 6.21). Also
   notice that your work area is now blank.

Playhead

Figure 6.21

*The playhead is on
Frame 2.*

Blank keyframe

Note

Click Frame 1, and you will see the globe image again. Then click Frame 2, and
your work area goes blank because there is nothing in Frame 2 on the work
area. You are going to re-create the globe image in Frame 2, but you will need to
be able to see the original artwork.

4. To accurately re-create the globe, you need to turn on the onion-skinning feature of Flash so you can see the globe graphic in Frame 1. Click the Onion
   Skin button (see Figure 6.22), and a vague image of the globe appears. Frame 2
   now acts like a sheet of acetate that allows you to trace the graphic underneath.

→ For more information on the onion-skinning feature of Flash, **see** Chapter 10, "Animating the
Movie," **p. 211**.

5. Create an outline of the globe shape. Use the Oval tool for the outline of the
   globe and the meridian lines. Delete extra lines and line segments as you go
   along. Use the Pencil tool to re-create the continents.

6. Fill in the water area with blue and the land area with green. Use off-white for
   the scroll that surrounds the globe.

7. Create individual text blocks for the letters W, A, and T, which represent
   Whirlwind Adventure Travel. Do this by clicking the Text tool and typing one
   letter at time as its own text block. Position the text blocks in the banner on the
   globe. Your image should now look similar to Figure 6.23.

Onion Skin button

Onion Skin markers

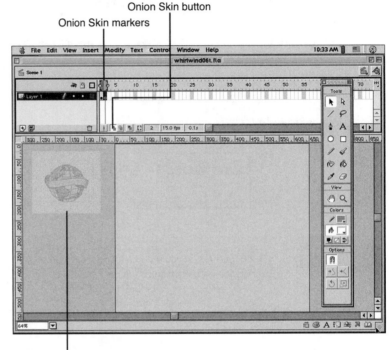

Figure 6.22

The Onion Skin markers indicate that you are viewing both Frame 1 and 2. That allows the image on Frame 1 to show through on Frame 2.

Light image of the globe

Figure 6.23

The recreated globe looks more like the other graphics you have on your site. It is also much smaller in file size than any of the previous attempts at converting the globe to vector format.

➔ For more information on using the Flash tools, **see** Chapter 5, "Creating and Editing Graphics for the Travel Company Web Site," **p. 93**. For more information on creating text blocks, **see** Chapter 7, "Using Text in Flash," **p. 153**.

With the globe re-created, all you need to do is delete the original globe graphic in Frame 1 of the Timeline:

1. Click Frame 1 of the Timeline and then click the globe graphic. Delete this graphic.

2. Click Frame 2 and then select the entire globe image that you created. Group its elements using the **Modify**, **Group** menu command.

3. With the grouped globe image active, copy it. Then click Frame 1 and paste the image onto the Stage. Position it in the top center of the white rectangular area.

4. Next you want to delete Frame 2 because we are done using it. Click Frame 2 and then choose **Insert**, **Remove Frames**.

5. Turn off the onion-skinning feature of Flash by clicking the Onion Skin button again.

Your Stage area should now resemble Figure 6.24. The globe matches the other graphics on the Stage and helps integrate the Whirlwind Adventure Travel company logo with the feeling of the site. Plus the file size is as low as it can be for this image because you created it from scratch.

Figure 6.24

Your Timeline now has one keyframe and holds all the elements on the Stage.

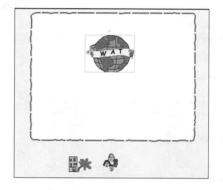

Vector Graphics

Your movie is coming together; all you need now is a few more graphics for your buttons. This section covers importing an Adobe Illustrator file to represent the Honeymoon button.

Importing into Flash

Flash handles importing of Illustrator files beautifully. You will see that the layers used to create the imported graphic are supported in Flash.

1. Choose **File**, **Import** and locate the Fish.ai graphic in the Chapter 6 folder on the CD-ROM that accompanies this book (see Figure 6.25). Import this file into your movie.

Figure 6.25

The Fish.ai *file was created in Adobe Illustrator 6.0.*

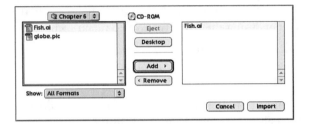

 Note

You will also find this fish graphic in the Flash Common Library named Movie Clips.

2. The file imports on its own layer in your movie. The new layer is named Layer 1 just like the original layer of the movie. Notice that you don't see it when you first import. That is because it came into the movie on a new layer that is located under your Layer 1, which holds all your movie images up to this point (see Figure 6.26). The original Layer 1 is covering up the new Layer 1 content.

New Layer with fish graphic

Figure 6.26

Your Layer 1 white rectangular area is covering the new Layer 1 fish graphic.

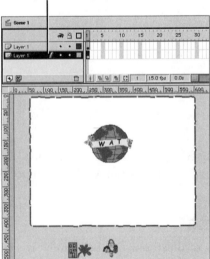

3. Click the dot in the Eye column of the top Layer 1 (see Figure 6.27). The fish becomes visible.

Eye column

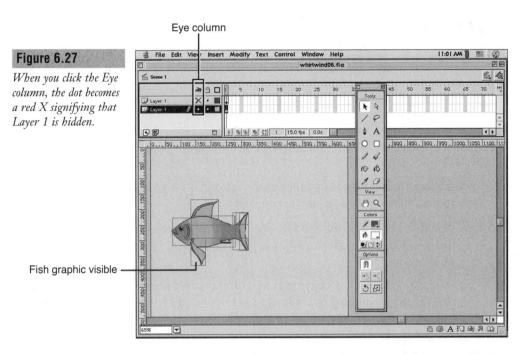

Figure 6.27

When you click the Eye column, the dot becomes a red X signifying that Layer 1 is hidden.

Fish graphic visible

6

→ For more information on creating and using layers in Flash, **see** Chapter 9, "Using Layers to Organize the Movie," **p. 197**.

4. Using your Arrow tool, click a part of the fish. Notice that the fish graphic comprises the various pieces that were used to create it. Because it is a vector graphic, it retains the layers that were used to create it (see Figure 6.28).

Figure 6.28

The fish graphic is made up of many individual shapes.

5. Marquee the fish graphic to select it all and group its elements through the **Modify**, **Group** menu command. Now the fish is one image.

6. Cut the grouped fish graphic from the new Layer 1.

7. Click the top Layer 1 and click the red X in the Eye column to toggle back to seeing the layer. All images on the Stage are now visible. Paste the fish with the **Edit**, **Paste** menu command. It appears on the original Layer 1.

8. Delete the new Layer 1. Click it to select it and then click the Delete Layer button in the lower-right corner of the Layer area of the Timeline (see Figure 6.29).

Figure 6.29

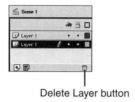

The trash can is the Delete Layer button.

Delete Layer button

The new Layer 1 disappears, and you now have only Layer 1 in the Layer area of the Timeline.

Focusing on the fish graphic, you'll want to change it into a button image for representing the Honeymoon area of your movie:

1. You first need to shrink the fish graphic in size to match the other button images. Click it to select it and use the Arrow tool's Scale option to resize the fish smaller.

2. Add two more fish by copying and pasting the fish image so that it looks like the fish are swimming in a school. Then resize and rotate the two new fish so that your image looks similar to Figure 6.30.

Figure 6.30

The Honeymoon button is represented by the three fish vector graphics.

➔ For more information on scaling and rotating an image, **see** Chapter 5, "Creating and Editing Graphics for the Travel Company Web Site," **p. 93**.

3. Group the fish to make them one image.

You have now added a vector graphic to your movie.

Tips for Graphics

As stated earlier, you must import artwork from other applications in a format that Flash recognizes. The process for importing is the same no matter what graphic format the images are in. Here are some overall tips for importing artwork that will help guide you in the creation of these images:

- If you can create the image in Flash, do so. It will be small in size and play faster as an animation. Remember, it does not matter what size the Flash (.FLA) file is—the Flash Player (.SWF) file is the one that your visitor will be viewing.

- Do not try to import images with a gradient fill created outside of Flash. Always create gradient fills in Flash for all images. Flash has a very powerful and flexible gradient fill feature.

→ For more information on gradient fills, **see** Chapter 5, "Creating and Editing Graphics for the Travel Company Web Site," **p. 93**.

- Try to import any image created in the actual size you want for the movie. You do not want to have to resize the image in Flash if you can avoid it.
- Always crop an image before importing it into Flash.
- For the cleanest conversion of a FreeHand image, always import a FreeHand file exported from FreeHand in SWF format.
- Tracing a bitmap using the **Modify**, **Trace Bitmap** menu command should be used only on simple images. Otherwise files will be very large in size.
- If you are planning to animate an image, it needs to be simple in design, not complex.
- Import all JPEG, PNG, and GIF files without compression. Flash has a great compression feature when it publishes a movie. Let Flash compress these file types.

Adding a Flash Movie Clip

We still need to create two more button graphic images for the movie—the Airfares button image and the Contact Us button image. We can use a previously created image that is supplied by Macromedia with the Flash program. Flash ships with Libraries of graphics, movie clips, buttons, and sound. To access these Libraries, choose **Window**, **Common Libraries**, **Movie Clips**. This opens the Movie Clips Library. Locate the Biplane movie clip and click it to select it. You will see an example of the movie clip in the Library preview window (see Fig 6.31).

Figure 6.31

Click the Play button to see the movie clip animation.

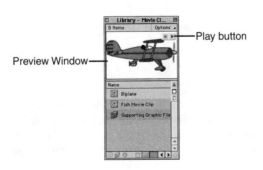

Play button

Preview Window

To use this graphic in your movie, drag it from the Library onto your Stage (see Figure 6.32).

Figure 6.32

You can use any of the Flash Library symbols in your movie by dragging from the Library onto your Stage.

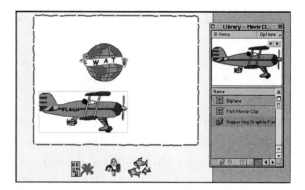

Resize the graphic so that it matches the other button images and move it to be the first button on the left side of the Stage.

To keep the branding of the site, let's use the globe image as the Contact Us image. Select the globe and copy it. Paste it to make another image of the globe and resize it so that it matches the other button images on your Stage. Your Stage should now look similar to Figure 6.33.

Figure 6.33

Do not worry about aligning your buttons and images on the Stage at this point. You will learn to use the Alignment panel in the following chapters.

 Tip

You will not see your Biplane movie clip instance animate in the Flash development mode. You need to test your movie in the Flash Player mode by choosing **Control**, **Test Movie** to see any movie clip animation. You will learn more about movie clips in Chapter 14, "Advanced Animation Techniques."

Save your Web site movie to save all the changes you have made. You will find an example of the Web site up to this point on the CD-ROM that accompanies this book. Open the Chapter 6 folder and locate the file whirlwind06.fla if you need to see an example of the project Web site.

Where You've Been!

This chapter has covered the skills needed to import and convert artwork created in other software packages into vector format. You also learned skills for optimizing an imported graphic to bring down its file size. You should have an idea of how other applications can work with Flash when you create your graphics for a Flash movie.

What's Next?

The next chapter covers creating and using text in Flash. You will learn how to create text blocks and how to manipulate and format the text. You will also learn how to convert the text into graphics so that you can apply special effects to it.

6

Chapter 7

Using Text in Flash

As was discussed in Chapter 1, "Why Use Flash?," Flash offers an advantage over HTML code in the area of text. If you create a fully flashed Web site, you can use any font you want for your text and it will display on all browsers exactly as you intended; correct font, and in the correct size and proportion no matter what size browser window the viewer is using.

→ For more information on the advantages of working with text in Flash, **see** Chapter 1, "Why Use Flash?," **p. 9**.

Creating Text

When creating text in Flash you'll find that most of what you need can be found in your toolbox and in your Character panel. Select the Text tool from the toolbox and then open your Character panel by choosing the **Window** menu and selecting **Panels, Character**. Notice the options that are associated with the tool in both the toolbox and the Character panel (see Figure 7.1).

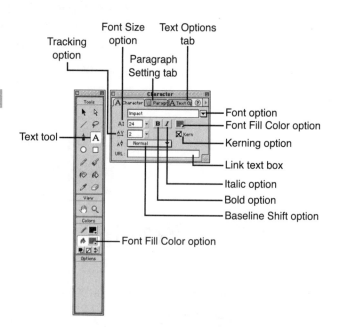

Figure 7.1

You can select the Text tool by pressing the T key on your keyboard. This is the keyboard shortcut for activating this tool.

Tip

You can also click the Character button on the Launcher Bar to quickly access the Character panel.

You can also set your Paragraph settings for text by clicking the Paragraph tab on the Paragraph panel (see Figure 7.2). You can access this panel through **Window, Panels, Paragraph**.

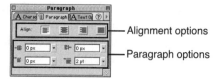

Figure 7.2

You can set the paragraph alignment, margins, indentation, and line spacing using the Paragraph panel.

You can set your Text Option setting for any text by clicking the Text Options tab on the Character panel (see Figure 7.3). You can also access this panel through the **Window, Panels, Text Options** menu command.

Figure 7.3

You can set the Text Type such as Static text for display, or input text for forms.

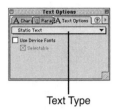

Text Type

 Tip

If you click the Use Device Fonts option on the Text Options panel, you set the OBJECT and EMBED HTML tags to True. These tags are used to display fonts in a browser. If you turn on Use Device Fonts, any Windows-based machine will substitute antialiased system fonts for fonts that are not installed on the user's system.

The combination of these panels and the Text tool on the toolbox allows you lots of freedom to create and use text in Flash. Once you have your text settings determined, move your mouse onto the Stage. The mouse now is represented by crosshairs with a small "A" in the lower-right corner (see Figure 7.4).

Figure 7.4

Use the new mouse tool to create a text block.

If you click, you will set an extendable text block. This type of a text block will extend to the right based on the amount of text being input. An identifiable feature is the round handle in the upper-right corner (see Figure 7.5).

If you click and drag a text block to a set size you create a fixed text block. It is identifiable by the square handle in the upper-right corner. Any text that you type into this block will automatically format itself to the size of the text block, wrapping any text that might extend past the right side of the block by creating a new line below (see Figure 7.6). The fixed text block will extend down based on the amount of text input into it.

Figure 7.5

An extendable text block is sized by the amount of text input into it.

Figure 7.6

The fixed text block can be resized by clicking and dragging the square handle in the upper-right corner to a new size.

> **Tip**
>
> You can change a fixed text block into an extendable text block by double-clicking on the square handle in the upper-right corner. The text block resizes to the full length of the text extended on one line. The handle changes to a circle.

> **Tip**
>
> You can change an extendable text block into a fixed text block by clicking and dragging the round handle in the upper-right corner to the left. As you drag, you are creating a fixed text block, and the text inside is wrapped downward, adjusting to the new size of the text block. The handle changes to a square.

These are the two types of text blocks that can be created with the Text tool. For this book's project, you need to create the Whirlwind Adventure Travel logo for the home page of your site. This logo will be used throughout the site.

1. Click on your Text tool and open the Character panel.

2. From the Character panel, click the arrow to the right of the Font option box and then click **Comic Sans MS** from the list of fonts.

3. Also from the Character panel, click the arrow to the right of the Font Size option box and slide the disk so that **24** shows in the Font Size box.

4. Click the Font Fill Color option on either the toolbox or the Character panel to display the color palette and click the green color that you used for the line in the white area of the site.

5. Move your mouse onto the Stage above the Globe logo and click to set your cursor and create an extendable text block. Type `Whirlwind Adventure Travel`. Your movie should look like Figure 7.7.

Figure 7.7

Do not worry if your text block is not in the correct location; you will fix that later in this chapter.

 — Extendable Text Block

Now you need to create your button text. Focus first on the Airfares button, which is represented by the Airplane graphic:

1. Click your Text tool and open your Character panel. Set your option settings to a **Comic Sans MS** font. Set the font size to 14 points and the color to `black`. Leave the other option attributes at the default settings.

2. Position your mouse tool under the Airplane graphic. Click and type `Airfares`. Don't worry about the location of the text block. Click anywhere on a blank area of your Stage to set the Airfares text block.

3. With the Text tool still the active tool, click under the Accommodations graphic to set another text block. Type `Accommodations`. Click anywhere on a blank area of your Stage to set this text block.

Repeat this process to create the Tours/Groups button text, the Honeymoons button text, and the Contact Us button text. Do not worry about positioning the text blocks precisely under the button graphics (see Figure 7.8).

Figure 7.8

Your button graphics should now have a text label under them. Your screen should look similar to this.

Modifying Text

Once you create a text block, you can modify it. You can edit the actual text, or change any of the attributes of the text. Your Whirlwind Adventure Travel text is too small; you'll want to make it larger.

7

Click your Arrow tool in the toolbox and then click the logo text block to select it. You should see a marquee around the text block indicating that it is selected.

In the Character panel, click the arrow to the right of the Font Size option. Adjust the slider so that it shows a 36-point font as the Font Size option. Because you selected the entire text block, all the text in the text block changes to the new font size. This looks better with the company name extending across most of the white area.

You can change any font attributes of an entire text block by selecting the text block with the Arrow tool and then selecting the new Character, Paragraph, or Text attribute options to be applied.

You can change individual words in a text block by selecting your Text tool and then clicking inside the text block containing the word or words you want to change. This sets your cursor in the text block. Using traditional word processing techniques, highlight the word or words to be changed and select the new font attribute option settings that you want.

A text block can be rotated or transformed using the Arrow tool's Rotate option or the Scale option. Click the text block to select it. Then you can use the menu commands **Modify**, **Transform**, **Scale and Rotate** to modify it. A text block behaves the same as an object on the Stage when these features are applied and, even though you have altered it, it still retains its text block features. Therefore, you can still edit and change the text in the altered text block. Neat feature!

Now you need to center the logo text block in the white area of your movie above the Globe logo. Click your Arrow tool in the toolbox and then click the text block to select it. Click and drag the text block so that it is positioned above the Globe graphic in a location that looks good. To exactly center the Whirlwind graphic horizontally on the Stage, you need to use the Alignment feature of Flash. Choose the menu command **Window**, and select **Panels**, **Align**. This displays the Align panel. Click the Align setting of Align horizontal center and the Align/Distribute to stage (see Figure 7.9).

Click the close box in the Align panel title bar. Now your movie should resemble Figure 7.10.

Align horizontal center

Figure 7.9

You can set many types of alignment for graphics through the Align dialog box.

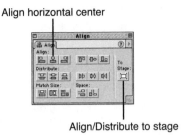

Align/Distribute to stage

Figure 7.10

The Whirlwind Adventure Travel text block is perfectly aligned horizontally on the Stage.

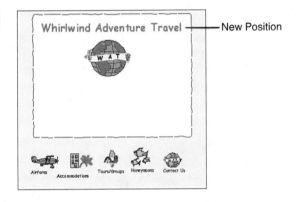

Aligning the Button Graphics

Now you want to align all your button graphics and text blocks, using different techniques for each. You will align the button graphics using a Guide, and you will align the text blocks using the Align panel.

Flash 5 now has *Guides* that can be pulled from the rulers and used to align objects on your Stage. This is similar to other page layout and graphic design programs. Before you begin this process, you need to display your rulers for the movie by choosing **View**, **Rulers** and then show your Guides by choosing **View**, **Guides**, **Show Guides**. Finally, turn on your Snap feature by choosing the menu command **View**, **Guides**, **Snap to Guides** so that Stage objects will adhere to the Guide.

The **View**, **Guides**, **Show Guides** and the **View**, **Guides**, **Snap to Guides** menu commands are toggle switches. Notice that, once you select the command, you have a check mark by it in the **View**, **Guides** menu. This means it is turned on. You can turn it off by reselecting it.

Once you have your rulers displayed and your movie set up to display Guides, click on the lower edge of the top ruler and drag a Guide onto your Stage (see Figure 7.11).

Top edge of ruler

Figure 7.11

Position the guide in the approximate location in which you want the bottom edge of the graphics to be aligned.

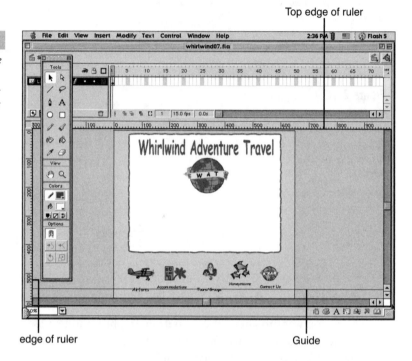

edge of ruler   Guide

 Tip   You can pull a vertical Guide from the left edge of the ruler.

 Note   You can pull out as many Guides as you need for any movie.

Next you need to move the Airfares button graphic so that the bottom edge aligns with the Guide. The Snap to Guide feature is a bit tricky in Flash 5. You must click and drag on the edge or in the center of the figure you want to snap to a Guide. You will see a small circle appear either on the object's edge that you clicked or in the center of the object where you clicked as you move the object and align it to the Guide. Click the bottom edge of the Airfares graphic so that it is selected and drag it so that a circle appears on the bottom edge of the graphic. It will then snap to the Guide (see Figure 7.12).

Using the same process of selecting the graphic on the bottom edge and then clicking and dragging the graphic so that the bottom edge and circle snaps to the Guide, position all the button graphics to the Guide (see Figure 7.13).

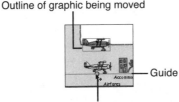

Outline of graphic being moved

Figure 7.12

When positioned correctly with the Guide, you will notice a small pull as the graphic snaps to the Guide.

Guide

Bottom edge of the graphic and circle

Figure 7.13

All button graphics align along their bottom edge to the Guide.

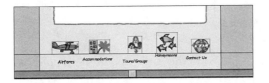

Pull out a second Guide from the top ruler and position the Guide below the buttons so that you can align the button text blocks under the button graphics. Repeat the alignment process by moving the bottom edge of each text block so that it snaps to the Guide (see Figure 7.14). Do not worry about aligning the text block horizontally under the appropriate button. We will do that next.

7

Figure 7.14

All text blocks align along their bottom edge to the second Guide. All graphics align along their bottom edge to the first Guide.

Aligning the Text Blocks with the Button Graphics

The button text blocks can now be aligned with the button graphics. You will use the Align panel to align the text blocks.

1. Select the Airfare graphic button first and then Shift-click the Airfares text block. A marquee appears around the graphic and the text block indicating that they are selected.

2. Choose **Window, Panels, Align** to display the Align panel. Click the Align horizontal center option as indicated in Figure 7.15. Your Airfares graphic and the text block now are vertically aligned on the Stage.

Align horizontal center

Vertically aligned

Figure 7.15

The Align horizontal center option aligns objects by their center points vertically.

3. Next you want to group the Airfares button graphic and the aligned text block to prevent them from getting out of alignment. With both objects selected, choose **Modify**, **Group**. A rectangular marquee will appear around both objects indicating that they are now one object.

Repeat the Align horizontal center alignment and grouping process with the rest of the button graphics and their associated text blocks (see Figure 7.16). When grouped, they become their own unique shapes locking in the new alignment.

Figure 7.16

Grouping many individual shapes creates one larger shape.

 Note

The Snap to Guides feature makes use of an invisible pull from the Guides. When an object gets close to the Guide, there is an invisible pull from the Guide that grabs the object. You can compare this to pieces of metal and their attraction to a magnet. When a piece of metal is placed close to the magnet, the magnetic pull of the magnet grabs the metal. The closer the object is to the magnet—or the Guide—the stronger the attraction is.

EXCURSION

Working with Grouped Objects

Grouping is a very important and functional feature for any graphics program. It allows you to assemble many smaller objects into one large item. You can then easily move, position, and resize the big object without losing the positioning and relationship between the smaller objects. If you want to alter any of the smaller objects that make up the larger object, you can do so by double-clicking the object. This takes you into the Group Mode of Flash. You will see the Stage dim except for the active grouped object, and a new tab appears in the upper-left corner of your Flash window (see Figure 7.17).

Figure 7.17

You can work with the individual objects that make up the grouped figure in the Group Mode of Flash.

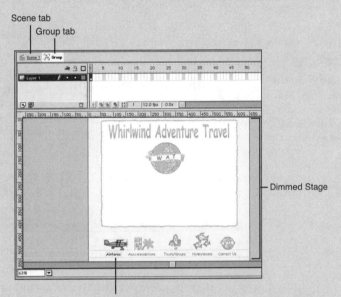

Scene tab
Group tab

Dimmed Stage

Active grouped object with individual graphic elements accessible

Once in the Group Mode, your grouped shape appears with each individual graphic element accessible. You can make your edits and changes to the individual graphic elements now. When you are through, simply click the Scene tab in the upper-left corner to return to the Flash development mode.

 Note

A common error made by beginning Flash users is to double-click a grouped object on their Stage by accident, which enters them into the Group Mode of Flash. When in this mode, you can only access the active grouped elements of the grouped object. If you try to access one of the dimmed objects on your Stage, you will not be able to. Many beginners do not realize that they are in the Group Mode and can become extremely frustrated when they cannot make any new changes to their Stage. If you are having trouble accessing items on your Stage, look in the upper-left corner of your screen to see if you are in the Group Mode.

Now you are ready to position the grouped buttons graphics so that they are equally distributed across the page. Shift-click on the buttons to select them all (see Figure 7.18).

Figure 7.18

A marquee appears around all button graphics.

Open the Align panel and select the options as show in Figure 7.19.

Figure 7.19

These options will align your button graphics so that they are evenly distributed in relation to each other.

Align bottom edge

Space evenly horizontally

Your button graphics are now evenly distributed in relation to each other. Now center them on the Stage, as follows:

1. To group them as one object, use the **Modify**, **Group** menu command.

2. Click the Align/Distribute to Stage and the Align horizontally center options (see Figure 7.20). This will center them as a group on the Stage.

3. Return the buttons to their own individual shapes by choosing the ungroup command, **Modify**, **Ungroup**, and then close the Align panel. Because the graphics are buttons, they need to be their own object (see Figure 7.21).

You are finished with your Guides, so you can drag them back up into the ruler to remove them from your Stage. If you need a Guide again later, just pull one from the ruler.

Align horizontal center

Figure 7.20

You must group the buttons as a whole so that they will be centered vertically on the stage as one object, not losing the even space around each button.

Align/Distribute to Stage

Figure 7.21

Your movie should resemble this figure.

Converting Text to Graphics

If you want to alter or edit the individual letters of a text block, you must first convert the text to a graphic. You can then edit and reshape or recolor individual letters. The logo text would look better with a gradient applied to it, and this must be done before the text is animated in Chapter 10, "Animating the Movie." To apply a gradient fill to the individual letters, you must first convert the text block to a graphic.

You need to move your text block onto the work area because you will be converting the text to a graphic. If you don't, once it is a graphic, it will merge with the white area behind it. Therefore, before you start this converting process, move the Whirlwind Adventure Travel text block into the work area next to the movie. This will make it easier to work with the text.

Breaking Apart Text

To convert a text block to a graphic, you must break it apart. Select the text block by clicking it with the Arrow tool. Then choose **Modify**, **Break Apart**.

 Tip You can also use the keyboard shortcut of (Cmd-B) [Ctrl+B] to activate the **Modify**, **Break Apart** command.

The text block becomes individual letters indicated by the marquee fill in each letter (see Figure 7.22). You have now converted your text block to a graphic—each letter is its own separate graphic. At this point all text features are no longer accessible through the Text tool. You cannot edit the text any more as you could when it was a text block. The editing features that you have available to you now are the same as you would use with any graphic or object in Flash.

Figure 7.22

Each letter is now its own graphic.

Whirlwind Adventure Travel

Special Effects with Text

Once the text has been converted to individual graphics, you can work with it as you would with any graphic object. You could fill each letter with a different color, reshape individual letters, or scale or rotate the text. For our project, you want to apply a gradient fill to the letters as a whole. To do this, marquee all the letters so that they are selected. Click the Paint Bucket tool in the toolbox and then open the Fill panel by choosing **Window**, **Panels**, **Fill**.

For the logo text, you want to create a gradient that is a linear fill with a combination of the colors of the forest green and black:

1. Click the Fill Style option and select Linear Gradient to display the Edit Gradient Range Bar (see Figure 7.23).

2. Click the Beginning Pointer above the Edit Gradient Range Bar to select it. Then click the Fill Color option to display a color palette (see Figure 7.24).

3. Select the green color chip that you have used before for the Whirlwind Adventure Travel text block. The Beginning Pointer changes to the green color.

4. Click the Ending Pointer to select it. Then click the Fill Color option to redisplay the color palette. Select the black color chip. The Gradient Definition Bar reflects a linear gradient that is comprised of green and black.

Edit Gradient Range Bar

Fill Style option

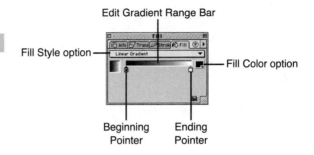

Fill Color option

Beginning Pointer   Ending Pointer

Figure 7.23

You can change your type of fill through the Fill Style drop-down menu.

Hex value

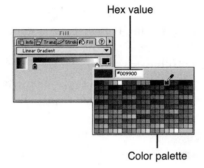

Color palette

Figure 7.24

You can identify the Hex value, or hexidecimal equivalent value, for any color in the upper-left corner of the color palette.

5. You can adjust the amount of each color to be displayed in the Gradient fill. To do this, move the Beginning Pointer to the right so that the fill is mostly green with a little black color (see Figure 7.25). Click the Save button and then close the Color dialog box.

Figure 7.25

Your Color dialog box should match the settings of this figure.

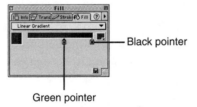

Black pointer

Green pointer

→ For more information on creating gradient fills, **see** Chapter 5, "Creating and Editing Graphics for the Travel Company Web Site," **p. 93**.

Notice that as you are setting the Beginning and Ending Pointers, you are changing the color of the selected text graphics in your work area. Your text graphic should look like Figure 7.26.

Figure 7.26

The gradient fill flows through the text graphic, filling each letter with the green/black linear gradient.

Click in a blank spot in the work area to turn off the selection, so that you can see the new fill. It flows from left to right through each letter.

The gradient fill looks okay at this point, but what if you want to have it flow from the top to the bottom instead, with the top being green and the bottom being black? You need to rotate the gradient fill to achieve this look. Click the Paint Bucket tool and select the Transform Gradient option. Move your mouse to the first letter of Whirlwind Adventure Travel and click once. This displays the gradient adjustment handles (see Figure 7.27).

Figure 7.27

You now have a round handle for rotating the fill and a square handle for adjusting the flow of gradient fill.

To adjust the gradient flow from horizontally to vertically through the letter, click and drag the right-corner round handle toward the bottom of your text. This will rotate the gradient so that it will flow from top to bottom (see Figure 7.28).

Figure 7.28

You can rotate the gradient flow to occur at any angle through the graphic text.

Repeat rotating the gradient for all letters in the logo. When you have all letters' gradients changed, click the Transform Gradient option again to turn this feature off and look at your Whirlwind logo. Your image should be similar to Figure 7.29.

Figure 7.29

The gradient should now flow from top to bottom throughout the graphic text as a whole.

Whirlwind Adventure Travel

EXCURSION

Special Effects with Text Graphics

Once you convert text to a graphic, you can then work with each individual letter as a graphic. You can apply a drop shadow behind the letter by copying the letter and then changing the color to a shadow color and moving the letter behind the original letter. You can fill the letter with any type of fill, and this includes a bitmap graphic fill. In fact, if you select all the letters and then apply the bitmap graphic fill, you will tile the bitmap graphic throughout all the letters as a whole, keeping the bitmap graphic image visible through each letter. Adding gradients and alpha effects also offers interesting effects that cannot be achieved without converting the text to a graphic. You also can alter each letter by distorting its shape through various techniques you've already learned in Chapters 3, 4, and 5. These are just a few special effects that can be added to text graphics.

Grouping Graphic Text

With the gradient fill set for the Whirlwind logo, select all the letters and then group the shape.

1. Click your Arrow tool and select all letters of the graphic text.
2. Select **Modify**, **Group** from the menu bar. The Whirlwind Adventure Travel text is once again one shape.

Your Whirlwind logo is now back to one image; any changes to it will occur to the image as a whole.

Transforming and Scaling Graphic Text

Next you want to scale the graphic text so that it is taller. Follow this process to transform the logo:

1. Using your Arrow tool, click the graphic text image to select it.
2. Open your Transform panel by choosing **Window**, **Panels**, **Transform**.
3. In the Transform panel, change the height scale to 120% (see Figure 7.30) and then press Enter on your keyboard. The text graphic will appear at its new height.

Double arrow tool

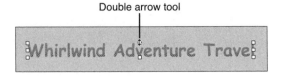

Figure 7.30

You can constrain the proportions of any image as you adjust it by clicking the Constrain option.

You can precisely scale or skew an object through the Info panel. To access this panel, choose **Window, Panels, Info**. You can set the exact height and width of an object as well as set the precise location on your Stage (see Figure 7.31).

Figure 7.31

By clicking a new point in association with a position on the object, the x and y coordinates will adjust to reflect these coordinates on the Stage.

Height and width in pixels

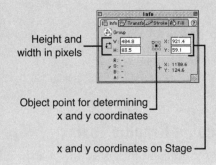

Object point for determining x and y coordinates

x and y coordinates on Stage

You can also rotate and skew graphic text using the Rotate option of the Arrow tool. Select the graphic text to be modified and then select the Rotate option. Click and drag a corner handle to rotate the image or click and drag a middle handle to skew the image. You can scale an object through the Arrow tool's Scale option, too.

EXCURSION

Editing Text as Curves

Once you have converted text into a graphic, you can edit the individual letters, transforming them into new shapes. Use your Arrow tool to select one of the letters and then position your mouse over the edge of it. Click and drag the line or end point to reshape the text graphic (see Figure 7.32). When you click and drag the edge of a line, you get the Arrow tool with a curve under it, which enables you to edit the line itself. If you click and drag a corner of the shape, you will get the Arrow tool with an angled line under it, which enables you to adjust an end point or corner point.

Figure 7.32

You must have the converted graphic text object ungrouped to display as individual graphics for each letter.

➔ For more information on reshaping an object, **see** Chapter 5, "Creating and Editing Graphics for the Travel Company Web Site," **p. 93**.

Repositioning the Text in the Movie

Now that you have your logo text set up with a gradient fill and resized, you will need to move it back onto your Stage:

1. Click and drag the image back onto the Stage.
2. To align the logo text on the Stage so that it is centered, click the **Window**, **Panels**, **Align** menu command to open the Align panel. Set your settings to match Figure 7.33.

Align horizontal center

Figure 7.33

When you click the Align/Distribute to Stage option, any of the other alignments will adjust from a focus on just the selected objects to aligning all selected objects with the Stage, too.

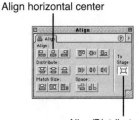

Align/Distribute to Stage

➔ For more information on using the Align dialog box, **see** Chapter 5, "Creating and Editing Graphics for the Travel Company Web Site," **p. 93**.

EXCURSION

Filling Text with a Bitmap Image

You can fill graphic text or any vector object with a bitmap image. You might want to create a new layer before you begin the process to keep your bitmap image and the object to be filled separate. To do this, follow these steps:

1. Import the bitmap image you want to use for the fill through **File**, **Import**.

2. With the bitmap image active, open the Fill panel through **Window**, **Panels**, **Fill**.

3. Click the Fill Style option and choose **Bitmap** from the list. The image appears under the Bitmap Fill Style in the Fill panel and it becomes the Fill Color option in the toolbox.

4. Click the Paint Bucket tool and fill the shapes you want with the Bitmap fill. Delete the Bitmap object from your Stage if you are finished with it.

Your movie should look similar to Figure 7.34. Now is the time to save your Web site movie to save all the changes you have made. You will find an example of the Web site up to this point on the CD-ROM that accompanies this book. Open the Chapter 7 folder and locate the file whirlwind07.fla to if you need to see an example of the project Web site.

Figure 7.34

By now your movie should look similar to what you see here.

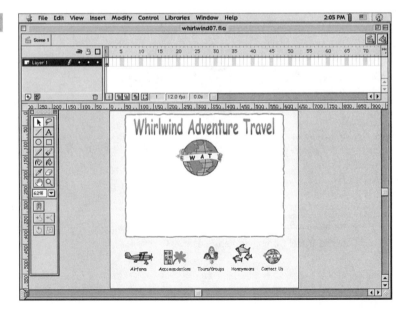

Where You've Been!

This chapter covered many of the skills you need to create, edit, format, and manipulate text. You learned how to convert text to a graphic and applied some interesting special effects to it.

What's Next?

In the next chapter, you will learn about symbols, instances, and the Library. These are key features for creating movies with low file size. You will convert your button graphics into button symbols and place instances of these buttons on your Web site.

7

Part III

Experience the Power of Flash: Create the Movie

In this chapter

- *Using Symbols in Flash*
- *Working with the Flash Library*
- *Creating and Using Instances*
- *More Features of Instances and Symbols*

Chapter 8

Using Symbols, Libraries, and Instances to Recycle and Organize Graphic Elements

Much of the power of Flash comes from the use of symbols. A *symbol* is any graphic, picture, sound, button, or movie clip that you create or import into Flash. Each symbol is a complete description of the item, which includes its size, shape, color, and behavior. When a Flash file is viewed in a browser, the symbol is downloaded to the browser just once and then can be reused many times as the Flash movie plays.

Overview of Symbols, Instances, and the Flash Library

You can create the symbols to be used in your movie. Once created, a symbol is automatically placed in the movie's *Library*. Each Flash file has its own Library. You can think of the Library as an area for grouping and storing symbols for use in a movie, accessible at any time. Typical of a Public Library, the Flash Library can hold many items and can have these items grouped in folders to create common classifications and easy access.

You can also open other Libraries from other Flash movies and use symbols from them. After you use a symbol instance from another movie's Library, that symbol is automatically placed in your Flash movie and the movie's Library. Thus, it becomes an *asset* or object of your Flash movie.

After a symbol is created, it can be placed in the movie as an instance. An *instance* is really just a copy of the symbol that points to the original symbol. Therefore, an instance is very small in memory because it's a reference to the symbol that contains all the information on the item's composition. You can use instances as many times as you need to in a movie. Your ability to do so again allows for very limited memory usage because the instance is just an occurrence of the original symbol.

See Figure 8.1 for examples of the concepts to be discussed in this chapter.

Figure 8.1

Using symbols in your movie makes download time shorter and more efficient for the site visitor.

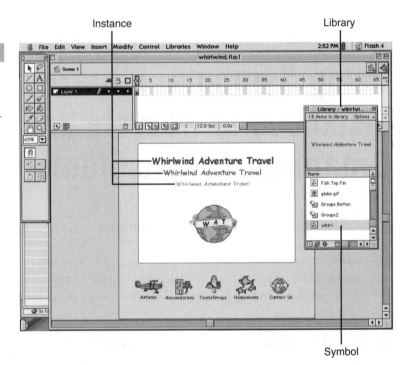

Using Symbols in Flash

As you begin to use Flash, you will probably want to create many of your graphics and artwork within the application. You also might need to import graphics into Flash from other programs. How you get your artwork into Flash is up to you, but to use the power of Flash, you need to convert these items into symbols.

Converting Existing Artwork into Symbols

Converting existing artwork that you have on your Stage into symbols is easy. Just follow these steps:

1. Select the Airfares button graphic by clicking it with the Arrow tool. It becomes the active item on your Stage. Then choose **Insert**, **Convert to Symbol**.

2. In the Symbol Properties dialog box that appears, type `Airfares Button` in the Name box for the symbol name. Select the behavior of **Graphic** for now (see Figure 8.2).

3. Click OK to close the dialog box. Your symbol then appears in the Library window. You have now converted your first graphic to a symbol.

Figure 8.2

Naming and defining the behavior of a symbol will help you begin to organize your assets in the Library.

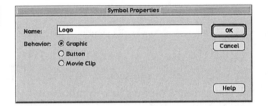

> **Tip**   You can also press the F8 keyboard shortcut to convert a selected object to a symbol.

Designating Symbol Behavior

When you create a symbol, you can designate three symbol behaviors—Graphic, Button, and Movie Clip. Each symbol behavior has its own function in a Flash movie:

- **Graphic**—This symbol behavior is used for static images or graphics. A graphic symbol can be reused many times in a Flash movie.

- **Button**—This symbol behavior is used for interactive buttons in a movie. A button symbol responds to regular mouse events such as *rollovers* (when the user moves the mouse cursor over a button but does not click it) or clicking. When you create a button symbol, you need to create images of the three button states for the button, such as Up, Over, and Down. You can also assign actions to the button states.

- **Movie Clip**—This symbol behavior is used to create reusable animation that will play separately from the Flash movie's Timeline. A *movie clip* symbol can be compared to a mini-movie that is animated according to its own Timeline within the main movie. Movie clip symbols can contain sound, interactivity, and other movie clip instances. Movie clip instances can be part of a button so that the button is animated too.

8

> Imagine the power and low file size of a movie clip symbol that is placed inside another movie clip or a button symbol. Instead of duplicating file size for repeated use of the movie clip, you are referring to a copy of an already defined movie clip within the new movie clip or button symbol.

The remainder of this chapter focuses on the graphic and button symbol behaviors for the Travel Web site. The movie clip symbol behavior is covered in more detail later in this book.

→ For more information on the behavior of movie clip symbols, **see** Chapter 10, "Animating the Movie," **p. 211**.

Using steps 1 through 3 described in the section "Converting Existing Artwork into Symbols," convert the remaining graphics into symbols that you can use for your buttons. Give these symbols the following names and behaviors:

- **Tour/Groups Graphic**—Groups Button; use the Graphic behavior
- **Company Graphic**—Logo; use the Graphic behavior
- **Honeymoons Graphic**—Honeymoons Button; use the Graphic behavior
- **Accommodations Graphic**—Accommodations Button; use the Graphic behavior
- **Contact Us**—Contact Button; use the Graphic behavior

EXCURSION

Creating a Symbol from Scratch

You don't always need to create artwork or a graphic on the Stage and then convert it into a symbol. Flash also allows you to create a symbol from scratch. This way, you can keep your Stage less cluttered and avoid problems or confusion that can arise from having too many unnecessary items on your Stage.

You can create a symbol from scratch by following these steps:

1. Activate *symbol-editing* mode by choosing **Insert, New Symbol**. The symbol-editing mode allows you to create or edit symbols. Any changes you make to a symbol in this mode is reflected in any instance of the symbol used on the Stage.

2. In the Symbol Properties dialog box that appears, type a name for the symbol in the Name box and set the behavior to either Movie Clip, Button, or Graphic. Click OK, and a new window appears (see Figure 8.3).

Figure 8.3

In the empty window of this symbol-editing mode, you can create a symbol without having other images or symbols distract your development process.

New tabs

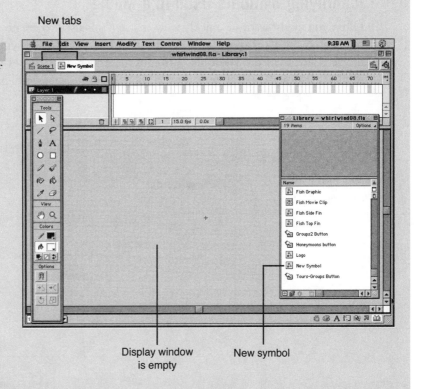

Display window is empty   New symbol

3. Now that you've switched to symbol-editing mode, notice that the screen is slightly different from the typical Flash screen. Two tabs are present in the top-left corner labeled with the name that you entered for the new symbol and Scene 1. The Library now houses the new symbol, and the Library Preview display of this symbol is empty. Now you can create a new symbol by using the Flash drawing tools or importing an existing graphic into symbol-editing mode.

4. After you create a symbol in the symbol-editing mode, you need to exit this mode and return to your movie window. You can choose from two techniques to exit this mode:

   • Choose **Edit**, **Edit Movie**.

   • Click the Scene 1 tab in the upper-left corner of the symbol-editing window.

Either method returns you to your movie window. Notice that the Library contains your new symbol, and you can now access this symbol to create instances of it in your movie.

8

 Note

When you create a symbol in symbol-editing mode, you don't need to group your images. When you use an instance of this symbol, it is automatically grouped as a symbol.

Identifying Symbols Used in a Movie

Often you might want to quickly view the symbols used to create a movie. Flash offers an easily accessible button on the Timeline that lists all symbols used in a movie. Click the **Edit Symbols** button in the upper-right corner of the Timeline to display a list of all the symbols used in the current movie (see Figure 8.4).

Edit Symbols button

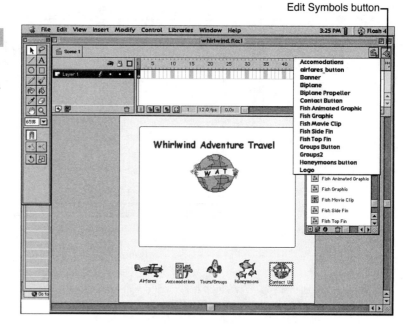

Figure 8.4

The Edit Symbols button displays a list of all symbols used in a movie.

 Tip

Selecting one of the listed symbols from the Edit Symbols button launches the symbol-editing mode so that you can edit that symbol.

Working with the Flash Library

The Flash Library has many features and is very flexible to use. It stores all the symbols, sounds, and bitmapped images used in a movie. As I stated earlier, you can compare this Library to your local Public Library. The Flash Library allows you to group and organize your files just as a public library groups and organizes books.

Features of the Library

Every movie has one and only one Library attached to it. You can open another movie Library if you need to access symbols stored in that Library. Every Library has features, buttons, and menus for organizing and manipulating the Library's objects. Figure 8.5 points out these features.

Features, buttons, and menu items of the Library.

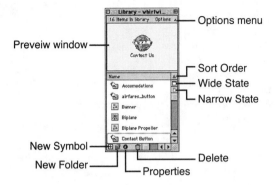

You can explore your movie's Library by clicking each of these features:

- **Options menu**—Contains many of the menu commands you need to organize symbols and use the Library features.
- **Preview window**—Previews the selected symbol.
- **Sort Order button**—Sorts the symbol list in descending or ascending order.
- **Wide State button**—Maximizes the Library window.
- **Narrow State button**—Restores the Library window to its default size.
- **Delete button**—Deletes the selected symbol.
- **Properties button**—Opens the Properties dialog box for the selected symbol. There, you can change any of the properties of the selected symbol.
- **New Folder button**—Creates a new folder.
- **New Symbol button**—Creates a new symbol and launches symbol-editing mode.

→ For a more detailed description of the Shared Library feature of Flash, **see** Chapter 2, "What's New with Flash 5," **p. 25**.

 Note

A new feature of Flash 5 is the Shared Library (see Figure 8.6). This Library was developed for use with multiple projects by teams of developers. The Shared Library allows multiple people working on a project to access the objects in a common Library. The Library is stored outside the Flash movie file, unlike a movie's Library, which is attached to the movie. Any changes made to an object in the Shared Library are reflected in all instances of this symbol used in any project file. You can open a Shared Library by choosing **File**, **Open as Shared Library**.

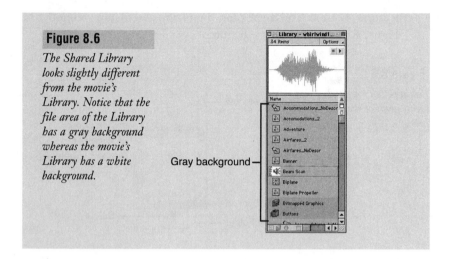

Figure 8.6

The Shared Library looks slightly different from the movie's Library. Notice that the file area of the Library has a gray background whereas the movie's Library has a white background.

Gray background —

Identifying Library Objects

Each movie Library houses all the bitmapped graphics imported into the movie as well as all symbols, buttons, movie clips, and sounds created for the movie. Remember that a symbol can have the behavior of a Graphic, Button, or Movie Clip. Notice that each of these symbol types and even the imported bitmapped images are represented by different symbols in the Library. You can easily identify an object's type by looking at the associated icon next to the object name (see Table 8.1).

Table 8.1   Symbol Icons

Icon	Type	Description
	Bitmap graphic	Anytime a graphic is imported into Flash, it automatically appears in the Library as an object.
	Graphic symbol	You must create or convert a graphic or item to a symbol and then assign it the Graphic behavior.
	Button symbol	You must create or convert a graphic or item to a symbol and then assign it the Button behavior.
	Movie clip symbol	You must create or convert a graphic or item to a symbol and then assign it the Movie Clip behavior.
	Smart clip symbol	Smart clips are special, intelligent movie clips that have parameters associated with them. You can create your own smart clips from an existing movie clip so that you can use this functionality in any movie. A smart clip appears as a smart clip symbol in your Library.
	Sound symbol	You can import any MP3, WAV, or AIFF sound file into Flash, and it will appear as a sound symbol in your Library.

Note

When you select a movie clip symbol in the Library, the Preview window displays the movie clip as well as a control panel. You can click the Play button to preview the animation of the movie clip (see Figure 8.7).

Figure 8.7

A control panel for playing movie clip symbols in the preview window of the Library.

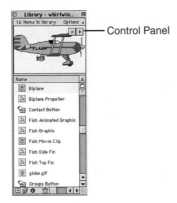

Control Panel

Using the Library to Organize Objects

The procedure for organizing your Library objects is similar to the way you organize your folders and files at the operating system level of your computer. You need to set up a few folders to group your symbols. The first folder you need to create is the `Bitmapped Graphics` folder. To create this folder, follow these steps:

1. Make your Library active by clicking it.
2. Click the New Folder button in the lower-left corner of the Library. A new folder appears with a highlight on the untitled folder name (see Figure 8.8).

Figure 8.8

Creating folders in the Library helps you organize the assets you're using in your movie.

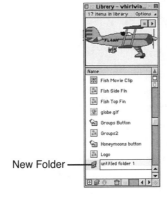

New Folder

3. Flash is ready for you to name your new folder. Type the name `Bitmapped Graphics`.

Next, you need to put symbols for all bitmapped graphics into the `Bitmapped Graphics` folder. By doing so, you can quickly locate your symbols from the bitmapped versions of the symbols. Select by clicking the first Bitmap symbol and drag it on top of the `Bitmapped Graphics` folder. When you release the mouse button, the symbol moves into the folder. Repeat this process to move all bitmapped symbols into the folder.

 Tip To close or open a folder in the Library, double-click the folder icon.

Using this process for creating a new folder and moving symbols into the folder, further organize your Library by creating a new folder called `Buttons` and move all your button symbols into this folder.

Renaming Library Objects

Often you might want to rename a symbol that you have created. For example, you can rename the Groups Button symbol to "Tours/Groups Button." To rename a symbol, follow these steps:

1. Select the Groups Button symbol in the Library and then click the Properties button at the bottom of the Library window. The Symbol Properties dialog box opens with the symbol name highlighted in the text edit box.

2. Type the name `Tours/Groups Button` and click OK. Your symbol is renamed in the Library.

 Tip You can also double-click the text (not the graphic) of the Library symbol to access the text edit box and then type a new name for the symbol.

Changing a Library Object's Behavior

You can change the symbol behavior for any existing symbol, such as a graphic symbol to a button or movie clip symbol. For example, you created your button graphics with a Graphic behavior. Now you need to change to a Button behavior because you will be making the graphics into buttons in Chapter 11, "Creating the Movie's Scenes and Buttons." You can change a symbol's behavior by doing the following:

1. Select the Airfares Button symbol in the Library.
2. Click the Properties button at the bottom of the Library. The resulting Symbol Properties dialog box displays three symbol behaviors.
3. Click the Button behavior and click OK.
4. Repeat steps 1 through 3 and change the other button symbols—that is, Tours/Groups Button, Honeymoons Button, Contact Button, and Accommodations Button—to the Button behavior.

 Tip

> You can (Control-click)[right-click] the symbol in the Library to access the short-cut menu and choose **Behavior**, **Button**. Then you can choose the behavior from the shortcut menu.

EXCURSION

Opening Additional Libraries

As I stated earlier in this chapter, you can open Libraries from other movies and use any symbols in these Libraries in your Flash movie. To open another Library, choose **File**, **Open as Library** and select the movie that contains the Library that you want to use. When the second Library opens, you can drag any symbol from this new Library onto your Stage. Any instance of a symbol you use from another movie's Library is automatically added as a symbol to your movie's Library.

Creating and Using Instances

After you create your artwork and convert it to symbols, you can begin to use instances of the symbol in your movie. Keep in mind that the power of Flash comes from the use of symbols and instances.

Creating an Instance

To add an instance of a new symbol on your Stage, you simply click and drag the instance onto the Stage. An instance of the symbol appears. You can then position it in the location that you want on the Stage. By doing so, you create a new instance of this symbol. It is linked to the symbol in the Library. Therefore, if you change this Library symbol, the linked instance also changes. Pretty neat!

Altering Instance Properties

After creating an instance, you can alter certain features of that instance. You can change the color effects applied to it, as well as alter the shape by skewing it, or change the size and rotation of the instance. You can also change the color of an instance. And finally, you can change the assigned symbol linked to an instance. This flexibility gives you the control you need to develop your movie and easily make changes and edits when you need to achieve a certain effect. You will change the size of the Whirlwind Logo as well as change the color effects of the Whirlwind symbol in the next section.

Changing the Shape, Size, and Rotation of an Instance

To make the Logo instance a little bigger than the actual symbol that it's linked to—without changing the original symbol—click the Logo instance on your Stage. Changing the size makes the Logo on the home page stand out and draws the visitor's eyes to the Travel company identity, but any other instance of the logo used in the site remains the original symbol size. Select the Logo instance and choose **Modify**, **Transform**, **Scale and Rotate** to open the Scale and Rotate dialog box (see Figure 8.9).

Figure 8.9

*The **Scale and Rotate** menu command enables you to change any instance or graphic to a precise size. Using the Arrow tool's Scale modifier, on the other hand, you must eyeball the size as you resize the graphic.*

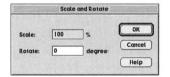

To make the logo about 20 percent larger, enter 120 in the Scale box. The logo is then enlarged by 20%, making it stand out on the page.

You can rotate any instance or graphic by using the Scale and Rotate dialog box. Because you enter exact numbers or degrees, you can get very precise and uniform when altering any instance or graphic on the Stage.

You can also use the Transform panel to precisely alter shapes. To open the Transform panel, choose **Window**, **Panels**, **Transform**.

Changing an Instance's Color Effects

You also can change the color effects applied to an instance. This capability allows you to vary the color of an instance on the Stage to add some variety to the Stage content. Next, you will adjust the Whirlwind logo with a slight transparency to achieve more of a wind effect. To do so, follow these steps:

1. Click the Whirlwind logo on the Stage. Open your Effect panel by choosing **Window**, **Panels**, **Effects** (see Figure 8.10).

Figure 8.10

By clicking the Color Effect drop-down menu, you can change the brightness, tint, or alpha of an instance.

2. Click the **Color Effect** drop-down menu and select **Alpha** (see Figure 8.11).

Figure 8.11

The default setting for an instance effect is None.

3. Enter 80% in the box and press the Enter key on your keyboard. Your Logo now has a slight transparency to it, which will look great when you animate it.

As you can see, the Effect panel has one menu—the **Color Effect** menu. The following list describes each of the menu choices for creating new color effects for an instance:

- **Brightness**—Adjusts the brightness of the instance (see Figure 8.12). You can type a percentage for lightness, or you can adjust the slider to set the lightness.

Figure 8.12

Use the Brightness slider or enter a number for the percentage that you want to adjust the brightness of an instance.

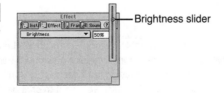

- **Tint**—Adjusts the overall color balance of the instance (see Figure 8.13). Click the Color Palette button and choose a new color. Or you can use the Tint slider or type a number in the Tint box to adjust the color.

Color palette button

Figure 8.13

You can also use traditional RGB values to create a new tint color.

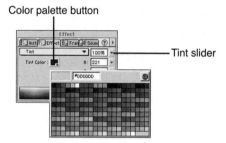

Tint slider

- **Alpha**—Adjusts the transparency of the image (see Figure 8.14). Enter a percentage to change the transparency.

Figure 8.14

You can also use the Alpha slider to change the transparency or alpha effect of the image.

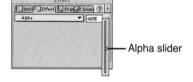

Alpha slider

- **Advanced**—Controls the brightness, alpha, and tint of an instance (see Figure 8.15). This option allows you to access all settings in one panel.

Figure 8.15

You can adjust all three color effect settings for an instance either by typing the new setting in the input box or adjusting the associated slider.

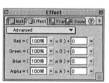

 Tip

You can use the Instance panel to change an instance's behavior (see Figure 8.16). This process is different from changing a symbol's behavior because you are changing the instance's behavior, not effecting the symbol's behavior. First, you must select the instance for which you want to change the behavior on the Stage. Then open the Instance panel by choosing **Window**, **Panels**, **Instance**. Click the **Behavior** drop-down menu and select the new behavior from the list.

Figure 8.16

On the Instance panel, you can set your instance options to designate how you want the instance tracked in the movie.

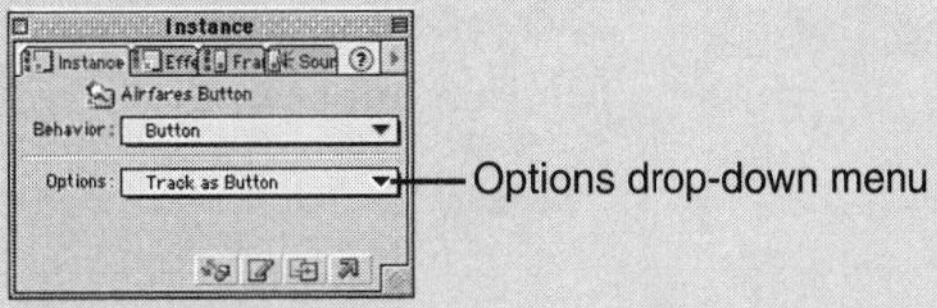

Options drop-down menu

EXCURSION

Breaking the Link Between an Instance and a Symbol

Sometimes you might want to break the link between an instance and its symbol. For instance, you might need to alter one instance's shape to convey a new concept or to make it really stand out. You don't want to change all the instances linked to this symbol by changing the symbol's shape, so you need to break the link between this instance and the symbol. To do so, select the instance you want to de-link on the Stage and choose **Modify**, **Break Apart** to break the instance/symbol link. Any changes made to the symbol do not affect the instance after this link has been broken. The instance is its own graphic; therefore, the file size of the movie increases by the graphic size.

More Features of Instances and Symbols

You will also want to use other features of symbols and instances that appear in your movie. As you learned earlier, you can alter an instance to appear different from a symbol, but what if you want to alter the symbol? You can do so through the symbol-editing mode of Flash. After a symbol is changed, all instances of this symbol reflect the new changes.

Editing a Symbol

You can use various techniques to edit a symbol and, based on where you are in your development of the movie, you might need to use one technique instead of another to perform the edit. For instance, if you need to make a lot of changes to a symbol, you might want to isolate the symbol so that it's the only item in a window. Other times, you might want to add a quick change to a symbol and see the change in relation to other objects on your Stage. You would perform this edit to your symbol directly on the Stage. The following are the symbol-editing techniques you can use to edit a symbol. Each activates symbol-editing mode.

Note

After you edit a symbol, any instances of the symbol that you have used in your movie are updated with the new features you have added. Remember, an instance is just a pointer or reference to the symbol and, therefore, reflects any new changes that are added to the symbol.

Next, you will adjust the Honeymoons Button to add your own gradient fill to the fish to make them appear different from one another. Follow these steps to edit the Honeymoons Button symbol:

1. Select the instance of the Honeymoons Button symbol on the Stage.

2. (Control-click)[Right-click] to access the shortcut menu. Select the **Edit** command from the shortcut menu (see Figure 8.17).

Figure 8.17

The shortcut menu allows quick access to commonly used commands. You will use the shortcut menu often to edit symbols.

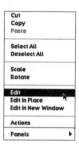

3. The symbol-editing mode is launched, and the window that appears is identical to the window for creating a new symbol from scratch (see Figure 8.18).

4. To add a new gradient to the Honeymoons Button's fish, select and delete the existing fill for the body of the large fish. Using the Paint Bucket tool and the Fill panel, which you open by choosing **Windows**, **Panels**, **Fill**, create a new gradient fill that goes from a red to a yellow to a reddish-brown color. Apply this new gradient fill to the Honeymoons Button symbol.

→ For a more detailed description of how to create new gradients, **see** Chapter 5, "Creating and Editing Graphics for the Travel Company Web Site," **p. 93**.

5. Change one of the smaller fish's gradient fills so that it goes from a red to a blue to a yellow-orange color. Adjust the direction of the gradient fill to flow from the top-left side to the bottom-right side of the fish (refer to Figure 8.18). Now the fish appear to be of a different variety.

When clicked returns
to movie

Figure 8.18

You can modify a symbol's shape, color, and size in symbol-editing mode.

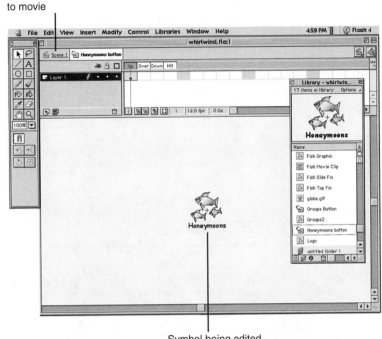

Symbol being edited

 Tip

Another technique to edit a symbol in symbol-editing mode is to double-click the symbol in the preview window of the Library or double-click the icon next to the symbol in the Library. You can also double-click the instance of the symbol on the stage to launch the symbol-editing mode.

8

 Tip

You can use layers to help isolate an instance on your Stage. By hiding other layers in your movie, you can focus on this instance to make changes. But if you want to alter the actual symbol, you still need to edit the symbol in symbol-editing mode through any one of the previously covered techniques. More information on layers and their use is presented in Chapter 9, "Using Layers to Organize the Movie."

EXCURSION

Editing a Symbol on the Stage

Another useful symbol-editing technique is to use the **Edit in Place** command. This command allows you to edit a symbol on the Stage in relation to all other items on the Stage. To activate this command, select the instance of the symbol you want to edit on the Stage and (Control-click)[right-click] to access the shortcut menu. Then select the **Edit in Place** command (see Figure 8.19).

Figure 8.19

*Use the **Edit in Place** command to edit a symbol directly on the Stage.*

This command causes other graphics or instances on your Stage to dim. The two tabs in the upper-left corner of the Flash window indicate that you have switched to symbol-editing mode even though your Stage is still visible but dimmed. Make your changes to the symbol and then choose **Edit**, **Edit Movie** to exit symbol-editing mode.

→ For a more detailed description of how to use the **Edit in Place** command to edit symbols, **see** Chapter 12, "Attaching Actions and Sounds to the Buttons and Frames," **p. 265.**

Switching a Symbol

Sometimes you might need to replace an instance of a symbol with another symbol, thus changing the symbol that the instance is linked to. Although you have a symbol created for the Tours/Groups button instance, as you develop the site, you might find a new image that would represent this button better. You therefore need to swap the present instance symbol with the new symbol. Flash offers this capability, and it's referred to as *switching a symbol*.

Symbols can be switched through the Instance panel. To switch a symbol for an instance, follow these steps:

1. Click the instance that you want to switch with a new symbol to make it active.

2. Choose **Windows**, **Panels**, **Instance** to open the Instance panel (see Figure 8.20).

Figure 8.20

You can use the four buttons in the lower-right corner of the Instance panel to work with symbols.

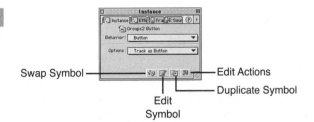

Swap Symbol

Edit Actions

Duplicate Symbol

Edit Symbol

3. Click the Swap Symbol button to launch the Swap Symbol dialog box (see Figure 8.21).

Preview window   Symbol list

Figure 8.21

You can swap any symbol in your Library with another symbol through this dialog box.

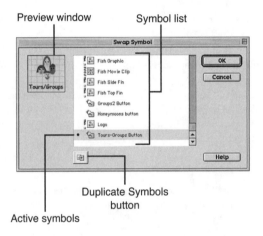

Duplicate Symbols button

Active symbols

4. Notice that a dot appears next to the active symbol in the symbol list. This active symbol also appears in the Preview window. Click the name of the symbol that you want to swap and then click OK. The new symbol replaces the active symbol that is linked to the instance on the Stage.

 Tip

You can also access the Instance panel by clicking the Show Instance button on the Launcher Bar in the lower-right corner of the Flash window. This is a toggle switch button. Clicking it again hides the Instance panel.

8

EXCURSION

Nesting a Symbol Inside an Existing Symbol

A neat trick and a memory-saving technique that Flash offers is to nest a symbol inside another symbol. You reduce the size of the movie and the new symbol by nesting an existing symbol inside it. You can take this one step further and create a new symbol by using many existing symbols. In essence, you are creating a reference loop from a new symbol to existing symbols and therefore barely adding any new data to the symbol memory size. You can create a nested symbol by doing one of the following:

- Place all the symbols that you want to use to create your new symbol on the Stage. Make any additions or changes to the instances and then select all these instances by Shift-clicking to make them active. Then convert them to a symbol by choosing **Insert**, **Convert to Symbol**. Your new symbol comprises all the instances that you selected from the Stage.

- Select an instance of a symbol that you want to nest and convert it to a new symbol by choosing **Insert**, **Convert to Symbol**. Drag all the symbols you want to use to make the new symbol from the Library window onto the symbol-editing mode window. The converted instance combined with the instances of the symbols you drag from the Library window make up your new symbol.

- Select all the instances and graphics that you want to make up the new symbol from your Stage by Shift-clicking and convert them into a symbol by choosing **Insert**, **Convert to Symbol**. You have a new symbol composed of instances and graphic images.

- Create a new symbol by choosing **Insert**, **New Symbol** to launch symbol-editing mode. Open your Library and drag any symbols from the Library to the empty Stage of the symbol-editing mode.

Where You've Been!

This chapter covered a great deal of ground concerning the principles and powerful features of Flash. You learned how to create and edit symbols. You should now feel comfortable with using the Library as well as organizing your symbols through the Library's features. The chapter also covered how to create and alter instances, as well as how to swap one symbol for another and, therefore, change all instances of this symbol with the new symbol.

What's Next?

In the following chapter, you'll learn how to further organize your movie and your movie's assets, symbols, and instances by creating and using layers. Layers are another powerful and useful feature of Flash. They are fundamental to creating animations in Flash.

Chapter 9

Using Layers to Organize the Movie

Layers are a key component of Flash, both for organizing graphics used in a movie as well as for creating animation and special effects. A layer can be compared to a transparency in that a layer enables you to position a graphic on your Stage and still see the background or other layers and their content behind it. You can better organize your movie elements by putting graphics on their own layers. Because objects are on their own layers, you can make changes to parts of your movie more quickly and efficiently. You do not need to re-create entire elements of your movie. In addition, layers are a must for animations. The only limitation is that you can create only one animation per layer.

→ For more information on using layers with animation and special effects, **see** Chapter 10, "Animating the Movie," **p. 211**.

Creating Layers for the Distinguishing Graphic Areas of Your Web Site

The layer functionality of Flash is located to the left of the Timeline. You might have noticed that any new Flash movie automatically has one default layer in it (see Figure 9.1). Your movie up to this point has one layer, and all the graphics you have created are located on this layer. You have four distinct areas with objects on your home page: the button area, the white rectangular area for presenting information, the globe area, and the area with the company logo Whirlwind Adventure Travel that you will animate later in the book. You will need to use four layers to help separate and further arrange the graphics on your Stage.

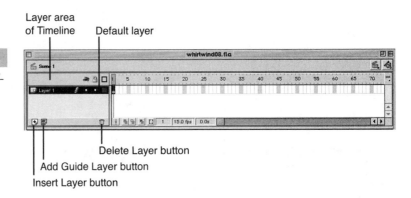

Figure 9.1

All the layer functionality and features can be accessed in the Layer area of the Timeline.

→ For additional information on layers, layer icons, and the Timeline, **see** Chapter 3, "Introduction to the Flash Workspace," **p. 43.**

To create a new layer, click the Insert Layer button in the lower-left corner of the Layer area of the Timeline.

 Tip

You can also create a new layer by choosing **Insert**, **Layer**.

A new layer is then added above Layer 1. By default, it is named Layer 2. Notice that your Stage does not change. This new layer is empty, and you can still see your Layer 1 graphic objects behind it (see Figure 9.2).

 Note

To the right of the layer name is a pencil icon. It lets you know that you can edit the active layer.

Pencil icon

Figure 9.2

The new Layer 2 is highlighted, indicating that it is the active layer.

Placing or Creating Stage Objects on a New Layer

Now that you have a new layer, you can move some of the existing objects on your Stage onto this layer. By moving the objects onto their own layer, you can edit these objects more easily. You'll also be able to animate them later in the book. For this project, move the Globe logo onto this new layer. To do so, you must first switch from Layer 2 to Layer 1, where the Globe logo is located.

Making a Layer Active

Using the Layer area, you can easily switch between layers, making a new layer the active layer. Simply click the layer that you want to be the active layer. The highlight and the pencil icon move to the selected layer, indicating that it is now the active layer ready to be edited. You must activate a layer before you can begin to create or relocate graphics on it. Now click Layer 1 to make it the active layer (see Figure 9.3).

Moving Graphics from One Layer to Another

Now you are ready to move the Stage objects to their own layers so that they are divided into four distinct areas—the button area, globe area, background area, and logo area. To do so, follow these steps:

9

1. Using your Arrow tool, click the Stage in an empty area to deselect the active graphics. Then click the globe object to make it the only active graphic on the Stage.

2. Choose **Edit, Cut** to cut the graphic from Layer 1.

3. Click Layer 2 to make it the active layer and choose **Edit, Paste in Place** (see Figure 9.4).

Figure 9.3

Layer 1 is highlighted in the Layer area, and all Stage objects positioned on this layer become highlighted.

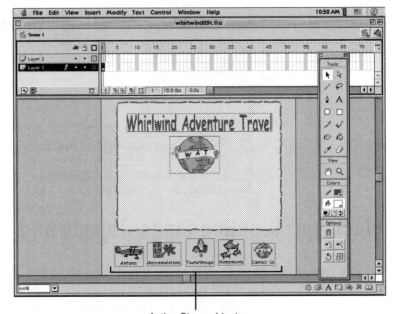

Active Stage objects

Figure 9.4

*The **Paste in Place** menu command positions the Globe graphic in the same location that it was placed on Layer 1.*

Tip
You can also use the keyboard shortcuts (Cmd-Shift-V) [Ctrl+Shift+V] to use the **Paste in Place** menu command.

 Warning
If you use the **Paste** menu command instead of the **Paste in Place** menu command, your cut or copied object will appear in a random location on the Stage.

4. Click the Insert Layer button to create two more layers.

5. Repeat steps 1 through 3 to move each of the existing graphics from Layer 1 to the new layers. Set your layers as follows:

   • Cut the five button graphics from Layer 1 and paste them in place on Layer 3.

   • Cut the Whirlwind Adventure Travel logo from Layer 1 and paste it in place on Layer 4.

You now should have four layers, with Layer 1 holding the white rectangular area, Layer 2 holding the Globe logo, Layer 3 holding the five button graphics, and Layer 4 holding the Whirlwind Adventure Travel text. Your Stage should look the same as before—all graphics in the same location as you started with, except that now they are all on their own layers.

 Tip
If you make a mistake in creating your layers and positioning the objects on the indicated layer, simply close the file without saving and reopen it. Work through the preceding steps again to re-create the layered Web site.

Renaming a Layer

To lessen any confusion over which graphics are located on a certain layer, you need to rename your layers as follows:

1. To rename Layer 4, click it to make it active.

2. Double-click the Layer 4 name in the Layer area. A text box appears with the Layer 4 text highlighted and editable (see Figure 9.5).

3. Replace the default layer name by typing Whirlwind. To accept this name and turn off the highlight, click once anywhere in a blank area on your Stage.

Highlighted text box

Figure 9.5

This text box indicates that you now can change the layer name.

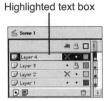

4. Repeat the layer-renaming process and rename Layer 3 to Buttons, Layer 2 to Globe, and Layer 1 to Background. Your layers should look like the ones in Figure 9.6.

Figure 9.6

If necessary, you can use multiple words to name a layer.

EXCURSION

Deleting a Layer

You can delete a layer as easily as you can create a layer. To delete a layer, select the layer by clicking it, and then click the Delete Layer button located at the bottom of the Layer area of the Timeline (see Figure 9.7). The layer is then deleted from your movie.

Figure 9.7

All graphics and objects on the layer are also deleted from your movie when you delete a layer.

Delete Layer button

 Tip

You can also (Control-click)[right-click] the layer to be deleted and click the **Delete Layer** command from the shortcut menu (see Figure 9.8).

Figure 9.8

The shortcut menu contains many useful commands for layers.

Hiding and Showing a Layer

As you add more and more layers to your movie, you will find that sometimes you need to hide certain layers so that you can focus on specific objects that appear on other layers. In the top-right corner of the Layer area, you will find three buttons. The first button, the Show/Hide All Layers button, appears as an Eye icon (see Figure 9.9). Under the Eye icon are little dots in a column, which is referred to as the Eye column. Each dot is associated with hiding or showing a layer.

Show/Hide All Layers button

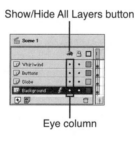

Figure 9.9

The Show/Hide All Layers button allows you to show or hide all layers at once, but if you click the dot associated with a layer, you can show or hide only that layer.

Eye column

By clicking the layer's dot in the Eye column, you hide that layer. A red X appears where the dot was, indicating that the layer is hidden (see Figure 9.10). Also, notice that all objects located on the Stage for that layer are hidden.

 Note

If you hide an active layer, a red X strikes through the pencil indicator to the right of the layer name. This means that because you have hidden the active layer, you can no longer edit it.

Figure 9.10

The Eye column dot is a toggle switch. By clicking it multiple times, you can turn the feature on or off.

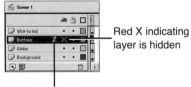

Red X indicating layer is hidden

Red X through pencil indicating you cannot edit the active layer

Tip

Clicking the Show/Hide All Layers button at the top of the Layer area hides all layers in the movie. If you click this button again, all layers in the movie reappear.

If you click the red X in the Eye column, the dot reappears, indicating that the layer is now visible, and all objects on the layer reappear on your Stage.

For your project, the next step is for you to edit the background layer by adding some footer information. You want to be able to focus on this layer in relation to the five buttons on the Buttons layer, so you need to hide the Globe and Whirlwind layers. To prepare for this edit, click the dot in the Eye column for those two layers (see Figure 9.11).

Whirlwind and Globe layers are hidden

Background layer is active

Figure 9.11

The Stage now reflects only the objects on the Background and Buttons layer.

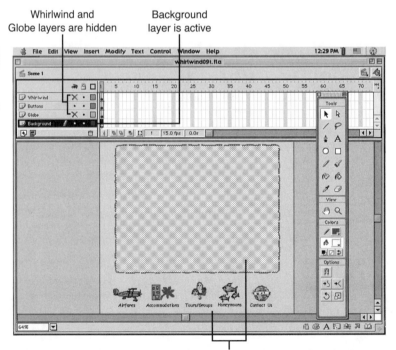

Buttons and white rectangular area on the Stage are visible

You can drag through the Eye column of dots to hide or show multiple layers.

If you (Option-click) [Alt+click] in the Eye column to the right of a layer's name, you hide all other layers. This shortcut is a quick way to hide all but the layer you want to work on.

Locking and Unlocking Layers

You can also lock and unlock layers in a movie. As with the Show/Hide All Layers button, the Lock/Unlock All Layers button is located in the upper-right corner of the layers area (see Figure 9.12).

Lock/Unlock All Layers button

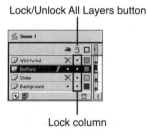

Lock column

Figure 9.12

The Lock/Unlock button allows you to lock or unlock all layers, but if you click the dot associated with a layer, you can lock or unlock only that layer.

By clicking a Lock column dot, you lock that layer. A lock icon appears where the dot was, indicating that the layer is locked. After a layer is locked, you can no longer edit items on the layer.

Focusing on your project Web site, you need to lock the Buttons layer because (even though you need it visible to create the footer information) you do not want to move or change any of the buttons on the Stage (see Figure 9.13). To lock this layer, click the dot in the Lock column of the Buttons layer. A Lock icon then appears in the Lock column of this layer, indicating that it is now locked.

As with hiding and showing layers, clicking the Lock/Unlock All Layers button at the top of the Layer area locks all layers in the movie. If you click this button again, you unlock all layers in the movie.

9

Figure 9.13

The Lock column dot is a toggle switch. By clicking it multiple times, you can turn the feature on or off.

Buttons layer is Locked

Tip   You can drag through the Lock column of dots to lock or unlock multiple layers.

Tip   If you (Option-click) [Alt+click] in the Lock column to the right of a layer's name, you lock all other layers. This shortcut is a quick way to lock all but the layer you want to work on.

Editing Objects on a Layer

You are now set to edit the Background layer. The Whirlwind and Globe layers are hidden, and the Buttons layer is locked.

1. Click the Background layer to make it active and select the Text tool.

2. Click under the five buttons and create a footer text block that will contain the Company name, a toll free number, and an email address. Open your Character panel and use the Comic Sans font, 9-point, bold, and the same green color you used for the Whirlwind text to create the Company information line of text.

3. Now create a text block that gives credit to the Web development company for the Web site. Use the Comic Sans font, 9-point, and black color for the Web development line of text.

4. Center both lines in the text block.

5. Also, add a black, 1-point, solid line above the footer information (see Figure 9.14).

→ For more information on creating and editing text blocks, **see** Chapter 7, "Using Text in Flash," **p. 153**.

With this edit completed, show all layers again by clicking the red X in the Eye column on both the Whirlwind and Globe layers. Then unlock the Buttons layer by clicking the Lock icon in the Lock column.

Figure 9.14

Footer information added to the home page.

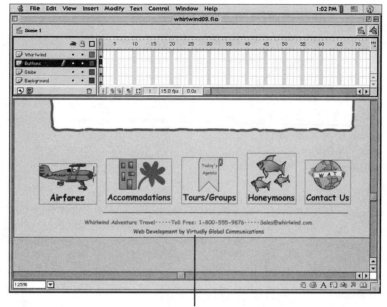

Footer information

Rearranging Layers

You now have your layers created and the appropriate graphics and text positioned on each layer. You need to do one more thing: You need to arrange your layers in a different order. For this project, position your Buttons layer above your Background layer. Arranging layers in Flash is as easy as dragging a graphic to another location. Just click the Buttons layer and drag it below the Globe layer (see Figure 9.15).

Figure 9.15

A horizontal line indicates the location of the rearranged layer.

Line

Your layers are now in a new order, as shown in Figure 9.16.

Figure 9.16

Your Layer area should match this figure.

EXCURSION

Using the Layer Properties Dialog Box

Flash offers another technique for editing layers and setting layer features. For this method, double-click the Document icon to the left of a layer name (see Figure 9.17).

Figure 9.17

Document icons appear to the left of layer names.

Document icon —

Double-clicking this icon displays the Layer Properties dialog box (see Figure 9.18). You can set multiple layer features in this dialog box. For example, you can rename a layer in the Name box. You can show or lock a layer by clicking the appropriate check box. You can set the layer type, and you can even set the outline color by clicking the Outline Color button to display the color palette and click a new color. You can also change the layer height.

Figure 9.18

You might want to change a layer's height if you have lots of information in the layer. This change causes the layer to appear in double or triple the default height.

Rename a layer

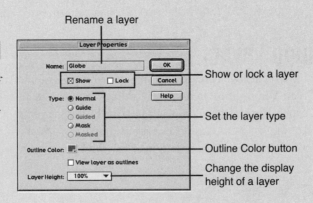

Show or lock a layer

Set the layer type

Outline Color button

Change the display height of a layer

EXCURSION

Viewing Layer Content in Outline Form

Another nice feature of Flash is the ability to see a layer's content in just an outline view. This way you can clearly see what is happening on each layer in a movie. This feature is particularly beneficial for troubleshooting multiple animations that are located on several layers. You can change to an outline view of all the objects on the Stage by clicking the Show All Layers as Outlines button in the upper-right corner of the Layer area (see Figure 9.19).

Show All Layers as
an Outline button

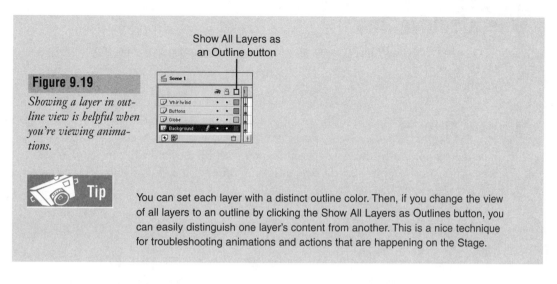

Figure 9.19

Showing a layer in outline view is helpful when you're viewing animations.

Tip

You can set each layer with a distinct outline color. Then, if you change the view of all layers to an outline by clicking the Show All Layers as Outlines button, you can easily distinguish one layer's content from another. This is a nice technique for troubleshooting animations and actions that are happening on the Stage.

Your movie should now look similar to Figure 9.20. Now is the time to save your Web site movie to avoid losing all the changes you have made. You will find an example of the Web site up to this point on the CD-ROM that accompanies this book. Open the Chapter 9 folder and locate the file whirlwind09.fla if you need to see an example of the project Web site.

Figure 9.20

Your movie should look similar to what you see in this figure.

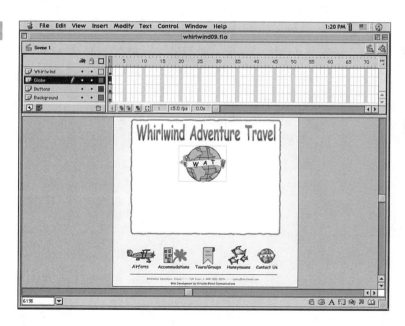

9

Where You've Been!

This chapter covered the layer features of Flash. You rearranged your travel company Web site so that the layers and layer objects are in the order that you will need them for the rest of the book.

What's Next?

The next chapter introduces you to animation with Flash. You will learn how to create motion and shape tweens, as well as create some special effects with color tweening and size tweening.

Animating the Movie

As you probably know by now, symbols and instances are where much of the power of Flash is, but animation is where the fun is! Next we will explore how to create and use animation to add some excitement to the project Whirlwind Adventure Travel Web site.

From the planning stage of your project you know that you need to create animation on the home page that is engaging and represents the company's name, Whirlwind Adventure Travel. We have planned the home page to show the Whirlwind text move on the Stage and then swirl up to its location at the top of the Stage. But how about some other ideas for animation to add excitement to the site? We could make the dot of the second "I" of Whirlwind roll down next to the Whirlwind text and then transform into Adventure. After this occurs, the Travel piece of the text can fly from right to left onto the Stage, ending next to the Adventure text. This additional animation will add more excitement and visual interest to the home page and will also give you a chance to learn more about the animation features of Flash.

➔ For more information on planning the Web site, **see** Chapter 4, "Planning Your Travel Company Web Site," **p. 59**.

Working with the Timeline

So far you have used the Timeline for creating different pieces and parts of your movie. In Chapter 6, "Importing Graphics for the Travel Company Web Site," you used the Timeline and keyframes to created a graphic from scratch by tracing the outline of the scanned globe graphic. Now you will begin to use the Timeline for animation.

Anytime you create animation, you need to work with frames. The Timeline is the holding area for all frames, and it allows you to sequence the frames so that you develop a progression of time. Animation is really a trick of the eye. As the *playhead* moves from one frame to the next, your Stage changes in its content, creating the illusion of motion. There are two types of frames in Flash, keyframes and frames. Your Timeline holds both in *photoframes* (see Figure 10.1).

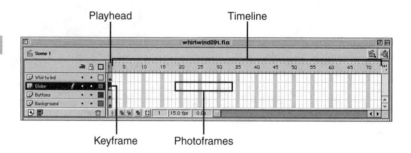

Figure 10.1

The Timeline is the key to creating animation. Your layers display different animations for your movie. When they are viewed together, you have a complex movie comprising a series of animations, some occurring at the same time and others, by themselves.

- **Timeline**—Controls and organizes a movie's content in layers and frames. As the Timeline moves from frame to frame, the illusion of motion is created.
- **Playhead**—Indicates where the movie is at in its flow of frame-by-frame animation.
- **Photoframes**—A frame placeholder in the Timeline for frames and keyframes.
- **Keyframe**—A frame in which you determine changes in the action on the Stage, or changes necessary for applying actions and labels in a movie.

 Note

When you create a new layer, Flash automatically creates a keyframe in Frame 1 of the Timeline for that new layer. A circle designates this keyframe.

Preparing for the Animation

Flash allows one object to be animated per layer. Therefore, you need to create three new layers for each of the words that you plan to animate in the company name. You need to insert three new layers above the Whirlwind layer:

1. Click the Whirlwind layer to make it active and then click the Insert Layer button.

2. A new layer appears above the Whirlwind layer. Rename the new layer to Whirl.

3. Repeat this process for creating and naming the Adventure and Travel layers.

Tip You can increase the area of the Timeline by clicking and dragging the lower Timeline border (see Figure 10.2).

Figure 10.2

The double arrow tool appears when you position your mouse on the lower border of the Timeline.

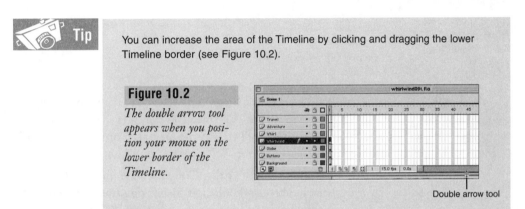

Double arrow tool

Because you want to make the Whirlwind text swirl onto the Stage and the other text to follow after that, the first thing that you must do is break the company name, Whirlwind Adventure Travel, into three separate symbols. Flash allows only one animated item per layer, and you have three different animations planned, one for each word in the company name. To prepare your text for animation, follow these steps:

1. Select the Whirlwind layer and then (Option-click) [Alt+click] on the lock symbol in this layer to cause all the other layers to be locked. You will be working with this layer's objects and do not want other layer objects to be accessible (see Figure 10.3).

Figure 10.3

The company name, Whirlwind Adventure Travel, becomes the active object on the Stage when you (Option-click) [Alt+click] the Whirlwind Text layer.

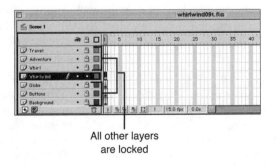

All other layers
are locked

10

2. If the Whirlwind Adventure Travel symbol is not selected on the Stage, click it to make it active. Choose **Modify**, **Break Apart** to break the link from this symbol and the instance on the Stage. The company name is broken into individual letter shapes that are highlighted (see Figure 10.4).

Figure 10.4

The company name becomes individual letters as shown by the highlight.

Whirlwind Adventure Travel

3. Click anywhere in a blank area of the Stage to deselect the highlighted company name. Then marquee the word Whirlwind so that it is the active object on the Stage. Convert it to a symbol by choosing **Insert**, **Convert to Symbol**. Name the symbol Whirlwind and set its behavior to Graphic.

4. Copy the Whirlwind symbol using the **Edit**, **Copy** menu command. Click the Whirlwind layer to make it active and unlock it by clicking the lock icon in the lock column. Use the **Edit**, **Paste in Place** menu command (Shift-Cmd-V) [Shift+Ctrl+V] to paste this text directly on top of the copied text on the Whirlwind layer.

5. On the Whirlwind layer, select the Adventure text by marqueeing it and convert it to a symbol. Name the symbol Adventure and set its behavior to Graphic. Then copy the Adventure symbol. Click the Adventure layer to make it active and unlock it by clicking the lock icon in the lock column. Use the **Paste in Place** menu command (Shift-Cmd-V) [Shift+Ctrl+V] to paste this text directly on top of the copied text of the Whirlwind layer.

6. On the Whirlwind layer, select the Travel text by marqueeing it, and then convert it into a symbol. Name the symbol Travel and set its behavior to Graphic. Then copy the Travel symbol. Click the Travel layer to make it active and unlock it by clicking the lock icon in the lock column. Use the **Paste in Place** menu command (Shift-Cmd-V) [Shift+Ctrl+V] to paste this text directly on top of the copied text on the Whirlwind layer.

You must convert any graphic that you are going to animate with a *motion tween* into a symbol. This helps reduce the overall movie size because you are not duplicating the graphic in each frame of the animation. Instead, you are pointing to a symbol for each frame of animation. If you forget to convert a graphic into a symbol when you apply a motion tween to it, Flash will automatically create a symbol of the graphic. Flash will generically name the symbol Tween1 (or 2, 3, 4, and so on) depending on the number of times you forget to create a symbol for a motion tween.

Your Stage should look exactly as it did before, but there are three new layers with the individual symbols of the company name pasted directly on top of the Whirlwind layer contents (see Figure 10.5). You will use the Whirlwind layer as a guide for positioning your animated text so that, when the movie finishes, all text will be located in the exact position as in the original Whirlwind symbol. The final step for your movie is to delete the Whirlwind layer since it is duplicate information. For now, click the lock icon for the Whirlwind layer to lock the layer.

Figure 10.5

Your Stage looks the same as before you created the three new layers.

EXCURSION

History of Animation and Keyframe Terminology

A *keyframe* is a frame that designates a major change in movement or motion on the Stage. The terminology of keyframe came from the early cartoon animation days. Back then there were two types of animators:

- Experienced, higher-paid professionals, who created the frames that only showed major changes in the cartoon or characters. These frames were called *keyframes*.

- Less experienced, lower-paid professionals, who created the in-between frames from one keyframe to another. These frames were called *tween (in between)* frames.

Flash uses this terminology and the above keyframe/tween frame concepts for its animation functionality.

Creating a Keyframe

Now that the layers have been created for each of the three text animations, it is time to focus on creating the Whirlwind animation. Remember that this animation will show the Whirlwind text swirl onto the Stage and then position itself in the top-left corner of the white rectangular area.

To begin this animation you must designate the start and finish keyframes for the swirling Whirlwind text. When you created the new Whirl layer, a keyframe was automatically created in Frame 1. Then you paste the Whirlwind text into this layer. Now you want to create a keyframe for the ending position of the swirling

Whirlwind text. Click in Photoframe 30 in the Whirl layer. Choose the **Insert, Keyframe** menu command. A keyframe is inserted in Photoframe 30 (see Figure 10.6).

Figure 10.6

When you insert a keyframe in Photoframe 30, only Whirlwind displays; all other Stage content disappears.

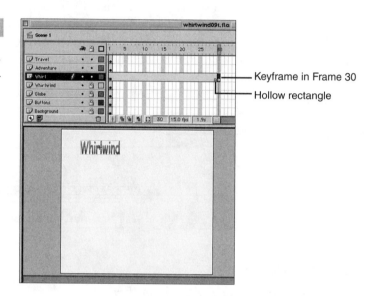

— Keyframe in Frame 30
— Hollow rectangle

Notice that the Stage has the Whirlwind text in the same location as before, and all other Stage content disappears. This is because the Timeline for each of these layers after Frame 1 is empty, therefore, no content is displayed. You will fix this problem in the next section. Also notice that your Timeline for the Whirl layer now has a gray shading between Frame 1 and Frame 30. You will see a hollow rectangle in Frame 29. This shading and hollow rectangle indicate that the frames from 1 to 30 contain the same content on the Stage.

Because you chose **Keyframe** instead of **Blank Keyframe** from the **Insert** menu, you duplicated the contents of the Stage from Keyframe 1 to all frames up through Keyframe 30.

You can use the keyboard shortcut of F6 for inserting a keyframe.

You can also (Control-click) [right-click] the frame or photoframe that will hold the keyframe to display the shortcut menu. Click **Insert Keyframe** from the shortcut menu to insert a keyframe into this location on the Timeline.

To prepare for the animation, you need to move the Whirlwind text into the start and finish positions for Keyframes 1 and 30:

1. Click Frame 1 of the Whirl layer to make it active, and then click and drag the Whirlwind text to the bottom right outside of the Stage area, aligned with the white rectangular area (see Figure 10.7). This is the starting location for the animation.

Figure 10.7

Position your Whirlwind text outside of the Stage area.

 Tip

> If you position an object outside the Stage area, it will not appear in your final movie. This technique can be used for the animation effect that shows objects flying into and out of the movie. Position the object outside the Stage area and then create the animation for moving the object onto the Stage.

2. Leave Keyframe 30 with the Whirlwind text in its location at the top of the white rectangular area. This will be the ending position of the text.

10

By creating the start and end position of your Whirlwind text animation, you have designated the major changes in animation for this part of the movie. You are now ready for the lower-skilled animators to fill in Frames 2–29 with the in-between frames showing this movement. Flash will do this for you with a motion tween. But before you create the motion tween, you need to create the frames showing the Stage content from Frame 2 through 30 for all other layers of the movie.

Creating a Frame

A frame is different from a keyframe. A frame is used to show static content on the Stage, or objects that are stationary during animation. You need to create all the frames for the Globe, Buttons, and Background layers. Since the Stage objects will not move on these layers, you need to insert frames in Photoframe 30 for each of these layers (see Figure 10.8). To do this, click in Photoframe 30 of the Globe layer and choose **Insert**, **Frame**.

Figure 10.8

All frames between 2 and 30 are filled with the contents of Frame 1 of the layer. Frame 30 now has a hollow rectangle indicating that the frames content is the same as Frame 1.

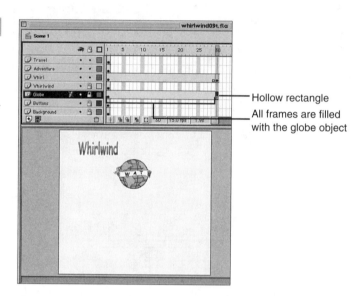

— Hollow rectangle

— All frames are filled with the globe object

The globe appears on your Stage even though you are in Frame 30. Click any of the frames between Frames 1 and 30 in the Globe layer, and you will still see the globe.

 Tip   You can use the keyboard equivalent of F5 for inserting a frame.

 Tip   You can also (Control-click) [right-click] on the photoframe that will hold the frame to display the shortcut menu. Click **Insert Frame** from the shortcut menu to insert a frame into this photoframe.

Using any of the above techniques, insert a frame in Photoframe 30 for the Whirlwind, Buttons, and Background layers.

Using Tweening

You are now ready to create the tweening frames for the swirling Whirlwind text. As stated earlier, Flash will create the tweening frames for you.

Creating Motion Tweening

Click the Whirl layer so that it is the active layer. Notice that you have selected the layer as well as all the frames from 1 to 30. You will now create the tweening frames between the start position of the Whirlwind text in Frame 1 and the end position in Frame 30 (see Figure 10.9).

Figure 10.9

When you select a layer, you will also select all frames that have Stage content.

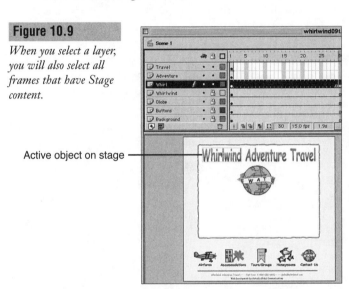

Active object on stage ——

Choose **Insert, Create Motion Tween**. This creates all the in between frames for showing the Whirlwind text moving from the start position to the end position (see Figure 10.10).

10

Figure 10.10

A blue fill with an arrow pointing from Frame 1 to Frame 30 appears in the Whirl layer to tell you that the frames containing the animated text now exist.

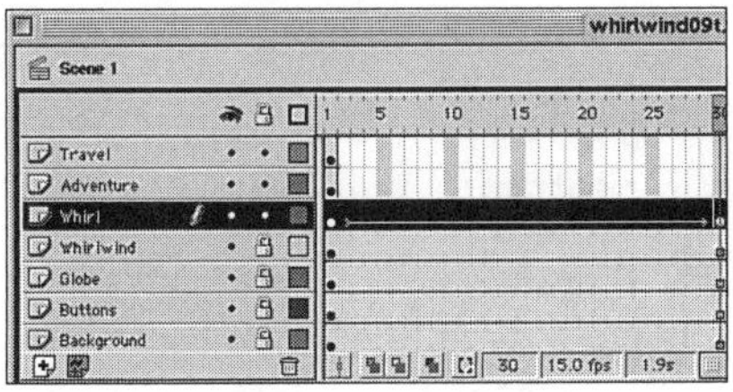

Note

When you create a motion tween in the Timeline, blue shading appears and there is an arrow pointing from the start keyframe to the end keyframe. This shading and the arrow designate that the animation for these frames on the Stage is a motion tween.

Playing Your Movie

 To test your animation you first need to rewind your movie by choosing **Control**, **Rewind**. The playhead moves to Frame 1 of the Timeline. To play the movie, choose **Control, Play**. You will see the Whirlwind text move from the lower-right corner to the ending position in the upper-left corner of the white rectangle area.

 Tip

You can also display your movie Controller by choosing **Window**, **Controller**. Use the buttons on it to rewind and play your movie (see Figure 10.11).

Figure 10.11

The Controller is a floating panel that can be moved to any location you want on the screen.

Move back one frame · Move forward one frame

Stop — Controller — Move to the end of the Timeline

Rewind to beginning of Timeline · Play

 Tip

You can use the keyboard equivalent commands of (Return) [Enter] to play a movie and (Option-Cmd-Return) [Alt+Ctrl+Enter] to rewind the movie.

You have created all the in between frames for moving the Whirlwind text from right to left on the Stage. But at this point, the animation is not swirling onto the Stage as you want. To create this swirling motion you need a guide layer to guide the animation in a swirling path.

Creating a Guide Layer for Motion Tweening

Flash offers the neat feature of a guide layer that allows you to designate a path for an animation to follow. To make your animation swirl on the Stage, follow these steps:

1. Click the Whirl layer to make it active and then (Control-click) [right-click] the new layer to display the shortcut menu.

2. Select **Add Motion Guide** from the list (see Figure 10.12).

Figure 10.12

*The **Layer** shortcut menu offers you many options for working with layers.*

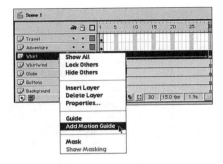

A new layer appears above the Whirl layer automatically labeled "Guide: Whirl" (see Figure 10.13). Notice that it has a different icon to the left of the layer name and that now the Whirl layer is indented slightly to the left. This designates that the guide layer is attached to the Whirl layer. Any path that you create on the guide layer will be associated with the Whirl layer and its animation.

Guide layer

Figure 10.13

The guide layer is connected to the Whirl layer as indicated by the indentation of the Whirl layer.

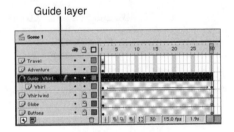

 **Tip**   A guide layer is only visible in the Flash development mode. When you publish the movie, the guide layer is not visible in the movie, but the path for the animation is still used to guide your animation in the published movie.

Creating a Path for Animation

10

After you have your guide layer set up, you can designate the path for the animation. It is easier to set the path if you can see your animation from start to finish, by turning on the Onion Skin feature of the Timeline. To do this, follow these steps:

1. Make sure the Whirl layer is active, and then click the first Onion Skin button that displays a default setting of three frames for your Whirlwind animation.

2. Reset the Onion Skin markers so that they encompass all frames from 1 to 30 by clicking and dragging the left marker to Frame 1. If needed, click and drag the right Onion Skin marker to Frame 30. Then click the Edit Multiple Frames button to turn this feature on. This allows you to edit multiple frames in an animation path (see Figure 10.14).

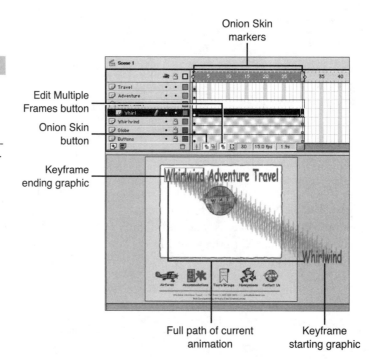

Figure 10.14

When you turn on the Onion Skin and the Edit Multiple Frames buttons, you can see the full path of your animation. Notice that darker shading represents the objects on the Stage for the keyframes of the starting and ending points.

Onion Skin markers

Edit Multiple Frames button

Onion Skin button

Keyframe ending graphic

Full path of current animation

Keyframe starting graphic

→ For more information on using the Onion Skin feature of Flash, **see** Chapter 6, "Importing Graphics for the Travel Company Web Site," **p. 127**.

 After you have the Onion Skin and Edit Multiple Frames buttons turned on, you can adjust the path of your animation by dragging the starting or ending keyframe graphic to a new location on the Stage. The full path of the animation will adjust its flow to the new positions of the starting and ending graphics.

 By locking the layers below the Whirl layer, you are not affecting any of the other objects on the Stage when you adjust the starting or ending point of an animation through the Edit Multiple Frames feature. However, you can adjust the entire Stage content by unlocking all layers and then turning this feature on and moving the individual Stage items.

With the two Onion Skin features turned on, you now can set your path with accuracy. Follow these steps to create a motion guide path:

1. Click Frame 1 of the Guide: Whirl layer (see Figure 10.15). Select the Pencil tool from the toolbox and click the Smooth option.

Frame 1

Figure 10.15

Click Frame 1 in the Guide: Whirl layer.

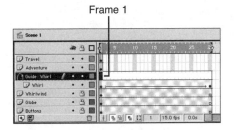

2. Begin to draw your path for the animation by starting it from the center of the beginning keyframe Whirlwind graphic in the lower-right corner. Start this path from the center point of the graphic and end your path in the center point of the ending keyframe Whirlwind graphic (see Figure 10.16).

Figure 10.16

If you want your animation to flow on and off the Stage, draw your path so that it exits the Stage into the work area in the positions that you want the animation to flow off the Stage.

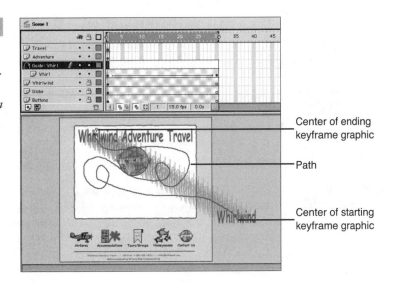

Center of ending keyframe graphic

Path

Center of starting keyframe graphic

10

3. When you release your mouse, you will see the animation path adjust to the pencil line guide. If you do not see this adjustment, you did not hit your center points for the starting and ending graphics. Undo the path and try again. Your screen should look similar to Figure 10.17.

Figure 10.17

You can adjust your path using the Arrow tool.

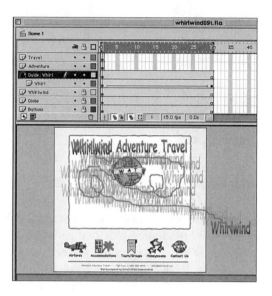

 Play your animation by choosing the **Control, Play** menu command (or any of the other Play techniques covered earlier in this chapter) to see the new flow of the Whirlwind graphic on the Stage. Now your Whirlwind text swirls onto the Stage.

> **Tip**
>
> It is always a good idea to play your animation when you create or make edits to it. It is easier to troubleshoot problems with animation by looking at each piece of the movie's animation as you are creating it.

> **Tip**
>
> If you want to hide the guide layer so that you can see your animation flow without out the guide line displayed, simply click the dot in the Eye column by the Guide: Whirl layer.

Creating Rotation Tweening

After you have created animation that follows a path, you can then add a rotating effect to the object being animated. The Whirlwind text would look more like it was blowing in the wind if it would rotate while it swirls onto the Stage. To create this effect, follow these steps:

1. Click the Whirl layer to select the layer and all frames. Then choose **Window, Panels, Frame**. This displays the Frame panel (see Figure 10.18).

Figure 10.18

You can create a motion tween through the Frame panel by selecting **Motion** *from the* **Tweening** *menu.*

2. To set the rotation of the animated object, click the **Rotate** menu and select **CW** from the menu. Click in the times box and type 2 for the number of times to rotate.

3. Next to Options, click the Orient to path box to more tightly align the animation of the path.

4. Set the Easing to -100 by either dragging the disk on the Easing slider to the up position or by typing 100 into the Easing box. Your settings should match Figure 10.19.

Figure 10.19

You can designate a shape tween instead of a motion tween by clicking the **Tweening** *menu and selecting* **Shape**.

Causes the animation to start slower and end faster

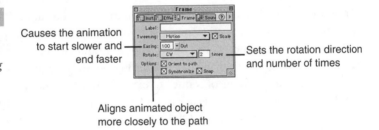

Sets the rotation direction and number of times

Aligns animated object more closely to the path

5. Close the Frame panel and play your movie. You should see your animation swirl and rotate onto the Stage to its resting position at the top-left corner. The playhead moves along the Timeline showing you the progression of your animation.

At this point, you no longer need the Onion Skin feature. Turn it off by clicking the Onion Skin and the Edit Multiple Frames buttons again. You also might want to hide the Whirlwind layer so that you can see your movie's animation without the ending position of the company name. Remember, you will delete this layer after you have completed your animation for each of the words.

10

Manipulating Frames and Keyframes

Next you are going to make the dot of the second "I" in Whirlwind text roll off and position itself next to the word Whirlwind. This dot will then morph into the word Adventure. Notice that you have only created Stage content in frames up to Frame 30. What you want to do will require additional animation in the Adventure layer that begins at Frame 30 and extends farther right in the Timeline. You set up your frames for the first four layers to only go to Frame 30, so now you will need to extend them.

 Tip
You can manipulate frames for all layers in the Timeline, whether the layers are hidden or locked.

To manipulate already created frames, you have several techniques. The easiest is to just click and drag the frame that you want to move to a new photoframe. Any Stage content or animation associated with this frame will automatically extend to fill the additional frames. You need to move the end frames of your Background, Buttons, and Globe layers farther to the right, beyond Frame 30. Click the Background layer to make it active, and then click and drag Frame 30 to Frame 70. Don't worry if this is not the correct number of frames to extend the Timeline; you can always adjust the number of frames that make up the layer at any time. Repeat this frame manipulation process for the Buttons, Globe, and Whirlwind layers. Notice that the gray shading in the Timeline extends to Frame 70. The gray shading designates static animation on the Stage.

 Tip
You can also cut, copy, and paste a frame or series of frames. First, select the desired frame or frames. Then choose **Edit**, **Cut Frame** or **Copy Frames**. Click the frame into which you want to paste the copied frames and choose the **Edit**, **Paste Frames** command.

 Warning
You cannot use the traditional cut, copy, and paste commands on frames. You must use the **Cut Frames**, **Copy Frames**, and **Paste Frames** commands found under the **Edit** menu. If you use the traditional cut, copy, and paste commands, you will be manipulating Stage content for those frames, not the actual frames.

Creating Multilayered Animation

As you know, you can only animate one object or group of objects on a layer at a time. So to create multiple objects moving at the same time on the Stage, you need to use multiple layers. In this section you will use a combination of a motion tween on one layer with a shape tween on another layer to accomplish this rolling dot and morphing animation.

Creating Shape Tweening

By now you should have your Whirlwind text swirling onto the Stage. Next you need to make the Adventure text appear. We've decided to make the dot of the second "*I*" break off and roll up over the "*d*" of Whirlwind, and then down to the bottom of the text and end up next to the Whirlwind text. When the dot is positioned, the word Adventure will morph out from the dot and assume its place next to the Whirlwind text. This type of animation involves a combination of motion animation to make the dot move, and then a shape tween to make the dot morph into the word Adventure. Let's first focus on the rolling dot.

First, you need to make a copy of the dot of the "*I*". To do this, you need to edit the symbol for the Whirlwind text:

1. Click in Frame 1 of the Whirl layer. The first instance of Whirlwind is visible in the lower-right corner.

2. (Control-click) [right-click] the instance and click **Edit** from the shortcut menu. This takes you to the symbol-editing mode.

3. If your Whirlwind text symbol is grouped, ungroup it (Shift-Cmd-G) [Shift+Ctrl+G], so that it appears as individual letters. Then select the dot of the second "*I*" only.

4. Copy the dot with the **Edit**, **Copy** menu command.

5. Now you want to create a new symbol for the dot because you will animate the dot with a motion tween. To create a new symbol while in the symbol-editing mode, make sure the dot is selected and then choose **Insert**, **New Symbol**.

6. The New Symbol dialog box appears. Type dot for the name of the symbol and select the behavior of Graphic. Click OK to close the dialog box. The dot is converted to its own symbol.

7. Exit the symbol-editing mode by choosing **Edit**, **Edit Movie** and return to the movie.

Open your Library if it is not already opened and notice that you have a new dot symbol (see Figure 10.20).

10

Figure 10.20

The dot is now its own symbol in the movie's Library.

You are now ready to create the motion tween of the dot. Follow these steps:

1. Click in Frame 30 of the Adventure layer. Insert a blank keyframe by choosing the **Insert**, **Blank Keyframe** menu command.

 Tip   You can also insert a blank keyframe by pressing the F7 key on your keyboard.

 Note   When you insert a blank keyframe, Flash does not copy the previous keyframe content into the new keyframe. You insert a blank keyframe and, therefore, a blank Stage displays at that point in the movie.

2. Drag an instance of the dot symbol from the Library onto the Stage. Position the dot over the dot of the second "*I*" of Whirlwind (see Figure 10.21). Close your Library.

Dot

Figure 10.21

You can use your arrow keys to position the dot exactly. The arrow keys move the dot one pixel at a time.

3. Click in Photoframe 35 in the Adventure layer and insert a keyframe by pressing F6 on your keyboard. Move the dot next to the "*d*". (Control-click) [right-click] any frame between 30 and 35 and choose **Create Motion Tween** from the shortcut menu (see Figure 10.22).

Figure 10.22

You must insert a keyframe and then move your object to the new location before creating the motion tween of the dot rolling.

10

Dot

4. Click in Photoframe 37 in the Adventure layer and insert a keyframe. Move the dot to the top of the "*d*" (see Figure 10.23). If the motion tween is not automatically applied to Frames 35–37, (Control-click) [right-click] any frame between 35 and 37 and choose **Create Motion Tween** from the list.

Figure 10.23

The blue shading and the arrow in the Timeline designate that a motion tween has been applied.

Dot

5. Click in Photoframe 40 in the Adventure layer and insert a keyframe. Move the dot to the bottom of the "*d*" (see Figure 10.24). If the motion tween is not automatically applied to Frames 37–40, (Control-click) [right-click] any frame between 37 and 40 and choose **Create Motion Tween** from the list.

Figure 10.24

This tween will cause the dot to appear to roll down the backside of the "d" of Whirlwind.

Dot

6. Click in Photoframe 45 in the Adventure layer and insert another keyframe. Move the dot to the center of the "*n*" of the word Adventure still visible from the Whirlwind layer below (see Figure 10.25). If the motion tween is not automatically applied to Frames 40–45, (Control-click) [right-click] any frame between 40 and 45 and choose **Create Motion Tween** from the list. Play your animation.

Figure 10.25

You will have the word Adventure morph out of the dot, so you want to position the dot in the very center of Adventure.

Dot

You have a copy of the word Adventure in frames 1–29 on the Adventure layer. Because you used a blank keyframe in Frame 30, Adventure is not in the next set of frames. We will use this word for our morph by cutting it from Frame 1 and pasting it in the frame we need for the morph.

To create the morph or shape tween, you need to know that shape tweening cannot occur with any objects that have been grouped or are a symbol. Therefore, you need to break the link between your dot instance and the symbol as well as break the link between your Adventure symbol and the Adventure instance. By doing this, the dot morphs into the word Adventure. Use the following steps to create a shape tween:

1. Click *Frame 45* of the Adventure layer to make it active. You will see the dot become that active object on the Stage. Copy this dot.

2. Click Photoframe 46 of the Adventure layer and insert a blank keyframe by pressing F7. Then use the **Paste in Place** command to paste the dot so that it appears in the exact location as the copied dot in Frame 45.

10

3. Now break the link between the instance of the dot instance on the Stage and the symbol by choosing **Modify**, **Break Apart**. The rectangular marquee around the dot disappears, and the dot fill becomes highlighted, indicating that it is now an individual shape of fill-color pixels (see Figure 10.26).

Figure 10.26

The dot has been broken into its individual pixel fills.

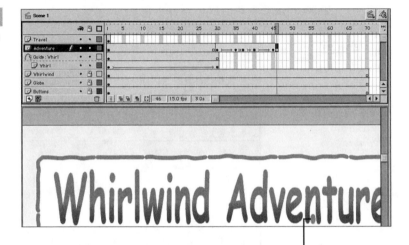

Individual pixel filled dot

4. Click Frame 1 of the Adventure layer so that the Adventure text becomes the active object on the Stage. **Cut** this text. Notice that Frame 1 becomes an empty keyframe, and all frames from 2–29 become empty frames because there is nothing on the Stage for these frames.

5. In the Adventure layer, click Photoframe 55 and insert a blank keyframe by pressing F7. **Paste in Place** the cut Adventure text (see Figure 10.27).

Blank photoframes   Static animation indicator

Figure 10.27

*The **Paste in Place** command positions the Adventure text exactly in the location of the original.*

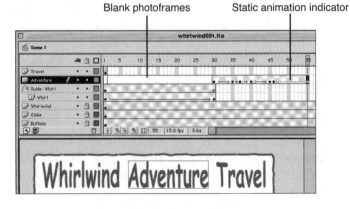

Note

Notice that there is a dotted line in frames 46–55. The dotted line means that these frames do not have any animation on the Stage—all objects for this layer are stationary for these frames at this point.

6. With Frame 55 still selected, you now want to break the link between the Adventure symbol and the instance on the Stage. If the Adventure instance is not active, click it and then choose **Modify**, **Break Apart**. The word Adventure becomes individual letters composed of a pixel fill.

7. You are now ready to apply the shape tween between the dot and Adventure. Click Frame 46 to select it. Choose **Window**, **Panels**, **Frame** to open the Frame panel (see Figure 10.28).

Figure 10.28

The Frame panel allows you to set the type of tween as well as specific settings for motion or shape tweens.

8. Click the **Tweening** menu and select **Shape** from the list. Leave all other setting at the default.

 TryIt You will see green shading in Frames 46–54 and an arrow pointing from keyframes 46 to 54, which indicate that you have applied a shape tween (see Figure 10.29). Close your Frame panel. Rewind your movie and play your animation. You might want to hide the Whirlwind layer by clicking the dot in the Eye column. Doing so allows you to more clearly see the animation that you have developed so far.

10

 Tip

If you adjust the Easing setting for a Shape Tween in the Frame panel, you can cause the shape tween to either begin fast and end slow (setting between 1 and 100), or begin slow and end fast (setting between –1 and –100).

Green shade and arrow

Green shading in the frames that have this animation applied designates a shape tween.

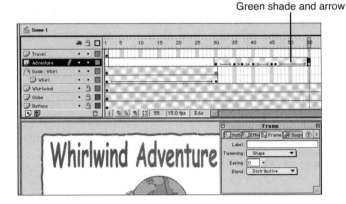

Tip

The Blend option allows you to set the type of morphing for the intermediate shapes that occur between the start and end shapes. If you select **Distributive**, the blend will be composed of intermediate shapes that are smoother and more irregular. If you select **Angular**, the blend preserves existing corners and the straight lines of the intermediate shapes.

Play your movie again. Everything looks great except that you need to make the Whirlwind and Adventure text remain on the screen after they complete their animations. Currently, they end on Frame 55, and the movie continues to Frame 70. You need to extend the frames for the Whirl layer and the Adventure layer through Frame 70 so they remain visible for the full animation as the other layers do. To do this, follow these steps:

1. Click Photoframe 70 of the Whirl layer and insert a frame. You can use the **Insert**, **Frame** menu command or F5 to do this.

2. Insert a frame in Photoframe 70 of the Adventure layer. Your Timeline should look like Figure 10.30.

Tip

You can use the < or > keys to advanced frame by frame, forward and backward, through the Timeline. (Actually, we are referring to the , or . keys. Do not use the Shift key in combination with the , or . keys to get the < or > keys for this keyboard shortcut.)

Figure 10.30

The dotted line in a series of frames indicates static animation on the stage for those layers. Green shading indicates a shape tween, and blue shading indicates a motion tween.

 Again, play your movie. Your movie animation should show the word Whirlwind swirling onto the Stage and then the dot of the second "*I*" of Whirlwind rolling off and down the "*d*" to land next to the word Whirlwind. Then Adventure expands out of the dot. Everything remains on the Stage through Frame 70 of the Timeline.

Next, you want to add one more effect to the Adventure text animation. You want to make the dot look more like it is rolling. You can accomplish this by applying a rotation to the motion tween:

1. In the Adventure layer, select all the frames between 30 and 45, including the keyframes, by clicking Frame 30 and then Shift-clicking on Frame 45 of the Adventure layer.

2. Open the Frame panel by choosing **Window**, **Panels**, **Frame** menu command. This displays the Frame panel.

3. In the Frame panel, click **CW** from the **Rotate** menu and in the times box type 6. Your Frame panel should look like Figure 10.31. Close the Frame panel and play your movie to see the rolling dot.

Figure 10.31

By Shift-clicking on frames 30–45, you selected all the frames that make up the rolling dot. Then you set the dot in these frames to rotate in a clockwise direction to create the full effect of rolling.

10

Finalizing the Company Text Animation

Now you need to finalize the company name by having the word Travel fly in from the right to land in its position next to Adventure. You will use a simple motion tween for this animation. If you hid the Whirlwind layer earlier when you tested your animation, make it visible again by clicking the red X in the Eye column of this layer.

Use the following steps to add animation to the Travel text:

1. Click in Photoframe 55 of the Travel layer. Insert a keyframe by pressing F6. This duplicates the Travel text (from Frame 1 in this layer) into Frame 55. It also includes this object in all frames between 1 and 55. Don't worry about that now. You will delete this Travel text from Frame 1 shortly.

2. Click in Photoframe 70 and insert another keyframe. All frames between 55 and 70 have the Travel text appearing in them.

3. Click in Frame 55 again and move the Travel text off the Stage to the right (see Figure 10.32).

Figure 10.32

By moving the Travel text off the Stage, you are setting up your starting and ending keyframes for a motion tween.

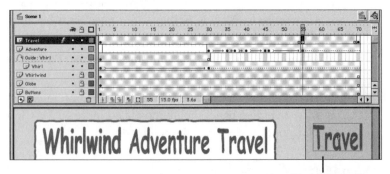

Move Travel off the stage

4. Click any frame between 55 and 70 in the Travel layer and then (Control-click) [right-click] in the highlighted frames to display the shortcut menu. Select **Create Motion Tween** from the shortcut menu. You have created the motion tween for moving the Travel text onto the Stage.

5. Click in Frame 1 of the Travel layer and delete the Travel instance from the Stage (see Figure 10.33).

Play your animation, and you will see the word Travel fly in from the right to land next to the word Adventure, completing the movie animation. Now you can delete the Whirlwind layer that contains the company name. You no longer need this layer for alignment. Click the Whirlwind layer and click the Delete Layer button in the layer area of the Timeline.

Blank frames

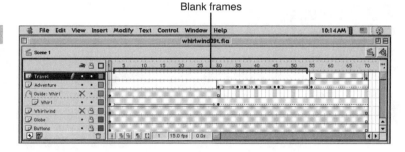

Figure 10.33

All frames from 1 to 54 contain nothing on the Stage. The company name is gone if you hide the Whirlwind layer.

→ For more information on layers and deleting a layer, **see** Chapter 9, "Using Layers to Organize the Movie," **p. 197**.

EXCURSION

Creating Size Tween Animation

You can create size tween animation, showing an object growing bigger or smaller, by following these steps:

1. Insert a keyframe by pressing F6 (or F7, if you want a blank keyframe). Create an instance of a symbol and scale it to the starting size that you want for the initial instance of the object.

2. Insert another keyframe in the Timeline. You can insert the keyframe any number of frames away from the first keyframe. The closer the second keyframe is to the first, the faster you will create the growth of the object in the size tween. The more frames between the two keyframes, the slower the growth of the object.

3. Scale the object to the size that you want for the final instance of the object. You can use the Scale option of the Arrow tool or the **Modify, Transform, Scale and Rotate** menu command. If you make the instance larger than the Stage area, only the part of the image on the Stage will appear in the movie. This can be an interesting effect.

→ For more information on scaling objects, **see** Chapter 5, "Creating and Editing Graphics for the Travel Company Web Site," **p. 93**.

4. (Control-click) [right-click] any frame between the first and second keyframes and choose **Create Motion Tween** from the shortcut menu. You will see an arrow appear between the keyframes, indicating that you have applied a motion tween.

5. Play your movie. You will see your object grow from small to large during the motion tween. This is size tweening.

 Tip

If you want to show an object shrinking, start with a large object in the first keyframe, and then create a small object in the second keyframe.

10

EXCURSION

Creating Color Tweening

You can create color tweening animation, which shows an object change in its color by following these steps:

1. Insert a keyframe by pressing F6 (or F7, if you want a blank keyframe) and create an instance of a symbol.

2. Insert another keyframe in the Timeline. You can insert the keyframe any number of frames away from the first keyframe. The closer the second keyframe is to the first, the faster you will create color tween between the two objects. The more frames between the two keyframes, the slower the color tween between the two objects.

3. Open your Instance panel by choosing **Window**, **Panels**, **Instance**. This displays the Instance panel. Adjust the color settings for the object until you have the new color for the object. Close the Instance panel.

→ For more information on altering an instance, **see** Chapter 8, "Using Symbols, Libraries, and Instances to Recycle and Organize Graphic Elements," **p. 177**.

4. (Control-click) [Right-click] any frame between the first and second keyframes and choose **Create Motion Tween** from the shortcut menu. You will see an arrow appear between the keyframes indicating that you have applied a motion tween.

5. Play your movie. You will see your object change in color from the first instance to the second. This is color tweening.

 Tip

If you adjust the Alpha of the instance, you can make the image appear to disappear or reappear, depending on which instance you apply the Alpha effect to.

Testing Your Movie

Now that you have your movie animation completed for the home page, you can test the movie in the Flash Player. So far, you have only played the movie in the Flash development mode, but now you can take this one step farther and see how it will look in SWF format.

 Choose **Control**, **Test Movie**. This causes Flash to export the movie to SWF format. You will see the Exporting Flash Player dialog box displaying the conversion process.

 Note

When you test a movie, Flash will create another document named the same as your Flash document. For example, you have named this file Whirlwind.fla. Therefore, Flash creates another document named Whirlwind.swf. It is created in the same directory as your Flash or FLA document. Check your directory for this file.

When the Export is finished, Flash opens the Flash Player with your movie playing in the window. You can control the movie playback by using the **Control** menu selection for **Play, Stop**, and **Rewind**. The **Play/Stop** command is a toggle menu command. You can also set the connection speed by choosing the **Debug** menu and selecting a connection speed at which to play the movie (see Figure 10.34).

Figure 10.34

*While in the Flash Player, you can also test the playback of the movie based on a user's connection speed by choosing the modem speeds in the lower portion of the **Debug** menu.*

 Note

Because you are in the Flash Player, you can resize the movie by clicking and dragging the lower-right corner of the window to a new size. Notice that the movie reproportions itself based on the window size. You are viewing the SWF format file of the movie, so you get the right proportion of all objects on the Stage as well as clean edges because all objects are vector graphics.

EXCURSION

Setting the Frames-Per-Second Rate for Your Movie

You can set a frames-per-second rate for your movie that includes all animations in the movie. The default setting is 12fps, which is recommended by Macromedia for Web use. Standard motion pictures use 24fps as the frame rate. To set the frames-per-second rate, you need to display your Movie Properties dialog box. Choose **Modify, Movie** to display this dialog box (see Figure 10.35).

10

Figure 10.35

Set your frame rate by typing in a number in the Frame Rate box.

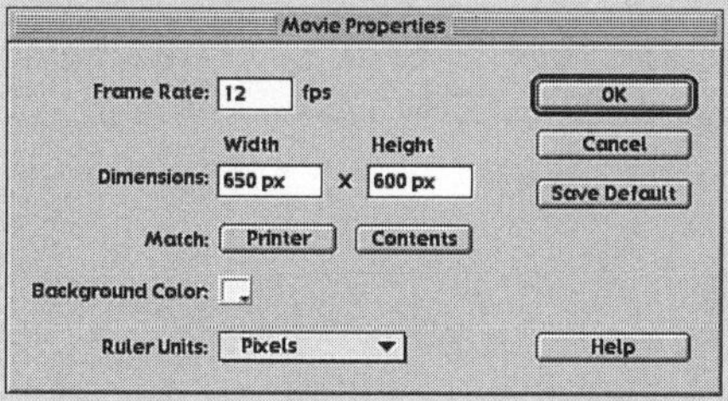

You can increase or decrease this setting as appropriate for your movie and your viewing audience. Simply type in a new number in the fps box. If your movie tends to stop and start while playing, your frame rate is too slow. If your movie tends to blur the animation details, your frame rate is too fast. You should set your frame rate at the beginning of creating your animation because this will be the frame rate that you use for the entire movie. You can only set one frame rate for your entire movie and all animation. We used the default setting since we are developing for the Web.

→ For more information on the Movie Properties dialog box, **see** Chapter 3, "Introduction to the Flash Workspace," **p. 43**.

Save your Web site movie to save all the changes you have made. You will find an example of the Web site up to this point on the CD-ROM that accompanies this book. Open the Chapter 10 folder and locate the file whirlwind10.fla if you need to see an example of the project Web site.

Where You've Been!

This chapter covers many of the animation techniques you can use to create your movies. You learned how to create a motion tween and a shape tween. Color tweening and size tweening were also covered. You will benefit if you practice these skills to gain a strong comfort level with animation. Your Whirlwind Adventure Travel movie is progressing. You now have your home page animation created for an engaging introduction to the site.

What's Next?

In the next chapter you will learn about using scenes in your movie. You will create the scenes you need to make your Web site display the second-level pages you have planned. You will link your buttons to go to these second-level pages and learn how to navigate to and from the movie scenes. You will create new buttons for the second-level pages, too.

Chapter 11

Creating the Movie's Scenes and Buttons

You should have your home page animation set and looking good. Now you need to start adding the other pages of your site as well as adding some interactivity. This requires the creation of scenes for the other pages and the development of your buttons. This chapter covers the creation of scenes and the creation of your buttons for these scenes.

Creating Scenes for Sublevels of the Travel Company Web Site

A *scene* in Flash is a series of animations or events that form a distinct division in a movie's content. Scenes segment a large project or movie so that it is easier to handle. In this chapter, you will use scenes to divide your movie into the second-level pages of your Web site. Every scene has its own Timeline and layers. This will allow you to use a different scene for each of the second-level pages of the site.

You will need to refer to your planning documents that you created in Chapter 4, "Planning Your Travel Company Web Site," for the structure and design of each of the second-level pages. You will use the symbols you created for the buttons on these pages, too. Because the button graphics are symbols, you will not be increasing your movie size much. Again, this is the beauty of symbols and instances!

Renaming an Existing Scene

The easiest way to create and modify a scene is through the Scene panel. You already have Scene 1, which represents the home page movie for the site. You now will rename Scene 1 as Home Page, following these steps:

1. Choose **Window**, **Panels**, **Scene** to display the Scene panel (see Figure 11.1).

Figure 11.1

The Scene panel allows you to create and work with scenes.

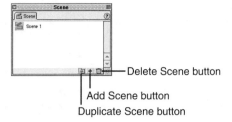

Delete Scene button

Add Scene button

Duplicate Scene button

2. Scene 1 displays in the Scene panel. This is the default scene that Flash creates for all new movies. Double-click "Scene 1" in the Scene panel to access the text box.

3. Delete the "Scene 1" name in the text box and type Home Page (see Figure 11.2).

Figure 11.2

You can name the scene any name that you want in the Scene Properties dialog box.

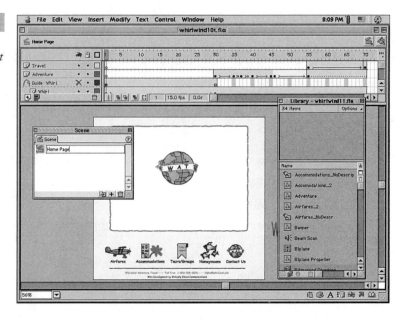

The Scene panel now displays Home Page instead of Scene 1. Notice that the tab in the upper-left corner above the layer area of the Timeline now also displays Home Page. You have renamed the scene. Leave the Scene panel open because we have more work to do with it in the next section.

 Tip   You can resize the Scene panel by clicking and dragging in the lower-right corner of the panel.

Creating a New Scene

Now you need to create the scenes for the second level of your Web site. You will use the Scene panel to do this, too, as shown in the following steps:

1. Click the Add Scene button in the Scene panel.
2. "Scene 2" appears under the Home Page scene (see Figure 11.3). Your Stage reflects the contents of this scene, which presently contains nothing.

Figure 11.3

All new scenes will be created below the selected scene.

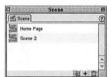

3. Rename "Scene 2" by double-clicking it to display the text box. Rename "Scene 2" as Int'l Airfares.
4. Repeat this process and create the other scenes for the rest of your second-level Web pages. Name the scenes Honeymoons, Accommodations, Tours/Groups, and Contact Us. Your Scene panel should look similar to the one seen in Figure 11.4.

Figure 11.4

These scenes will be used to represent the second-level Web pages of your movie.

11

 Tip   You can also create a new scene by using the **Insert, Scene** menu command.

Switching Between Scenes

After you have your scenes created, you will need to switch between them. To do this, simply click the scene name in the Scene panel. You will see your Stage change to the selected scene's content, indicating that you have moved to that scene. Notice that you see the scene name reflected on the upper-left tab above the layer area of the Timeline (see Figure 11.5).

Figure 11.5

Use your Scene panel to switch between scenes.

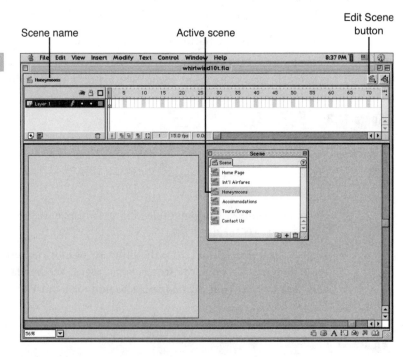

Creating New Scene Content on the Stage

After you have created your scene, you can set up your Stage for this scene. All new scenes have their own Timeline and layers. Therefore, you can create Stage content through the Timeline, adding the appropriate layers that you need. First, let's focus on the Int'l Airfares page of the Web site. You need to refer to your planning documents created in Chapter 4 for all second-level Stage content. Buttons on second-level Web pages appear on the left side of the Stage with the white rectangular area to the right. You will use your Library symbols to create most of the graphics on this page. The following steps guide you through this process:

1. Click the Int'l Airfares scene from the Scene panel to change to this scene.

2. Rename Layer 1 as Background. Create a new layer above the Background layer and name this layer Buttons.

→ For more information on creating and editing layers in Flash, **see** Chapter 9, "Using Layers to Organize the Movie," **p. 197**.

3. Click the Buttons layer to make it active and then place the button symbols from the Library onto your Stage. You will need to use the **Window, Panels, Align** menu command to align them vertically on the Stage. Duplicate the order of the buttons that you used on the home page (see Figure 11.6). (Click the Home Page scene in the Scene panel if you need to check the button order.)

Figure 11.6

Align horizontally all the buttons on your Int'l Airfares scene Stage through the Align panel.

→ For more information on using symbols to create instances in Flash, **see** Chapter 8, "Using Symbols, Libraries, and Instances to Recycle and Organize Graphic Elements," **p. 177**.

4. Re-create the white rectangular area using your Rectangle tool on the Background layer. Position the rectangle to the right of the buttons. Use the same stroke width and color for the rectangle as you did for the rectangle on the home page. Make the rectangle shape extend beyond the height of all buttons on the page. Leave a small blank area at the top and the bottom of the page.

11

5. While still on the Background layer, place an instance of the company name (the Logo symbol) above the white rectangular area. You will see Whirlwind Adventure Travel appear above the rectangle area, but it is too big. Resize the logo instance so that it fits better above the rectangle area.

6. Next you need to place the footer information below the white rectangular area. Click the Home Page scene from the Scene panel to change to the home page. Then copy the footer text block located at the bottom of the Stage. You might need to unlock the Background layer to copy the footer information.

7. Click the Int'l Airfares scene from the Scene panel. Your Stage changes back to the Int'l Airfares layout. Paste the footer information onto the Stage and position it below the rectangular area. Your Stage should look similar to Figure 11.7.

Figure 11.7

This is the initial layout for the Int'l Airfares page of the Web site.

→ For more information on creating and drawing graphics and images, **see** Chapter 5, "Creating and Editing Graphics for the Travel Company Web Site," **p. 93**.

Copying and Pasting Layers and Frames Between Scenes

After you start using scenes in your movies, you will find that to save some work you can copy frames and layers between scenes. Because you have the initial layout for the Int'l Airfares page developed, you could use this same layout for the other four scenes representing the second-level pages, as indicated in your planning documents. The only change that you need to make between the scenes is the color of the white rectangular area's outline. To duplicate the Int'l Airfares layout to the other four scenes, follow these steps:

1. Click the Int'l Airfares scene. Click the Buttons layer so that the layer and Frame 1 are highlighted.

2. Shift-click the Background layer to select this layer as well. Both Layers and Frame 1 of each layer should be highlighted (see Figure 11.8).

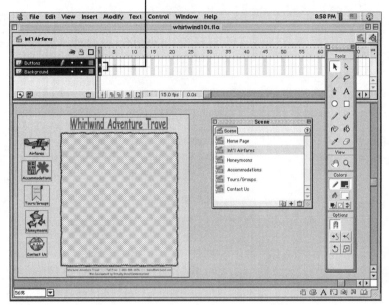

Figure 11.8

All objects on the Stage become highlighted because you have selected both of the layers that make up the scene.

3. Choose **Edit, Copy Frames** to copy both layers and all frames.

4. Click the Honeymoons scene from the Scene panel.

5. Click Frame 1 of the Honeymoons Layer 1 in the Timeline.

6. Choose **Edit, Paste Frames**. Both layers and their Frame 1 content are copied to the Honeymoons scene Timeline (see Figure 11.9).

7. Rename the layers to Buttons and Background as you did in the Int'l Airfares scene.

8. Repeat the previous steps and copy both layers and their Frame 1 to the Accommodations, Tours/Groups, and Contact Us scenes. Rename the layers to Buttons and Background for all scenes.

You now have set up your movie with the initial layout for all second-level Web pages.

11

Figure 11.9

The Stage reflects the objects used on the Int'l Airfares scene that have now been copied to the Honeymoons scene.

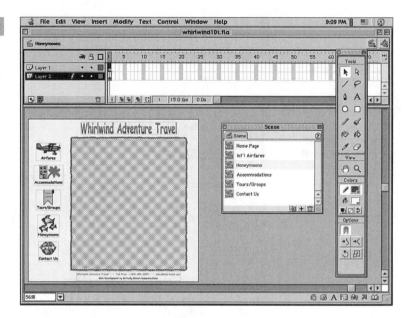

Customizing the Content for Each Scene

You have your second-level Web pages created. Now you need to customize the Stage to reflect each page's content. Using your planning documents from Chapter 4, re-create the preliminary information by following the steps below:

1. Click the Int'l Airfares scene in the Scene panel and click the Background layer to make it active. Using your Arrow tool and the Character panel, type `Listing of Weekly and Monthly Specials` in the white rectangular area. Use a Comic Sans MS, 20-point, black font for the text block. Position the text block in the white rectangular area (see Figure 11.10).

Figure 11.10

This second-level page will contain information specific to the Int'l Airfares area of the site.

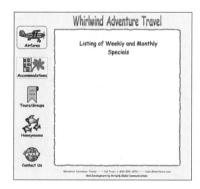

> **Note**
> You can use any font that you want for the text blocks on the second-level pages. The instruction calls for Comic Sans MS font, but, if you don't happen to have that one, you can use whatever font you want.

2. Click the Accommodations scene in the Scene panel and click the Background layer to make it active. Change the line color of the rectangle to blue. Do not add any text blocks to this page. You will be customizing and setting up this page's interface later in this book.

3. Click the Tours/Groups scene in the Scene panel and click the Background layer to make it active. Change the line color of the rectangle to red. Create a text block that reads `Listing of Advertised Tours`. Use a Comic Sans MS, 20-point, black font for the text block. Position the text block in the white rectangular area as you did with the Int'l Airfares page.

4. Click the Honeymoons scene in the Scene panel and click the Background layer to make it active. Change the line color of the rectangle to purple. Create a text block that reads `Description of Top Honeymoon Destinations, Happy Customer Comments`. Use a Comic Sans MS, 20-point, black font for the text block. Position the text block in the white rectangular area as you did with the Int'l Airfares page.

5. Click the Contact Us scene in the Scene panel and change the line color of the rectangle to aqua. Do not add any text blocks to this page. You will be customizing and setting up this page's Contact Us form later in this book.

Playing Your Movie and All Scenes

Even though you have broken your movie into scenes, Flash still recognizes all scenes as one movie. You can advance through the entire movie—one scene at a time—by playing your movie. To see all scenes advanced while in the Flash development mode, you must make sure you have a Play All Scenes feature turned on. Choose **Control**, **Play All Scenes** to turn this feature on.

 With your Scene panel visible, play your movie. Make sure you rewind the movie so you start at the beginning. Watch the movie progress through the scenes listed in the Scene panel, starting with the Home Page, which is at the top of the list, and then ending with Contact Us, which is at the bottom of the list.

→ For more information about playing or testing a Flash movie, **see** Chapter 10, "Animating the Movie," **p. 211**.

11

You can rewind your movie by clicking on the first scene in your Scene panel. Before you can play the movie, you must click Frame 1 of any of the layers that make up this starting scene.

If you test your movie in the Flash Player, all scenes are played, whether you have the **Control, Play All Scenes** menu command turned on or off in the Flash development mode. The **Control, Play All Scenes** menu command is for use in the Flash development mode. It allows you to play your movie and see all scenes without having to test the movie in the Flash Player mode. The movie will always play all scenes in the Flash Player mode but this is not true of the Flash development mode.

Reordering Scenes in the Movie

You can easily reorder your scenes in a movie. If you created the scenes following the order that the previous instructions and the figures represented, you will notice that your planning documents show the Honeymoons scene to be in the wrong order. It needs to be moved above the Contact Us scene. To do this, follow these steps:

1. In the Scene panel, click the Honeymoons scene to select it and then drag it above the Contact Us scene (see Figure 11.11).

Figure 11.11

You will see a horizontal line indicating the location of the reordered scene.

Horizontal line

2. When you release your mouse button, you drop the Honeymoons scene in the second-from-the-last position in the Scene panel.

 Now play your movie, and you will see that the Honeymoons page appears near the end of the movie.

Creating a Multi-State Button

After your scenes are created, you can begin to add some interactivity to the site. You will make your buttons active so that when they are clicked, the end-user can access the appropriate page of the Web site.

You converted your buttons to symbols in Chapter 8, "Using Symbols, Libraries, and Instances to Recycle and Organize Graphic Elements." Now you need to create the various button states for each button symbol used in your site. We will be creating buttons that display a message describing the area of the Web site that the button links to, when the end-user hovers his mouse over the button.

Then on the second level of the site, the buttons will be slightly different. They will have a different Stage appearance to help designate the page that the end-user is on. The other four buttons will simply link to their designated areas, without the hover descriptions. This will require two sets of fully developed buttons; presently, you have only one set of buttons that have not been fully developed yet. To fully develop a button, you will create the various *button states*—Up state, Over state, Down state, and Hit state—for full functionality. You will add functionality to the present set of buttons, and then create a new set of buttons and add functionality to them in this section of the chapter.

Creating the Airfares Button States

Click the Home Page scene from the Scene panel so that you are looking at the home page and its buttons. We will focus on these buttons first. Because the buttons are symbols, you need to go into the symbol-editing mode to edit them. Open your Library and then open the Buttons folder that contains all the buttons for the site. (Control-click) [Right-click] the airfares_button symbol in the Library and select the **Edit** menu command from the shortcut menu. This launches the airfares_button symbol in symbol-editing mode.

You should now have a new Timeline that is composed of the four button states used by Flash—Up, Over, Down, and Hit (see Figure 11.12). Next you will create the various graphics that will represent the button states of the Home Page buttons.

→ For more information about editing symbols in the symbol-editing mode, **see** Chapter 8, "Using Symbols, Libraries, and Instances to Recycle and Organize Graphic Elements," **p. 177**.

11

Up State

The Up state of a button is represented by the image of the button when it is sitting on the Stage. This is the first image of the button that you see. The Up state frame of the button Timeline already has a keyframe with the Airfares button image as the Stage content. You need to create the other three button states and images.

Figure 11.12

By default, the Up state of this button has a keyframe inserted. This keyframe holds the button image for the Up state.

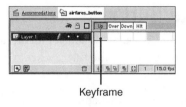

Keyframe

Over State

The Over state of the button is the button state that's triggered when the end-user moves his cursor over the button. The hover image of the button represents this state. You want the button's text to change color and display a description of the Web site area that the button links to on this page (see Figure 11.13). Follow these steps to change the button Over state:

1. Click the Over state frame and press F6 to insert a keyframe. This copies the Up state image on the Stage to the Over state's Stage.

Figure 11.13

The Over state of the button represents a different appearance of the button.

Green colored text for the button name

2. Click the button image. If the button image is grouped, you need to ungroup it because you need to change the text color in the text block. Choose **Modify**, **Ungroup** to ungroup the image from the text block.

3. Using your Arrow tool, double-click the text block to make it the only active element on the Stage. You will see a cursor in the text block. Select all the text in the text block.

4. From the toolbox, select the Text tool and set the Fill Color option to a green color (the same color used for the white rectangular area line for both the Home Page and the Int'l Airfares page).

The Airfares button text will now change to the green color whenever the end-user hovers his cursor over that button.

Down State

The Down state of the button is the button state that's triggered when the end-user clicks the button. He will see a quick image of this button as he presses down on the mouse button. To create this button image, follow these steps:

1. Click in the Down state frame and press F6 to insert a keyframe. This copies the Over state image to the Down state Stage.

2. Double-click the text block to make it the only active element on the Stage. You will see a cursor in the text block. Select all the text in the text block.

3. From the toolbox, select the Text tool and set the Fill Color option to a light green color. Your text will change to the light green color.

Now when the user clicks the Airfares button, the dark green text will turn to the new light green color you've just chosen.

Hit State

The Hit state of the button is the area around the button that is active, or the *hot spot* of the button. When clicked, this area will trigger an action. To create this button state, follow these steps:

1. Click the Hit state frame and press F6 to insert a keyframe. This copies the Down state image to the Hit state Stage.

2. From the toolbox, select the Rectangle tool. Using any settings for Line Height, Stroke Color, and Fill Color options, click and drag a rectangle around the Airfares image. You want to surround the image and the text block (see Figure 11.14).

Figure 11.14

You are defining the hot spot area around the Airfares image for activating the button with the filled rectangle.

 Note

Do not worry about what options you use for the Hit area; you are only determining the area around the button that will be the hot spot.

11

Tip

By creating different Over and Down state images, you can create very interesting buttons. You can even place a movie clip in either of these states to create an animated button. See Chapter 14, "Advanced Animation Techniques," for information on creating movie clips.

Testing the Airfares Rollover Button

After you have the button states created, you need to test them. Return to the movie by clicking the Home Page tab in the upper-left corner of the symbol-editing mode and perform the following test:

1. Choose **Control**, **Enable Simple Buttons** to enable your buttons in the Flash development mode.

2. Move your mouse over the airfares_button symbol and then click the button. You will see the three button state images that you just created: Up, Over, and Down. Notice that the button activates when you move your mouse into the area that you designated as the Hit state. The button does not link to anything because you have not created that interactivity yet.

3. You must turn off the **Enable Simple Buttons** command by selecting the menu command again, **Control**, **Enable Simple Buttons**. This command is a toggle switch. If you leave it on, you cannot edit your buttons because they are active.

Note

Notice that your mouse activates the button when it is within the Hit state area that you defined with the rectangle for the button. This is the hot spot area for the button.

Creating the Airfares Button Description

Now that you have the button states set with the appropriate images, you want to add the description of the Web area that the button links to. This description appears when the end-user hovers over the button. To do this you need to edit the button directly on the Stage. This allows you to make edits to the button states while viewing other Stage objects. You can precisely place your button elements in relation to other objects, as follows:

1. Make sure you are on the Buttons layer of the home page Timeline and that it is the active layer, ready to be edited. Click the airfares_button symbol to make it the active image on the Stage.

 **Warning**   You must turn off the **Control**, **Enable Simple Buttons** menu command to edit a button. Reselect this command to toggle it off.

2. (Control-click) [Right-click] the airfares_button symbol and click the **Edit in Place** command from the shortcut menu. You will see the rest of the Stage dim, and the Timeline with the four button states displays. You will also see the airfares_button tab in the upper-left corner, signifying that you are in the symbol-editing mode (see Figure 11.15).

Figure 11.15

The Edit in Place command causes other objects or instances on the Stage to dim when you access the symbol-editing mode.

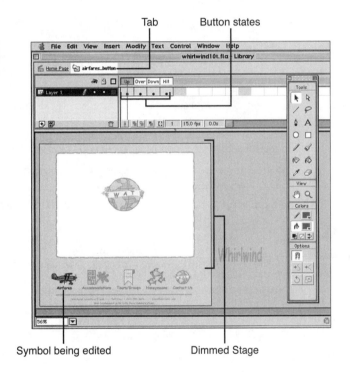

3. Click the Over state keyframe to make it active.
4. Click the Text tool from the toolbox and create a text block. Set your font to a 14-point, Comic Sans MS, black font. Type Check Out Our International and Domestic Airfares. Monthly and Weekly Specials Advertised!. Position the text block toward the bottom of the white rectangular area, centered horizontally in the rectangular area (see Figure 11.16). You can use your Align panel to center the text block on the Stage. Because we will be adding other button descriptions, you might want to pull out a Guide to help align all other text blocks that you will create next.

11

Figure 11.16

Create the description text in the Over state of the button.

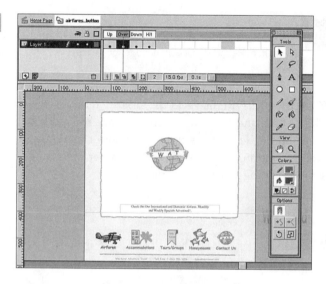

→ For more information about using Guides and the Align panel, **see** Chapter 5, "Creating and Editing Graphics for the Travel Company Web Site," **p. 93**.

5. Exit the symbol-editing mode by clicking the Home Page tab.

6. Test your button by turning on the **Control, Enable Simple Buttons** menu command. Notice that when you hover your mouse over the airfares_button symbol the description appears in the white rectangular area.

 Note

> The **Edit in Place** command allows you to precisely position buttons and elements for the buttons in relation to other objects on the Stage.

Creating the Other Rollover Buttons for the Home Page

Using the instructions in an earlier section, "Creating the Airfares Button States," create your other buttons for the home page. Use Table 11.1 for the settings relevant to each button on the home page.

Table 11.1   Home Page Button Features

Button	Button State	Button Description
Accommodations	Over	Blue text, same color as line used in the white rectangular area of the Accommodations second-level Web page. Black, Comic Sans MS, 14-point font for text description. Text block description: `We Offer Units and Housing all over the World! Use our Search & Find Feature to Locate Your Next Vacation Accommodations..`

Table 11.1   continued

Button	Button State	Button Description
	Down	Light blue text color for button name.
	Hit	Filled rectangle that covers the button image and text block to create the hot spot.
Tours/Groups	Over	Red text, same color as line used in the white rectangular area of the Tours/Groups second-level Web page. Black, Comic Sans MS, 14-point font for text description. Text block description: `We Can Custom Create a Tour for You and Your Group. Or Choose One of Our Popular Tours That Others Rave About!`.
	Down	Light red text color for button name.
	Hit	Filled rectangle that covers the button image and text block to create the hot spot.
Honeymoons	Over	Purple text, same color as line used in the white rectangular area of the Honeymoons second-level Web page. Black, Comic Sans MS, 14-point font for text description. Text block description: `See What We Have Planned for Others on Their Honeymoon. We Can Custom Design Your Honeymoon or You Can Choose from Our Top Destinations.`.
	Down	Light purple text color for button name.
	Hit	Filled rectangle that covers the button image and text block to create the hot spot.
Contact Us	Over	Aqua text, same color as line used in the white rectangular area of the Contact Us second-level Web page. Black, Comic Sans MS, 14-point font for text description. Text block description: `Please Feel Free to Contact Us if You Would Like to Talk with a Sales Representative or to Express Questions, Concerns, or Your Travel Experiences.`.
	Down	Light aqua text color for button name.
	Hit	Filled rectangle that covers the button image and text block to create the hot spot.

TryIt Test your new buttons on the home page to make sure they are functioning correctly.

11

Creating the Buttons for the Second-Level Web Pages

Now that you have your button images created for the Home Page scene, you need to adjust these buttons slightly for the second-level Web pages. Test these buttons on one of the second-level pages. Notice that you have the description of the second-level page appearing on the page. You do not want these descriptions displaying at this level, so you will need to delete them. You also want the button image for the

Up state to display with a rectangle around it for the second-level pages. This will visually help the end-user know what section of the Web site he is on. You need to re-create these buttons for the second-level pages of the Web site. You do this by creating a nested symbol of the original button in a new button symbol and then altering the button states.

→ For more information on editing symbols in the symbol-editing mode and for using the Instance Properties dialog box, **see** Chapter 8, "Using Symbols, Libraries, and Instances to Recycle and Organize Graphic Elements," **p. 177**.

Creating the Second-Level Button for Distinguishing the Page

To create a new image for the button that distinguishes the page you are on as second level, do the following:

1. Switch to the Int'l Airfares page of the Web site by using your Scene panel or the Edit Scene button in the upper-right corner of the Timeline. You can now edit this page and all its buttons (see Figure 11.17).

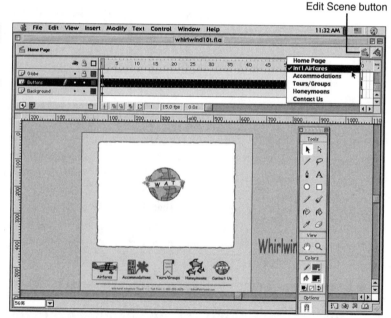

Edit Scene button

Figure 11.17

You can switch to any scene in your movie by choosing it from the Edit Scene button menu list.

2. Select the airfares_button symbol on the Stage and then (Control-click) [right-click] the button. Choose **Edit** from the shortcut menu to launch the symbol-editing mode.

3. Make sure the airfares_button symbol is the active symbol on the Stage in the symbol-editing mode by clicking it. Choose **Insert**, **Convert to Symbol**. Name this symbol `Airfares_2`. Set the button behavior to Graphic because this image will not really link anywhere. It will visually represent that the end-user is now on the Int'l Airfares page.

4. Notice that, even though you created a new symbol, you are still editing the airfares_button symbol. While still in the symbol-editing mode, you need to switch to the new button symbol you created. Open your Library, locate the Airfares_2 symbol, and double-click it. This switches to the Airfares_2 symbol in symbol-editing mode.

5. We want a rounded rectangle around the image so that it visually designates that the visitor is on the Int'l Airfares page. Click the Rectangle tool and open your Stroke panel. Set the option settings to a 1-point, ragged, green line (same as the white rectangle area line of this page), no fill color. Then click the Rounded Rectangle Radius option to display the Rectangle Settings dialog box. Type `10` in the Corner Radius box (see Figure 11.18).

Figure 11.18

Your toolbox and Stroke panel settings for the Rectangle tool should match this illustration.

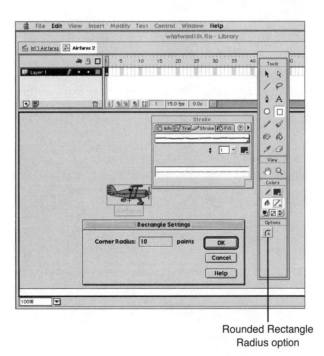

Rounded Rectangle
Radius option

6. Now create a rectangle that surrounds the Airfares button image and text block (see Figure 11.19).

Figure 11.19

Position the rectangle around the Airfares image. Don't make it too large; it should resemble this figure.

7. Exit the symbol-editing mode by clicking the Int'l Airfares tab in the upper-left corner of the Timeline.

8. Now you need to switch the current airfares_button instance that is on the Stage with the new instance of the new symbol you created. Click the airfares_button instance on the Stage and then open your Instance panel through the **Window, Panels, Instance** menu command (see Figure 11.20).

Figure 11.20

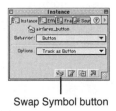

The Instance Properties dialog box allows you to switch, edit, and duplicate symbols.

Swap Symbol button

9. Click the Swap Symbol button to open the Swap Symbol dialog box (see Figure 11.21).

Replacement symbol

Figure 11.21

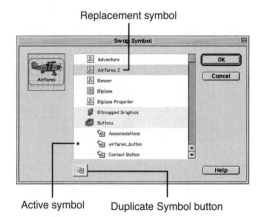

The Swap Symbol dialog box allows you to switch and duplicate symbols.

Active symbol   Duplicate Symbol button

10. Locate the Airfares_2 button in the list and click it.

11. Click OK to switch the instance's symbol to the Airfares_2 symbol, creating a new instance on your Stage.

12. Click the new Airfares_2 instance on your Stage. In the Instance panel, change the behavior to Graphic to match the behavior of the symbol you just created. Close the Instance panel.

Warning Make sure you do not have the **Enable Simple Buttons** menu command selected in the **Control** menu. You will not be able to edit your buttons with this feature on.

With this button set, you now can repeat the steps 1–12 to create a new symbol from the original button for the other four second-level pages of the Web site. Create the Graphic symbol for each of these pages so that it visually distinguishes the second-level page. Name each of these Graphic symbols in the format of the Airfares_2 symbol—Accommodations_2, Groups2_2, Honeymoons_2, and Contact_2.

Editing the Other Buttons for the Second-Level Web Pages

Now you need to edit the other buttons on each of the second-level pages so that they do not display the description when the end-user hovers his mouse over the button. This actually requires creating new buttons to replace the existing buttons. To do this, follow these steps:

1. Focusing on the Int'l Airfares page first, switch to this page by clicking the Edit Scene button and select **Int'l Airfares** from the menu list.

2. Make sure you do not have your **Enable Simple Buttons** menu command feature turned on; if it is, turn it off. Click the Accommodations_button symbol to make it active. Then (Control-click) [right-click] it. Choose **Edit** from the shortcut menu to launch the symbol-editing mode.

3. Click the Hit state keyframe and then Shift-click each of the other button state keyframes to select all of them for the Accommodations button. Make sure the playhead is on the Up state of this button with the other three states selected. Copy them using the **Edit, Copy Frames** menu command. You will use these keyframes in the new button symbol you will create in the next step.

4. Click the **Insert, Convert to Symbol** menu command. Name this symbol Accommodations_NoDescr. Select the Button behavior.

5. Notice that, even though you created a new symbol, you are still editing the airfares_button symbol. You need to switch to the new button symbol you created. While still in the symbol-editing mode, open your Library, locate the Accommodations_NoDescr symbol, and double-click it. This switches the symbol that you are editing into the symbol-editing mode.

11

6. The new symbol only has one keyframe in the Up state of the button. You want to copy the original button's keyframes into the new button's keyframe. With the Up state keyframe active, paste the previously copied keyframes into this symbol by choosing **Edit, Paste Frames**. This copies the button states to the new button symbol.

7. Click the Over state keyframe to make it active. Then click the description on the Stage to make it active and delete it.

8. Exit the symbol-editing mode by clicking the page name tab in the upper-left corner. This returns you to the second-level page.

9. Now you need to switch the current Accommodations_button symbol that is on the page with the new symbol you created. Click the Airfares button and open the Instance panel. Click the Swap Symbol button to open the Swap Symbol dialog box.

10. Locate the Accommodations_NoDescr button in the list and click it.

11. Click OK to swap the symbols. Close the Instance panel.

12. Test your new button by turning on the **Enable Simple Buttons** command from the **Control** menu.

13. Repeat steps 2–12 for the other buttons on the page: Group2_button, Honeymoon_button, and Contact_button. Create new button symbols named `Groups2_NoDescr`, `Honeymoon_NoDescr`, and `Contact_NoDescr`.

14. Now you need to create an airfares_button symbol with no description. Because you are on the Int'l Airfares page, you need to go to a page that needs this button. (You have the Airfares_2 image on this page now). Click the Edit Scene button and click **Accommodations**. This switches to the Accommodations scene of the second-level Web pages.

15. Click the airfares_button symbol and repeat steps 2–11 to create the Airfares_NoDescr symbol and swap it with the existing symbol on the second-level page.

You now have created all five buttons without a description in the Over state. With your Int'l Airfares page set, you need to switch out the original button symbols located on each of the other second-level pages with the new button symbol that doesn't have the description text. Using the previous steps 8–12, set up these second-level Web pages by swapping the existing button on the pages with these new buttons.

> **Tip**
>
> You might want to clean up your Library at this time. You have created new buttons that you can place in your Buttons folder in the Library.

Save your Web site movie to save all the changes you have made. You will find an example of the Web site up to this point on the CD-ROM that accompanies this book. Open the Chapter 11 folder and locate the file whirlwind11.fla if you need to see an example of the project Web site.

Where You've Been!

In this chapter you learned how to create, edit, and manipulate scenes. You used scenes to set up your second-level Web pages. You learned to use the **Edit in Place** command to add a button description to each button. You learned out how to swap out instances with other symbol instances. You have now created all your buttons for the Web site.

What's Next?

Next you will learn how to make your buttons functional by adding ActionScripting to them. You will make all your buttons on the home page link to the second-level pages. You will also add sound to your buttons to make them more engaging for the end-user.

11

Chapter 12

Attaching Actions and Sounds to the Buttons and Frames

Your Web site now has the necessary scenes for the first- and second-level pages. You have created the buttons for each of these scenes. Now you need to make these buttons functional. You will need to add this interactivity through *ActionScripting* programming language. The *ActionScript* commands will enable your site visitors to move from one scene of the site to the next, stopping where they want and moving on to where they are interested. This chapter will also cover adding sound to your site and to the buttons. This will enhance the site and make it more interesting for the end-user browsing your site.

Attaching Actions to Buttons

Now that buttons have been created on each page of your Web site, you need to make them link to the appropriate page. You will use the ActionScript programming language of Flash to do this.

Creating a Go To Action

Using ActionScripting, you will create the Go To action to make your buttons link to the appropriate pages. Focusing on the home page first, make it the active page by choosing the Home Page scene from either the Scene panel or the Edit Scene button. Now you need to insert the ActionScript to link your buttons to their Web pages by following these steps:

1. Click the Airfares button on the home page to make it active. Open the Actions panel by choosing **Window**, **Actions**. This displays the Object Actions dialog box (see Figure 12.1).

Add a Statement - Add button (+)

Delete a Statement - Delete button (-)

Figure 12.1

The Actions dialog box will be named either Object Actions or Frame Actions, depending on the element you have selected—an object or a frame.

Toolbox list

Actions menu

Actions list

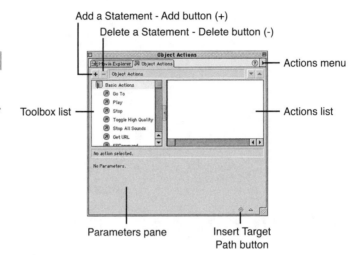

Parameters pane

Insert Target
Path button

2. To add an action, click the Add button (+). This displays a menu listing the many actions available in Flash. The actions are divided into six categories: Basics Actions, Actions, Operators, Functions, Properties, and Objects. Choose the **Basic Actions** menu command and then select **Go To** from the list of basic actions. The Actions list displays the Go To ActionScript commands. Notice that this command begins with on (release) {, which references a mouse event. After this command, you see gotoAndPlay (1), which refers to moving to Frame 1 and playing. The next line has the } command, which ends the mouse event (see Figure 12.2).

Figure 12.2

The Parameters pane lists the various parameters that you can edit and change for this Go To command.

3. Your Parameters pane changes to display the parameters of the Go To command. Click the arrow to the far right of the **Scene** box and choose **Int'l Airfares** from the list (see Figure 12.3).

Figure 12.3

You could choose <next scene> from this list but you will find that this is a programming practice that can cause errors. If you insert another scene before the Int'l Airfares scene, this Go To *action would be incorrect.*

 Tip   It is a good idea to always name scenes and refer to the actual scene name in an ActionScripting command. This will avoid mistakes that can occur if you reorganize your scenes or add new scenes.

4. Keep the Type option set to Frame Number. Click the Frame box and type 1.

5. Notice that the Go to and Play check box at the bottom of the Parameters pane is selected. If you turn this off, the scripting in the Actions list will change to gotoAndStop ("Int'l Airfares", 1);. Keep this option checked (see Figure 12.4).

Figure 12.4

You've attached an ActionScripting command to the Airfares button that instructs Flash to go to and play the Int'l Airfares scene, starting at Frame 1 when the end-user clicks the button.

6. Close the Object Actions panel.

 Test your button by turning on the **Enable Simple Buttons** feature and the **Play All Scenes** feature, and clicking the Airfares button. If you correctly added the action to your Airfares button, you will advance to the Int'l Airfares scene upon clicking that button.

12

Note
Your movie will continue to run after you click the Airfares button, advancing to the other scenes. This is because you have the **Play All Scenes** feature turned on in the **Control** menu and because you set your Go To action to Play from Frame 1 on in the scene. Click the **Control**, **Play All Scenes** menu command again to turn it off. In the next section of this chapter, you will learn how to add ActionScripting that causes the movie not to play continuously.

Attaching Actions to All Buttons in the Web Site

Attach the Go To action to all other buttons on the home page and the other buttons on the second-level scenes. Follow the previous "Creating a Go To Action" section's steps 1–6 to correctly program these buttons. Make sure that you link the button to the appropriate scene. Always test your buttons after attaching a script.

Tip
You can use the **Copy** and **Paste** keyboard equivalent commands (Cmd-C and Cmd-V) [Ctrl+C and Ctrl+V] in the Actions list of the Actions panel. If you highlight a completed Go To ActionScript for a button in the Actions list and copy it, you can then paste this in another button instance's Action list of the Actions panel, instead of re-selecting the parameters each time. You will have to select the **Go To** command in the **Basic Actions** menu and then reselect the appropriate scene that the command is pointing to in the Parameters pane to make the script correct.

With your buttons set, test your movie in the Flash Player. Notice that the movie continues to play from one scene to the next. You barely have time to click a button. You need to add some ActionScripting that adds a Stop action to cause the playhead to stop at the end of each scene. This allows you to click a button to navigate to the scene that you want.

EXCURSION
Using the Get URL Command

You can use the Get URL ActionScripting command similarly to the Go To command. You'll find this command under the **Basic Actions** category when you click the Add button (+) in the Actions panel.

If you attach Get URL to a button, and then enter the URL you want to link to in the Parameters pane (see Figure 12.5), the button will pull up the designated URL. This could be a URL for an HTML page, Web site, or any document on a server within an intranet.

Figure 12.5

You can designate a URL for accessing a document on the Internet or an intranet. Simply type the absolute path into the URL box of the Parameters pane.

You can also designate how you want the URL to open: in the current browser window, in a new browser window, or in a frame. You set the target in the Window box. Click the arrow to the far right of the Window box and choose the appropriate target.

Attaching Actions to Frames

With your buttons set to link to the appropriate page, now you need to add some ActionScripting to control the playhead as it progresses through your movie. Before you begin to create this scripting, turn on the **Enable Simple Frame Actions** feature in the Flash development mode. Choose **Control, Enable Simple Frame Actions** to turn this on. This will enable any of the scripting that you attach to frames to work in the Flash development mode.

Stop Action

For your movie to stop at the end of the Home Page scene, you need to insert an action in the very last frame of the scene. It is a good idea to create a new layer that holds all the actions that you will create for a frame. Click the Travel layer and then click the Insert Layer button to add a new layer above the Travel layer. Double-click the new layer and name it `Actions and Labels` (see Figure 12.6).

→ For more information on creating and editing layers, **see** Chapter 9, "Using Layers to Organize the Movie," **p. 197**.

You can now begin to create your ActionScripting that will cause the movie to stop at the last frame of the Home Page scene. Make sure you are on the Home Page scene and then follow these steps for creating the `Stop` action:

1. Click Frame 70 of the Actions and Labels layer of the Home Page scene.
2. Insert a keyframe by pressing F6.

3. Double-click the new keyframe in Frame 70. This opens the Frame Actions panel (see Figure 12.7).

Figure 12.6

By creating a new layer for all your labels and actions, you are making it easier to troubleshoot any problems that might occur in your ActionScripting.

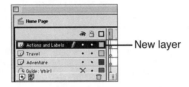

New layer

Figure 12.7

The Frame Actions panel should look familiar to you. It is very similar to the Object Actions panel that you used to attach an action to your buttons.

 Tip

You can also (Control-click) [right-click] a frame and click **Actions** from the shortcut menu to display the Frame Actions panel.

4. Click the Add button (+) and choose the **Basic Actions** menu and then select the **Stop** action from the list (see Figure 12.8). Close the Frame Actions panel.

Figure 12.8

The Stop action does not have any parameters associated with it.

Tip

Look at your Timeline. Notice that in Frame 70 of the Actions and Labels layer, you have a small *a* in the keyframe (see Figure 12.9). This designates that you have an action attached to this frame. Open your Actions panel through the **Window**, **Actions** menu command and click Frame 70. You will see the ActionScripting that is attached to this frame.

If you are using Flash on a PC computer, you will not see a circle in Keyframe 70. You will only see the *a* in this keyframe. This is a small difference between the Macintosh version of Flash 5 and the PC version of Flash 5 and how empty keyframes are handled.

Frame has an
action attached

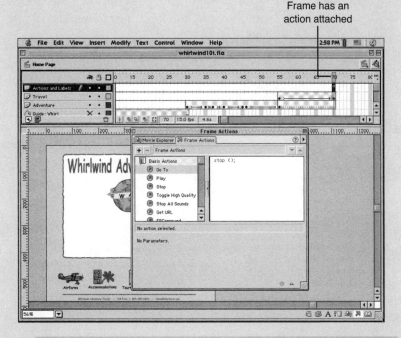

Figure 12.9

With the Actions panel open, you can click any frame that has an action attached and see the ActionScripting that is applied to that frame.

TryIt

5. Play your movie. Make sure you have the **Enable Simple Frame Actions** and the **Enable Simple Buttons** features turned on so that you can click a button and see your Stop action work.

12

When you test your movie, you will see your home page animate; at any time you can click any of your buttons on this page to go to that designated page. Click the Airfares button and notice that the movie again proceeds from the Int'l Airfares scene and advances through all other second-level Web page scenes.

Adding the Stop Action to All Second-Level Pages

To finish the interactivity for your site, you need to add the Stop action to the Timeline for all second-level pages. Now you need to stop your movie for each of the second-level scenes. Go to the Int'l Airfares scene and follow these steps:

1. Add a new layer for all actions and labels for the Int'l Airfares scene. Click the Buttons layer and then click the Insert Layer button to create a new layer above the Buttons layer.

2. Double-click the layer and name it to Actions and Labels.

3. Double-click the keyframe in Frame 1 of the Actions and Labels layer to access the Frame Actions panel.

 Note   By default, Flash creates a keyframe in a new layer, so you have a keyframe to work with. You do not need to insert one in the Timeline.

4. Click the Add Button (+), choose the **Basic Actions** menu command, and then click **Stop** from the list. Close this panel.

 5. Rewind your movie and play it. When the movie stops on the home page, click the **Airfares** button. The movie advances to the Int'l Airfares page and stops. You can now click any of the buttons on this page to advance to another scene. Notice that after the Int'l Airfares scene, the movie plays through all other scenes, assuming you have the **Play All Scenes** feature turned on.

6. Repeat steps 1–5 for each of the second-level Web pages and create an Actions and Labels layer. Attach the Stop action to the keyframe in Frame 1 of the new layers.

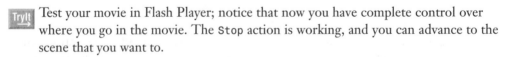 Test your movie in Flash Player; notice that now you have complete control over where you go in the movie. The Stop action is working, and you can advance to the scene that you want to.

EXCURSION

Creating and Using the Play *Action*

Similar to the Stop and the Go To action, you can add a Play action to a frame to cause a scene, frame, or movie clip to play. Like the Go To and Stop actions, the Play action controls the progression of the movie's Timeline. Insert a keyframe in the frame where you want to apply the Play action, and then double-click that frame. This displays the Frame Actions panel. Click the Add Button (+), choose the **Basic Actions** menu, and select **Play** from the menu list. The Play command is listed in the Actions list (see Figure 12.10). Close the Frame Actions panel.

Figure 12.10

There are no parameters for the Play *action.*

Adding Sound

Now that you have your movie set to be interactive, let's add one more effect to the movie. You are going to add some sounds to the opening animation on the home page and then a short sound clip for all buttons in the movie.

Two types of sound are used in Flash—*event sounds* or *streaming sounds*. An event sound is a sound that occurs due to a viewer's interaction with the movie, such as clicking a button or hot spot, or by an event in the animation. An event sound is short in duration. A streaming sound is a sound that occurs in the background or to accompany animation in the Timeline. Streaming sounds are longer in duration than the event sounds. You will use both in the following sections.

Importing Sounds

You import a sound just as you import graphics or artwork, through the **File**, **Import** menu command or by opening an existing Flash movie that has the sounds you want to use as a Library and adding the sound symbol to your movie's Library.

12

All sounds are housed in the Library. Flash imports sounds in either WAV (Windows format), AIFF (Macintosh format), or MP3 (New Internet Compression format good on either platform).

Flash is not a sound editing program. It cannot improve sounds that are imported into it. When importing sounds, you want to follow the same rules that apply to importing graphics:

- You must import most sounds in uncompressed file format. Let Flash compress the sound when you publish the movie. This does not include MP3 file format.
- Always edit sound files to be as short as possible before importing into Flash.
- Sounds take up large amounts of RAM and disk space. Keep your sounds small by importing them as 22kHz 16-bit mono sounds as often as you can.
- Stereo sound doubles the file size.
- Flash can import 8- or 16-bit sounds at sample rates of 11kHz, 22kHz, or 44kHz. Using the **File**, **Publish** or **File**, **Export Movie** command, you can lower these sample rates.
- Because sounds are stored in the Library, you only need one copy of the sound file. You will use the sound as an instance throughout your movie, therefore saving on file size.
- Flash cannot improve the quality of a sound. Always create the sound for the quality that you want before importing into Flash.
- Flash 5 can now import and publish/export a sound file with MP3 compression. Other versions of Flash could only publish or export a sound file with MP3 compression.

➔ For more information on sound compression and the publishing process of Flash, **see** Chapter 13, "Publishing the Movie for the Travel Company Web Site," **p. 287**.

Attaching Sound to an Event

To add a sound to a button, you will use an instance of the sound from your Library. In this project, you will attach some of the previously created sounds that come with Flash to your buttons. Follow these steps:

1. Click the **Window**, **Common Libraries**, **Sounds** menu command. This displays the Library-Sounds Library that comes with Flash.

2. Select the Plastic Button sound symbol in the Library- Sounds Library. Click the Play button in the Preview window to hear the sound. This will work well for all buttons in the movie (see Figure 12.11).

Play button

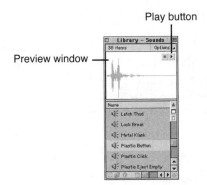

Preview window

Figure 12.11

You will find many other sounds in the Library-Sounds Library that accompanies Flash.

3. From the Home Page scene, (Control-click) [right-click] the Airfares button and click **Edit** from the shortcut menu. This launches the airfares_button symbol in the symbol-editing mode of Flash.

4. Create a new layer above the Button layer by clicking the Insert Layer button. Name this layer Sound.

5. Click the Down state of the Sound layer and then insert a keyframe by pressing F6.

6. Drag the Plastic Button sound from the Library-Sounds Library onto your Stage (see Figure 12.12). Do not worry about where you drop the sound on the Stage.

Figure 12.12

Nothing changes on your Stage, but the sound waveform appears in the Down state of the Sound layer.

 Note

Do not worry that the sound appears to extend into the Hit frame of the Button layer. The sound is really in the Down state frame, but, due to the Hit state not having a keyframe in it, the sound waveform flows into the adjacent frame.

7. Exit the symbol-editing mode, turn on **Enable Simple Buttons**, and test your button. You should hear the click when you click the button and then advance to the Int'l Airfares scene.

12

Add this same sound to all other buttons in your movie using steps 1–7 as a guide.

When you add a sound from another movie's Library, just like Flash's Library-Sounds Library, the sound will automatically be added to your movie's Library. Open your movie's Library, and you will see the Plastic Button sound now in this Library.

Notice that because you used an instance of the buttons labeled with _NoDescr throughout the second-level Web pages, you only have to add the sound to these buttons. It will be used in all instances of the button through the second-level pages.

If you click the Plastic Button sound in the Down state keyframe to select it and then open your Sound panel by choosing **Window**, **Panels**, **Sound**, you will see that this sound is set to a default setting of Event in the Sync option. You want all event sounds to have a Sync setting of Event in the Sound panel (see Figure 12.13). You will learn more about this feature later in this chapter.

Figure 12.13

The Sound panel helps you customize how a sound is heard.

Attaching a Streaming Sound

Next you will attach a couple of sounds to stream with the animation on the home page. As in attaching an event sound, you will need to create a sound layer that corresponds with the layer of animation you want the sound to be synced with. Follow these steps to attach a streaming sound:

1. Click the Guide: Whirl layer of the Home Page scene. Create a new layer and name it Sound.

2. Click the keyframe in Frame 1 of the Sound layer.

3. If the Library-Sounds Library is not opened, open it through the **Window**, **Common Libraries**, **Sound** menu command.

Note

You always need a keyframe for attaching a sound to the Timeline. Because the new Sound layer has a keyframe in Frame 1 and the animation you want the sound to be synced with begins in Frame 1, you do not need to create another keyframe for this layer.

4. Locate the Visor Hum Loop sound and drag it onto the Stage. It appears in your Sound layer (see Figure 12.14).

Visor Hum sound

Figure 12.14

Nothing changes on your Stage, but the sound appears in the Sound layer as a waveform.

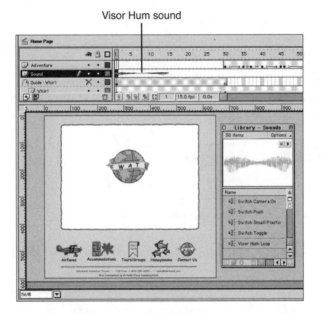

5. Rewind and play your movie. The sound plays for the first part of the Whirlwind animation.

This is good, but we want the sound to play through the entire animation of the Whirlwind text swirling on the Stage.

 Tip

You can click and drag the playhead of the Timeline to *scrub* through the animation. You can also rewind your movie to any point in the Timeline by positioning the playback head to where you want to begin.

12

Tip

Animation is subordinate to a sound. This means that the sound plays in sequence with the animation in the movie, but if the animation cannot keep up with the streaming sound, the animation will skip frames, causing it to be jumpy or jerky in its playback. This can occur if the end-user's machine is not powerful enough to play both the sound and the animation at the same time.

Controlling the Sound Duration and Setting Sound Streaming

You can control the amount of time a sound plays, but you must first know how long a sound is set to play. This could be in seconds or in frames. You can check the number of frames or the amount of time a sound plays through the Sound panel. To do this, follow these steps:

1. Click any frame in the Sound layer. This selects all the frames in this layer. Then open the Sound panel by choosing **Window**, **Panels**, **Sound**. This opens the Sound panel (see Figure 12.15).

Figure 12.15

Click the Edit button to edit a sound.

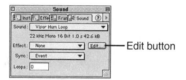

Edit button

2. Click the Edit button to open the Edit Envelope dialog box (see Figure 12.16).

Figure 12.16

You can determine the exact length of a sound through the Frames button or the Seconds button and the Time In Control feature.

Time Out Control   Time Control line   Time In Control

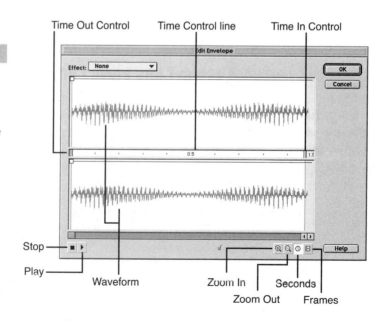

Stop

Play

Waveform   Zoom In   Seconds

Zoom Out   Frames

3. Click the Seconds button. The Time In Control feature displays the number of seconds the sound plays.

4. Increase your magnification of the Time Control line by clicking the Zoom In button. Zoom in on the exact number of seconds the sound plays. The Visor Hum Loop plays for almost one second.

5. Click the Frames button. The Visor Hum Loop plays for 15 frames. Your Whirlwind animation plays for 29 frames; therefore, you need to extend the length that this sound plays. Close the Edit Envelope dialog box.

To extend the time that a sound plays, you can loop it to make it play longer in the Sound layer. To do this, follow these steps:

1. You should still have the Sound layer active; if not, click any frame in the Sound layer. If your Sound panel is not opened, open it through the **Window**, **Panels**, **Sound** menu command.

2. Click the Loops box and change the 0 to 2. Click the **Sync** menu and select **Stream** from the list (see Figure 12.17). Close the Sound panel.

Figure 12.17

*You set the type of sound you want in the **Sync** menu. You want this sound to stream with the Whirl layer animation, so you click **Stream** from the **Sync** menu.*

3. Notice that your Visor Hum Loop sound now extends the full length of the Whirl layer animation (see Figure 12.18).

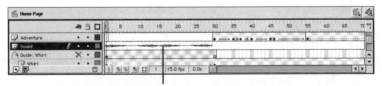

Figure 12.18

Your waveform of the sound now is doubled in length and extends through the entire length of the Whirl layer animation.

Visor Hum Loop sound

4. Rewind and play your movie. You will hear the sound throughout the animation of the Whirlwind text swirling on the Stage.

12

Tip

By setting your **Sync** menu to **Stream**, you are telling Flash to stream this sound in conjunction with the animation that occurs in all layers for the frames in which the sound occurs.

 Note

A streaming sound will stop after the animation is over, even if it extends farther in the Timeline than the animation.

Adding More Streaming Sounds to Your Home Page Animation

Next you want to add a sound for the dot rolling off of the Whirlwind text and the word Adventure morphing from the dot. This will be another streaming sound. Follow these steps to create this effect:

1. Click the Adventure layer and add a new layer. Name the layer Sound2.

2. Click in Photoframe 30 of the Sound2 layer and insert a keyframe by pressing F6.

3. From the Library-Sounds Library, locate and drag the Shutter Advance 35mm sound onto the Stage. You will see a wave example of this sound starting in the new keyframe of the Sound2 layer and flowing to the right (see Figure 12.19).

Shutter Advance 35mm sound

Figure 12.19

Your waveform of the sound extends just past the animation of the dot rolling that ends in frame 44.

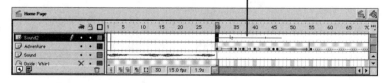

4. Click any frame between 30 and 44 in the Sound2 layer and then open the Sound panel by choosing the **Window, Panels, Sound** menu command.

5. Set the **Sync** menu to **Stream**. Close the Sound panel.

6. Click in Photoframe 45 of the Sound2 layer. You will select all frames in this layer but notice that your playhead is on Photoframe 45. Do not worry about not seeing just Photoframe 45 selected. Having the playhead in Photoframe 45 indicates that you are selecting this frame. Now insert another keyframe by pressing F6.

7. Locate and drag the Beam Scan sound from the Library-Sounds Library to the Stage. This attaches the Beam Scan to the Sound2 layer (see Figure 12.20).

Beam Scan sound

Figure 12.20

The wave example of the Beam Scan sound extends the full length of the animation for both the morphing of the Adventure and the Travel text.

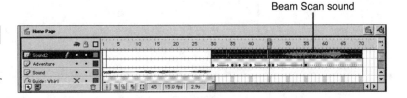

8. Click any frame between 45 and 70 in the Sound2 layer and then open the Sound panel by choosing **Window, Panels, Sound**.

9. Set the **Sync** menu to **Stream**. Close the Sound panel.

 Although you did not attach a sound for the flying Travel text, this combination of the Shutter Advance 35mm sound and the Beam Scan sound adds a nice effect for your animation and carries over into the Travel text entering onto the Stage. Rewind your movie and play it to hear the results of your work so far.

EXCURSION

More Features Using Sound in Flash

The Sound panel offers other nice features for working with sounds in Flash (see Figure 12.21). You can switch a sound that has been attached to a button or frame with another sound by clicking the **Sound** menu and choosing a new sound from the list.

Figure 12.21

The sounds listed in the Sound menu have been imported into your Library.

You can also apply an effect to a sound that you have attached to a button or frame. In this case, a special effect means how the sound is heard. Remember, you cannot improve a sound with Flash, but you can adjust the volume for both the left and right sound channels. Click the **Effect** menu and choose a new effect to apply (see Figure 12.22).

12

Figure 12.22

Although you cannot edit a sound in Flash, you can apply some special sound effects to it.

If you click the Edit button in the Sound panel, you can work with sounds even more in the Edit Envelope dialog box. You can also apply an effect from the **Effect** menu here, too. You can then take the effect one step further and edit the envelope lines for that sound. You can customize how the right and left channels of a sound play by clicking and dragging to adjust the envelope lines (see Figure 12.23).

Figure 12.23

If you click a volume setting on the envelope lines and drag, you can adjust the volume of the sound in that channel. The right and left sound channels do not need to have the same settings.

Effect menu

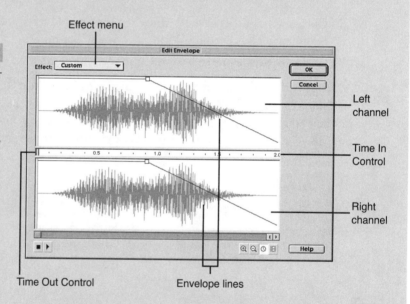

Left channel

Time In Control

Right channel

Time Out Control   Envelope lines

 Tip

The special effects of **Fade Left to Right** and **Fade Right to Left** create sounds that fade from one channel to the other. This creates the illusion of movement due to the sound being heard in first one ear and then the other.

 Warning

If you do not plan on using a portion of a sound, do not use the Time In or Time Out Controls to control the sound. Always edit the sound to the exact length that you need, prior to importing it into Flash.

Compression and Sound Files

You can set the type of compression for individual sound files used in your movie. You have a choice of ADPCM, MP3, or Raw compression. You would use the ADPCM compression for short sounds or your event sounds in the movie. You would use the MP3 compression for your longer background sounds or your streaming sounds in the movie. Raw compression exports a sound without any compression applied to it all. You apply the compression to individual sounds in your Library. To do this, follow these steps:

1. Open your Library and double-click the Plastic Button sound. This displays the Sound Properties dialog box (see Figure 12.24).

Figure 12.24

You can test sounds in the Sound Properties dialog box by clicking the Test button. You can also import new sounds and update existing sounds that you might have re-edited by clicking the Update or Import buttons.

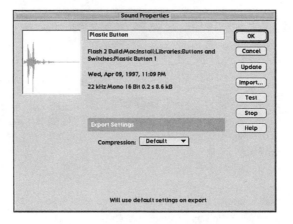

2. Click the **Compression** menu and select **ADPCM** from the list.
3. Click the **Sample Rate** menu and select **22kHz** from the list.
4. Click the **ADPCM Bits** menu and select **4 Bit** from the list (see Figure 12.25).
5. Test your sound by clicking the Test button.

Figure 12.25

The compression setting of ADPCM is the best choice for short event sounds for Web presentations. The compression setting of MP3 is the best choice for streaming sounds for Web presentation.

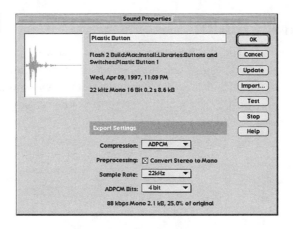

12

You have set your movie's button sounds to ADPCM compression. Because you have not set any of the other sounds in your movie, they will have the Default setting. When you publish the movie, you will set their compression rate through that command.

 Tip

You can also set the compression rate for all sounds in your movie when you export or publish your movie.

 Note

When you choose the bit rate of ADPCM, you can set your ADPCM Bits from a list of two to five. The higher compression rates create a smaller file size but poorer sound quality. Two is the lowest quality option, and five is the best quality option.

 Note

The Sample Rate for the ADPCM allows you to set the export rate for the file. Higher rates create better sound fidelity and larger file size. A setting of 22kHz is a common choice for Web playback. The standard compact disc (CD) sample rate is 44kHz.

→ For more information on globally compressing sounds used in your movie, **see** Chapter 13, "Publishing the Movie for the Travel Company Web Site," **p. 287**.

Save your Web site movie to save all the changes you have made. You will find an example of the Web site up to this point on the CD-ROM that accompanies this book. Open the Chapter 12 folder and locate the file whirlwind12.fla if you need to see an example of the project Web site.

Where You've Been!

You applied both button and frame actions to start allowing your movie to be controlled by the end-user. You added sound effects to the animations you used in the movie and to all the buttons in your Web site. Your movie is interactive, allowing the end-users to have control over where they go in your Web site, and therefore, control over their experience with your Web site.

What's Next?

In the next chapter you will learn how to set your publishing settings and how to publish your movie. You will learn how to set any sound compression rates globally as well as how to override any settings you applied individually. You will also view your movie in a browser to test it.

Publishing the Movie for the Travel Company Web Site

For your movie to be seen by visitors on the Internet or through other players, you must publish the movie. The Publish command in Flash is very powerful and helpful. You can create all types of formats for your movie as well as set up the HTML page for viewing the movie through a Web browser. This chapter covers how to set up and use the Publish command.

Publishing the Movie with the Publish Command

You know how to test a movie to see how it will look in the Flash Player but now we want to test the movie in a Web browser. This requires publishing the movie. When you publish a movie, you set up the exact settings for the file format or formats that you will need for viewing the movie on many different platforms. You use the **File, Publish Settings** command to customize the movie's output.

 Tip

It is always a good idea to save your Flash movie before you publish it.

 Tip

Just like the Test Movie command, which generates a SWF file in the same folder as the Flash file, the Publish command will generate files in this same folder. Make sure you have the Flash file in the folder location in which you want your published files to appear.

Setting Your Movie's Publish Settings

Since you are developing a Flashed Web site, you need to adjust your publish settings for viewing the Web site on the Internet. Choose **File**, **Publish Settings**. The Publish Settings dialog box appears (see Figure 13.1).

Default settings

Figure 13.1

When first accessed, the Publish Settings dialog box has three tabs, which allow you to determine the settings for your published movie.

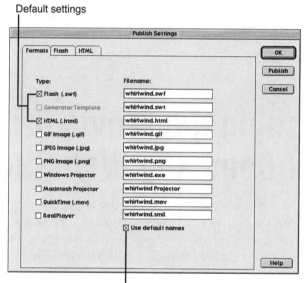

Causes all published formats to have
the same name as the original file

The Formats Tab

Focusing on the Formats tab first, here you need to set your settings for Internet viewing. The Flash (.swf) and HTML (.html) settings are turned on as a default. You must *embed* the SWF Flash Player file inside an HTML page for a browser to view it. To place a SWF file inside an HTML document, you need to use the OBJECT and EMBED HTML commands. These commands instruct the appropriate browser, Netscape or Microsoft Internet Explorer, to display the Flash file in the browser. Flash will generate the needed HTML page with all the coding required for viewing the site on both of the popular browsers.

The HTML code generated includes the OBJECT and EMBED tags, which are the commands needed by the two popular browsers for viewing a Flash movie in SWF format. OBJECT is the HTML tag that opens a Flash movie in Microsoft Internet Explorer, and EMBED is the HTML tag that opens a Flash movie in Netscape. Next you will set options for the other tabs that are present in the Publish Settings dialog box. These settings will further define the OBJECT and EMBED commands in the HTML document that Flash generates by setting their attributes.

Notice that there are many different format types that you can export or publish your movie to. Click the GIF Image (.gif) check box to turn that on, too. You will now have another tab labeled GIF in the Publish Settings dialog box.

Your Formats tab on the Publish Settings dialog box should resemble Figure 13.2.

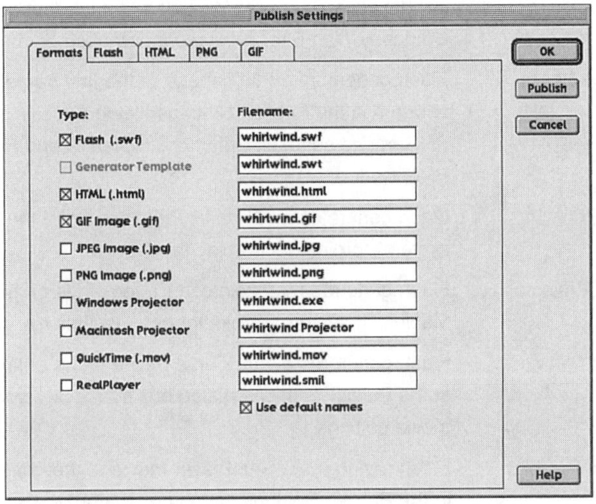

Figure 13.2

You should have the two default settings, Flash (.swf) and HTML (.html), and the GIF Image (.gif) setting selected.

By selecting the GIF Image (.gif) option, you will generate an image of the first frame of the movie. You want this image available for display, in case the site is viewed by someone with an older browser that does not have the Flash plug-in. This GIF file can be pulled up instead of the SWF file through the HTML code for browser viewing. You would need to create this HTML file and save it as a template in the Flash Template folder. Then you can use this as the template for the HTML tab, which we will cover later in this chapter. Creating a new HTML template is outside the scope of this book, but we will generate the GIF file that this template would call.

If you uncheck the Use default names check box, you can then name the generated file types any name that you want. You can type a new file name. You can also designate a directory/folder/file hierarchy by typing in the full path and the filename. For Windows, use a path such as this: `C:\Folder\filename.swf`. For Macintosh, use a path such as this: `HardDrive name:Folder:filename.swf`.

Table 13.1 provides you a description of the other settings that appear on the Formats tab.

Table 13.1   Other Formats Tab Settings

Format Type	Description
JPEG Image (.jpg)	Flash generates a JPEG image of the first frame of the movie. A new tab appears in the Publish Settings dialog box that allows you to determine JPEG image settings. Refer to Chapters 5, "Creating and Editing Graphics for the Travel Company Web Site," and 6, "Importing Graphics for the Travel Company Web Site," for more information on the JPG file format.
PNG Image (.png)	Flash generates a PNG image of the first frame of the movie. A new tab appears in the Publish Settings dialog box that allows you to determine PNG image settings. Refer to Chapters 5 and 6 for more information on the PNG file format.
Windows Projector	Flash generates a Windows Projector file of the entire movie. The Windows system's projector can play this file.
Macintosh Projector	Flash generates a Macintosh Projector file of the entire movie. The Macintosh system's projector can play this file.
QuickTime (.mov)	Flash generates a QuickTime movie of the entire movie. A new tab appears in the Publish Settings dialog box that allows you to determine QuickTime movie settings.
RealPlayer	Flash generates a RealPlayer movie of the entire movie. A new tab appears in the Publish Settings dialog box that allows you to determine QuickTime movie settings.

If you create a Macintosh Projector file using a Windows version of Flash, you must convert the Macintosh Projector file to appear as an application file in the Macintosh *Finder*. You can use a file translator such as BinHex to do this conversion. The Windows version of Flash uses an .hqx extension when it names a Macintosh Projector file, which will not work on the Macintosh system. Not all features of Flash 5 for standalone projector files are supported by the projectors. You might need to publish using a lower Flash version setting.

The Flash Tab

Next, let's focus on the Flash tab of the Publish Settings dialog box. Click the Flash tab, and you will see the publish settings for Flash (see Figure 13.3).

13

Figure 13.3

The Flash tab allows you to determine the settings for the Flash file itself.

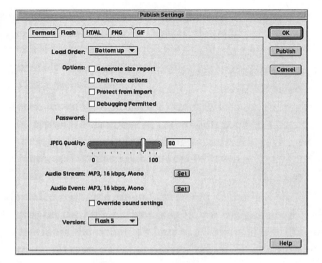

This tab allows you to set options for the Flash Player movie that you will generate. Notice you can set the image and sound compression for files in the movie. Select the following options for this tab:

1. Leave the **Load Order** menu on the default menu setting of **Bottom up**. This will cause your SWF movie to be loaded from the bottom to the top in the browser window. You have your buttons on the bottom of the page and then the animation at the top. This option lets the buttons display before the animation displays.

2. Click the Generate size report check box. This creates a report and statistics on the movie. You will find that this report provides you with a lot of information on your movie. This is where you can see the final file size for all graphics that you imported and optimized in your movie.

→ For more information on importing graphics into Flash, **see** Chapter 6, "Importing Graphics for the Travel Company Web Site," **p. 127**.

3. Leave the Omit Trace actions option unselected. This feature is for turning off the Trace feature in Flash. You have not used this feature yet but will learn about it later in the book.

→ For more information on using the Trace feature of Flash, **see** Chapter 16, "Creating the Accommodations Page," **p. 339**.

4. Click the Protect from import option. When this setting is applied to a movie, other people cannot import your movie back into Flash. This protects your work and ActionScripting from being used by others.

5. Do not choose the Debugging Permitted option. This option allows you to debug a movie remotely. If you select this option, you can then set a password for protecting your file.

6. Leave the JPEG Quality setting as is. You did not leave any imported bitmap images as bitmaps in your movie. You traced the globe bitmap, which converted it to a vector graphic. But this setting allows you to determine the amount of compression to be applied to all imported bitmap images used in the movie. The default setting is 80, but you can set this to whatever setting you want. 100 provides the highest quality and least compression to the bitmap images.

7. Click the Set button next to the Audio Stream option. This displays the Sound Settings dialog box for all streamed sounds in the movie. This setting applies to streamed sounds you have used as background music in the site. Since you are using this movie on the Web, you need to set your streaming sound settings for Web delivery. Click the **Compression** menu and select **MP3** from the menu list. Click the **Bit Rate** menu and choose **16kbps** from the menu list, which works well for Web viewing. Then click the **Quality** menu and click **Fast** from the menu list, which is recommended for Web streaming of sound. When you export music for other platforms, set the bit rate to 16kbps or higher for best results. Your dialog box should resemble Figure 13.4.

Figure 13.4

Since you chose 16kbps, the Convert Stereo to Mono option is not available. A rate of more than 16kbps allows this option to be accessible.

8. Returning to the Flash tab, click the Set button next to the Audio Event option. This displays the Sound Settings dialog box for all event sounds in the movie. This setting applies to event sounds you have used for your buttons in the site. Again, since you are using this movie on the Web, you need to set your event sound settings for Web delivery. Click the **Compression** menu and select **ADPCM** from the menu list. Click the **Sample Rate** menu and choose **22kHz** from the menu list, which is a popular choice for Web playback—this is also half the standard rate for CD-ROM playback. And then click the **ADPCM Bits** menu and click **3 bit** from the menu list. The greater the compression rates, the smaller the sound files but you also get poorer sound fidelity. The 2

bit option is the smallest, lowest quality option of the ADPCM Bits menu, and 5 bit is the largest, best quality option. Your dialog box should resemble Figure 13.5.

Figure 13.5

Because your event sounds are short in length, you chose the next-to-lowest ADPCM Bits setting.

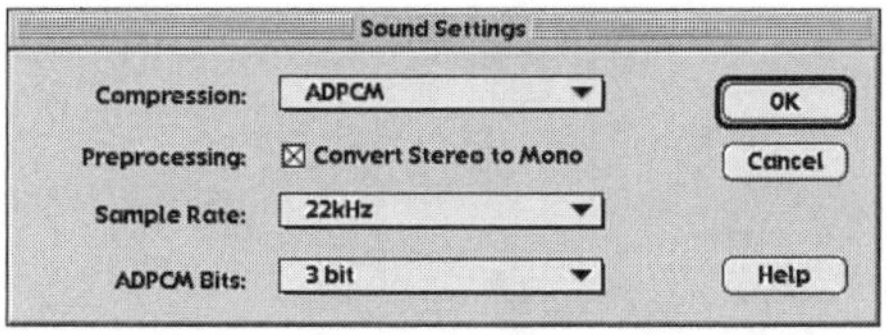

9. Do not select the Override sound settings check box in the Flash tab. This will override all settings that you have already applied to individual sounds, both event and streaming, with the Flash tab sound settings you have just set.

10. Keep **Version** at the default menu setting of **Flash 5**. Your Flash tab of the Publish Settings dialog box should look like Figure 13.6.

Figure 13.6

These are the options you should have set for your Flash movie settings for the published movie.

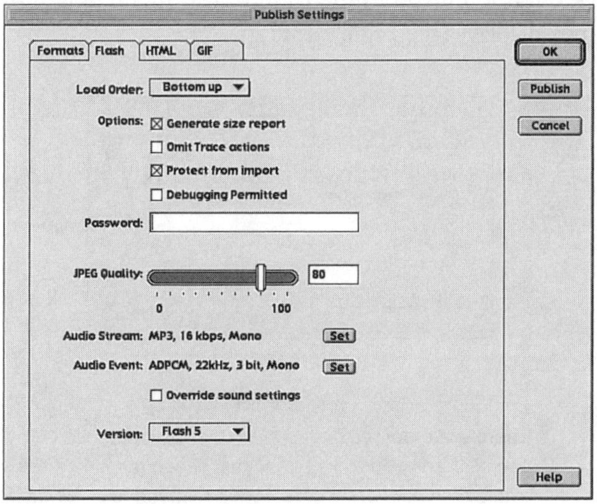

The HTML Tab

Now, let's look at the HTML tab for the Publish Settings dialog box (see Figure 13.7). This tab allows you to set your HTML settings for the HTML page that Flash generates.

Figure 13.7

All the options on this page determine the attribute settings for the OBJECT and EMBED commands used in the HTML code for embedding the SWF file.

1. Leave the **Template** menu at the default setting of **Flash Only (Default)**. Click the Info button to the right of this menu. The Html Template Info dialog box displays (see Figure 13.8).

Figure 13.8

The Template menu gives you a description of the template and its features.

 Note

> There are other templates available for you to use in the **Template** menu. You can also add your own templates. These templates are simply HTML documents with the OBJECT and EMBED codes required to show the SWF movie. Each HTML document has some variances in code that perform some new function in the browser.

2. Click the **Dimensions** menu and choose **Percent** from the menu list. The height and width change to 100%. This means that the movie will be displayed at 100% in the browser window, no matter what size the browser window is.

13

You can choose **Match Movie** from the **Dimensions** menu to have the movie appear in the size that you set in the Flash movie. You can also choose **Pixels** and restrict the size of the movie to appear in the browser. If you choose a size that is not in proportion with the original movie size, your movie will appear out of proportion.

3. Under Playback, make sure the Paused At Start option is not selected. Click the Display Menu check box to select it. This allows user to activate a Display menu through a (Control-click) [right-click] action. The user can then rewind, play, and pause the movie through the shortcut menu. Make sure the Loop check box is not selected. If you choose the Loop option, your movie will loop continuously in the browser window. And finally, make sure the Device Font option is not selected. This feature is a Windows-only feature. It sets the DEVICE FONT parameter to True and uses antialias fonts for any fonts that are not installed on the user's system. This feature, by default, is set to off.

If you choose the Paused At Start option, this will cause the movie to be paused when the movie first loads into a Web browser. The user must then click something to cause the movie to start. This could be a button, or they could click anywhere on the screen to initiate the movie's action. They could also initiate the movie's action through the shortcut **Display** menu and the **Play** menu choice.

4. Under **Quality**, select **High** from the menu list. Table 13.2 describes each of the Quality settings.

Table 13.2   HTML Quality Settings

Setting	Description
Low	When this is selected, the Flash Player gives preference to playback speed over appearance. Antialiasing is not used with this setting
Auto Low	When this is selected, the Flash Player first gives preference to playback speed, but will improve appearance when it can. The Flash Player checks the user's machine processor to see if it can handle more and then turns on antialiasing.
Auto High	When this is selected, the Flash Player emphasizes appearance and playback speed equally at first, but will forfeit appearance for playback speed if the end-user's processor cannot handle both. Antialiasing is turned on at first, but, if the playback speed drops below the determined frame rate, antialiasing is turned off. This will improve the playback speed.

Table 13.2 continued

Setting	Description
High	When this is selected, the Flash Player gives preference to appearance over playback speed. Antialiasing is always turned on, but, if the movie does not contain animation, any bitmap image is smoothed. If the movie does include animation, bitmap images are not smoothed. This is the default setting for Flash.
Best	When this is selected, the Flash Player always provides the best quality, ignoring playback speed entirely. All displays are antialiased, and all bitmaps are smoothed.

5. Under the **Window Mode** menu, select **Window**. This option is a Windows platform–only feature. It allows you to take advantage of a transparent movie, absolute positioning, and layering capabilities available in Internet Explorer.

6. Under the **HTML Alignment** menu, leave this setting at the **Default** menu choice. This option sets the ALIGN attribute for the OBJECT, EMBED, and IMG tags in the HTML code. This sets the position for the Flash movie window in the browser window. Table 13.3 describes each of the HTML Alignment settings.

Table 13.3 HTML Alignment Settings

Setting	Description
Default	Centers the movie window in the browser window. Affected edges are cropped if the browser window is smaller than the movie.
Left	Aligns the movie window along the left edge of the browser window. If necessary, the top, bottom, and right side of the movie window are cropped.
Right	Aligns the movie window along the right edge of the browser window. If necessary, the top, bottom, and left side of the movie window are cropped.
Top	Aligns the movie along the top edge of the browser window. If necessary, the bottom and right and left sides of the movie window are cropped.
Bottom	Aligns the movie along the bottom edge of the browser window. If necessary, the top and right and left sides of the movie window are cropped.

7. Under the **Scale** menu, leave the setting at **Default (Show all)**. This option determines how the movie is placed in the boundaries you specify in the Width and Height fields. Since we used Percent for this field, this setting does not apply to your movie.

8. Under the **Flash Alignment** menu, click **Center** from the lists for both Horizontal and Vertical options. This option sets the SALIGN parameter of the OBJECT and EMBED HTML tags. It determines how the Flash movie is placed in the movie window contained within your browser window.

13

9. Make sure the Show Warning Messages check box is selected. If not, click it to turn it on. This will display an error message if tag settings conflict. An example of this would be if you set a template that refers to an alternate image, and you failed to specify this image or upload it.

These are the HTML settings you want for your movie. Your HTML tab settings should match Figure 13.9.

Figure 13.9

Your HTML tab should resemble this figure.

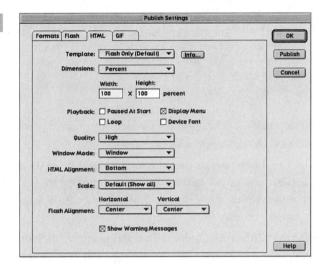

The GIF Tab

This tab appears only if you chose the GIF Image (.gif) check box on the Formats tab of the Publish Settings dialog box. The GIF tab provides an easy way to generate a GIF image. You could create your own HTML template that calls this GIF image to appear in the HTML document if the end-user's browser does not have the Flash plug-in. This avoids having the broken image document appear if the browser does not support Flash. As stated before, neither Netscape 3.0 nor Internet Explorer 3.0 or any earlier version come with the Flash Player. You can create either a standard GIF image or an animated GIF image. You will need to set the following settings:

1. Under **Dimensions**, click the **Match Movie** option to select it. Notice that the Width and Height settings are now 650×600—the size of the movie.

2. Under **Playback**, make sure the **Static** option is selected. This will generate a GIF image of the movie. Flash automatically uses Frame 1 of the movie for the GIF image.

If you choose the Animated option under Playback, Flash will generate an animated GIF of the movie. You would only use this for short, sequenced movies. Flash will generate only the frame-by-frame changes in the movie for the animated GIF.

You can also make the GIF image include an imagemap so that the buttons on the GIF image are functional. You must put the frame label of #Map ActionScript in the keyframe in which you want to create the image map. By default, Flash will use the very last frame to create an imagemap if you do not designate a keyframe.

3. Under Options, click Optimize Colors, Interface, Smooth, and Remove Gradients. Do not select Dither Solids.

4. Under the **Transparent** menu, click **Opaque** from the menu list. This makes the background of the movie opaque, as opposed to Transparent or Alpha. If you choose **Alpha**, the Threshold (0–255) becomes active, and you can set the transparency threshold.

5. Under the **Dither** menu, leave this menu setting at **None**. Since you did not specify dithering in the Options settings, this feature does not apply.

6. Under the **Palette Type** menu, click the **Web Snap Adaptive** menu command. This defines the color palette to use for the image.

7. Under **Max Colors**, type 216 to designate the 216 Web safe colors to be used for the GIF image. If you choose a smaller number, you will create a smaller GIF file. You can only set this option if you have selected **Web Snap Adaptive** or **Adaptive** under the **Palette Type** menu.

8. Your GIF tab should match Figure 13.10. Click OK to close the Publish Settings dialog box.

You can also choose the Publish button in the Publish Settings dialog box to publish the movie instead of closing the Publish Settings dialog box.

Figure 13.10

Your GIF tab should resemble this figure.

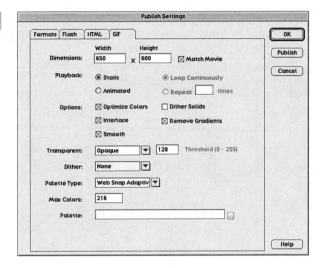

Publishing Your Movie

After you have your publish settings determined, you can publish your movie. Choose **File**, **Publish**. The Publishing dialog box displays, showing you the progress of the Publish command.

Tip

Flash combines all layers into one layer for the published movie. Any Guide or motion guide layers are not included in the published movie.

Note

Flash applies compression to sound and bitmap images based on the settings you select in the Publish Settings dialog box. If you compare the file size for the FLA Flash movie to the SWF Flash Player file, you will see a dramatic decrease in file size.

Viewing the Generate Size Report

Since you selected the Generate size report option on the Flash tab in the Publish Settings dialog box, you can now view this report. This file is a text file and can be opened either in SimpleText, if you are on a Macintosh, or in Notepad if you are on a Windows machine. You will find this file in the same folder as your whirlwind.fla file. Launch your text editor and then open the whirlwind.swf.txt (Macintosh-generated) or whirlwind.txt (Windows-generated) report file. This report provides you with data on your movie, frame by frame (see Figure 13.11), as well as information on the compression that has been applied to your bitmap files and sound files (see Figure 13.12).

Figure 13.11

Flash shows you, frame by frame, the memory size of each frame and then the running total of the file size under Total Bytes.

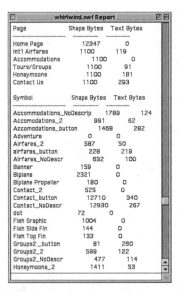

```
          whirlwind.swf Report

Movie Report
------------

Frame #   Frame Bytes   Total Bytes   Page
-------   -----------   -----------   ----
    1        47035         47035       Home Page
    2          239         47274       2
    3          135         47409       3
    4          239         47648       4
    5          135         47783       5
    6          239         48022       6
    7          135         48157       7
    8          240         48397       8
    9          240         48637       9
   10          136         48773       10
   11          240         49013       11
   12          135         49148       12
   13          239         49387       13
   14          240         49627       14
   15          134         49761       15
   16          240         50001       16
   17          135         50136       17
   18          240         50376       18
   19          240         50616       19
   20          136         50752       20
   21          239         50991       21
   22          135         51126       22
   23          239         51365       23
   24          237         51602       24
   25          136         51738       25
   26          240         51978       26
   27          135         52113       27
```

Figure 13.12

Flash shows each bitmap image/symbol in your movie with a breakdown of the Shape Bytes and the Text Bytes that make up the bitmap image/symbol.

```
          whirlwind.swf Report

Page                  Shape Bytes   Text Bytes

Home Page                12347          0
Int'l Airfares           1100         119
Accommodations           1100           0
Tours/Groups             1100          91
Honeymoons               1100         181
Contact Us               1100         293

Symbol                Shape Bytes   Text Bytes

Accommodations_NoDescrip   1789        124
Accomodations_2             991         62
Accomodations_button       1468        282
Adventure                     0          0
Airfares_2                  587         50
airfares_button             228        219
Airfares_NoDescr            692        100
Banner                      159          0
Biplane                    2321          0
Biplane Propeller           180          0
Contact_2                   525          0
Contact_button            12710        340
Contact_NoDescr           12930        267
dot                          72          0
Fish Graphic               1004          0
Fish Side Fin               144          0
Fish Top Fin                133          0
Groups2 _button              81        260
Groups2_2                   599        122
Groups2_NoDescr             477        114
Honeymoons_2               1411         53
```

 Tip

If the movie were to be printed out, each frame would be translated into a page. The Page heading designates this Frame to Page relation.

Testing the Movie in a Web Browser

After your movie is published, you can then test it in a browser. There are two methods to viewing your HTML document in a browser:

- You can open the HTML file directly in your browser by opening your browser and then, using the browser's **Open** menu command, open your movie file whirlwind.html from your local drive. You will find this file in the same directory or folder as your FLA file. This HTML file uses the OBJECT or EMBED command to display the SWF file in either Netscape or Microsoft Internet Explorer.

- You can open any of the generated files through Flash by choosing **File**, **Publish Preview**, **HTML** to launch your default browser and open the file.

You will see your movie displayed in a browser. Resize your browser window to test the percentage setting that you set for the movie display. You might also want to open the GIF file of the movie and check that, too. It is always a good idea to test any published movies and generated graphic files in both of the popular browsers (Netscape and Microsoft Internet Explorer).

Save your Web site movie to save all the changes you have made. You will find an example of the Web site up to this point on the CD-ROM that accompanies this book. Open the Chapter 13 folder and locate the file whirlwind13.fla if you need to see an example of the project Web site at this stage in the process.

Where You've Been!

This chapter covered how to set your publish settings using the Publish command. You now have published your movie and tested it in a browser. You also have generated a GIF image of frame 1 of your movie. After publishing your movie, you will find other files in your directory where the whirlwind.fla file resides.

What's Next?

In the next chapter of the book, you will learn advanced animation techniques and concepts. You will begin to build your gate page, which limits the visitor's entrance into your site until all files for the site have been streamed. The gate page assesses whether the site has been downloaded for the visitor before, and it allows the visitor to access the home page. You will also learn how to create and apply a mask in animation. You will learn how to create a movie clip symbol and how to create a transition between scenes.

Part IV

Putting It All Together: Creating the Fully Flashed Travel Company Web Site

Chapter 14

Advanced Animation Techniques

Now that you have your Web site basically designed, you want to add a *gate page* to display when the site first opens up. This page will allow the site and all its contents, sound, and animation to load or stream down before it allows the end-user to advance into the site. This gate enables a complete viewing experience for the end-user. All elements of the site will be streamed down before allowing the end-user to access the site's contents. You want this page to be entertaining while the rest of the site is downloading so you need to create a movie clip using the Biplane symbol and add a special transition effect to the page. This chapter will guide you through the creation of the gate page.

Creating a Gate Page

To create a gate page for your site, you first need to create a new scene and put that scene in front of the Home Page scene. Now you can create the animation, special effects, and ActionScripting that will cause this page to function as the governing gateway into your site.

Before you can create the gate page, you need to create a new scene. We are also going to add a new color to the Stage.

1. Click the **Window**, **Panels**, **Scene** menu command to display the Scene panel.

2. Click the Add Scene button, which creates a new scene in the Scene panel. Double-click the scene name and rename it to Preload.

3. Move the Preload scene above the Home Page scene (see Figure 14.1).

4. Create a new layer and name it Sky. Move it below Layer 1. Click your Rectangle tool and set your options to a blue fill for representing the sky and no line stroke. On the Sky layer, create a rectangle that is slightly larger than your Stage.

> **Tip**
>
> You can only set your Stage background to one color that will be used through-out your movie in every scene. If you want to change the Stage background color for a scene you need to create a rectangle slightly larger than the Stage and fill it will the new background color.

Figure 14.1

The Preload scene will be the gate page for the Web site.

New scene ——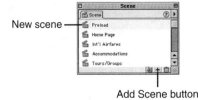

Add Scene button

→ For more information on creating and reorganizing scenes, **see** Chapter 11, "Creating the Movie's Scene and Buttons," **p. 241**.

Creating the Gate Page Animation

After you have a new scene created for the gate page, you can begin to create the scene content. You want to use the Biplane movie clip in this new scene and you need to create a banner with the word Loading blinking on it. This requires using a movie clip for the banner containing the word loading and then creating another symbol of the plane pulling the banner for the animation.

→ For more information, **see** Chapter 8, "Using Symbols, Libraries, and Instances to Recycle and Organize Graphic Elements," **p. 177**.

Creating the Loading Movie Clip

A movie clip symbol has its own Timeline that runs independently from the movie's Timeline. Therefore, we need to create a new movie clip symbol with a banner that contains the word Loading. We will animate the banner by including a series of blinking dots (an ellipsis) that follow the word Loading. Regardless of how the plane animates in the movie, this banner will also animate. Follow these steps to create the Loading banner movie clip:

1. Create a new symbol by clicking the **Insert**, **New Symbol** menu command. Name it Loading and click the **Movie Clip** behavior (see Figure 14.2). Click OK to close the Symbol Properties dialog box.

Figure 14.2

The Loading symbol will be a movie clip so that it will have its own Timeline for the blinking period animation.

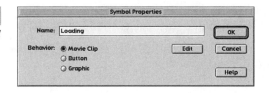

14

2. Using either the Pen tool or the Pencil tool, draw a banner with a black stroke and white fill. Group the banner shape.

3. Create a text block and type the word Loading. Use the following text attributes: Comic Sans MS, 28 points, black, bold. Place the text box in the banner (see Figure 14.3). You have your first frame for the Loading animation created at this time.

Figure 14.3

If need be, using the **Modify**, **Arrange**, **Send to Back** *menu command, move the banner to the back so that the text is displayed like this.*

4. Now you need to create the first blinking dot that will follow the word Loading. Create a keyframe in Frame 5. Using the Text tool, create a text block with a dot (period mark) in it. Make sure you are using option attributes that match the "Loading" text.

5. Position the dot after the word Loading and then align the dot and the word Loading using the Align panel; (Cmd-K) [Ctrl+K] is the keyboard shortcut for opening the Align panel and the Bottom Vertical Alignment button (see Figure 14.4).

Bottom Vertical Alignment

Figure 14.4

To align the word Loading and the dot, make sure both objects are selected and then click the Bottom Vertical Alignment button.

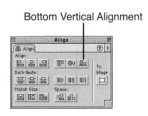

6. Insert another keyframe in Frame 10. The word Loading and the first dot are automatically copied onto this new keyframe Stage content. Copy the dot and paste the copy of the dot, positioning this second dot after the first dot. Then select the word Loading and both dots, and again, vertically align them based on the bottom edge of each object.

7. Repeat step 6 and create another keyframe in Frame 15 with a third dot.

8. Click Frame 20 and insert a frame using the F5 keyboard command. This frame extends the animation of the third dot for five frames allowing it to be seen for a longer period of time in the Loading animation.

9. Test your Loading movie clip in the Flash Player by choosing **Control**, **Test Movie**. You should see the word Loading appear and then one dot at a time displays to give the appearance that the dots are flashing.

10. Exit the symbol-editing mode by clicking the Preload tab in the upper-left corner of the symbol-editing window. This returns you to your main movie.

You have now created a movie clip that runs on its own Timeline.

Tip

If you play your movie in the Flash development mode, you will not see the movie clip symbol animate. Remember, it has its own Timeline and therefore you must test the movie in the Flash Player mode to see the movie clip symbol animate.

Creating the Airplane Animation

With the Loading movie clip symbol created, you now can create the animation for the airplane pulling the banner. The airplane and banner also need to be a symbol because you will be animating them. We also want to create a cloud symbol to add some interest to the page. After the symbols are created you can begin to animate your airplane pulling the banner.

Creating the Symbols to Be Animated

You will need to nest both the Biplane and the Loading movie clip symbols in a new graphic symbol. To do this, follow these steps:

1. Create a new Layer and name it Plane. Position the Plane layer above the Layer 1 layer. With the Plane layer active, open your Library and drag an instance of the Biplane symbol and the Loading symbol onto the Stage.

2. Position the Loading movie clip instance behind the airplane. Resize the Biplane movie clip symbol so that it is 60% of its original size. Use the

14

Transform panel to resize the plane (see Figure 14.5). Make sure you have the Constrain option clicked to retain the Biplane's proportions. If needed, resize the Loading movie clip symbol to be in proportion with the airplane symbol.

Figure 14.5

*You can access the Transform panel by clicking the **Window**, **Panels**, **Transform** menu command.*

3. Select both objects and choose **Insert, Convert to Symbol** to convert these two movie clip symbols into one new symbol. Name the symbol `Banner/Plane`.

You will need to create one more symbol for your airplane animation—the cloud.

1. Click the **Insert, New Symbol** menu command to launch the symbol-editing mode.
2. Name the new symbol `Cloud1` and set its behavior to Graphic.
3. Create a cloud shape using either the Pen tool or the Pencil tool.
4. Use a white fill and white line as the option settings (see Figure 14.6).
5. Exit the symbol-editing mode, returning to the movie.

Figure 14.6

You will use the Cloud1 symbol two times in the Preload scene.

Animating the Airplane and a Cloud

If you've followed all the steps so far, you should have the new symbol, Plane/Banner, on Layer 1 of the Preload scene. You can now begin to create the animation for the gate page:

1. Click Layer 1 and rename it `Cloud`. Do not worry about its position; you will position it later when you animate it.
2. Next you'll animate the Plane. Click Frame 1 of the Plane layer to make it active and move the plane to the left of the Stage, in the lower-middle portion of the Stage (see Figure 14.7).

Figure 14.7

Position the plane in a lower-middle portion of the Stage.

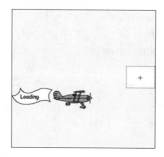

3. Click Frame 10 and insert a keyframe. Reposition the plane to be more in the center of the Stage (see Figure 14.8). Create a motion tween by selecting all frames between 1 and 10 and then (Control-click) [right-click] any of these frames and select **Create Motion Tween** from the shortcut menu.

Figure 14.8

Position the plane in the middle of the Stage.

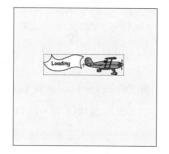

4. Click Frame 20 and insert a keyframe. Reposition the plane to be close to the right edge of the Stage and a little lower than the middle of the Stage (see Figure 14.9). Notice in the Timeline that the motion tween automatically applies to the Frames 11–20.

Figure 14.9

Position the plane to the right of the Stage just slightly lower than the middle of the Stage.

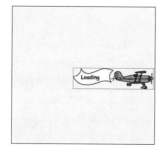

5. Click Frame 30 and insert a blank keyframe, F7. Click Frame 1 of the Plane layer and copy the Banner/Plane symbol. Then click Frame 30 and use the **Paste in Place** command to paste the Banner/Plane symbol (see Figure 14.10). Again, notice that your motion tween is automatically applied to the new frames and blank keyframe.

Figure 14.10

Because you are creating a conditional loop and replaying this animation over and over, you want to have the plane end in the same position as where it began. This gives the animation an ongoing flying effect.

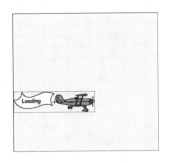

 Tip

You do not need to select the keyframes and frames before applying a motion tween in the Timeline. You can just (Control-click) [right-click] any frame that is between the two keyframes (not selecting any of the frames) and select **Create Motion Tween** from the shortcut menu. But this technique creates a vertical line on the last keyframe's left border in the Timeline (see Figure 14.11). This indicates that a motion tween will not be applied to any additional frames and keyframes that occur after the bordered keyframe. In the above instruction, you are selecting the keyframes and all frame between them before applying a motion tween. This tells Flash that you want to continue the same motion tween to any additional keyframes and frames you create in the layer.

Figure 14.11

You will need to apply any motion tweens or shape tweens to new keyframes and frames that occur after the bordered cell.

Bordered keyframe

6. Make sure you have the **Play All Scenes** command deselected in the **Control** menu and then play your animation in the Flash development mode. The plane appears to fly across your Stage and then repositions itself in its starting position.

7. Now we can make the cloud animate. Click in Frame 1 of the Cloud layer and position the cloud slightly above the airplane but to the far right of the Stage (see Figure 14.12).

Figure 14.12

By starting the cloud to the far right of the Stage and having the cloud move to the left, the plane will have the appearance of flying forward.

8. Click Frame 15 of the Cloud layer and insert a keyframe. Reposition the active Cloud1 instance to the center of the Stage, slightly below the airplane (see Figure 14.13). Highlight Frames 1–15 by Shift-clicking the two keyframes and choose **Insert, Create Motion Tween** from the shortcut menu.

Figure 14.13

The airplane will appear to be flying forward as the cloud moves closer to it.

9. Click Frame 30 of the Cloud layer and insert a keyframe. Reposition the active Cloud1 symbol to the far left of the Stage, slightly above the airplane (see Figure 14.14). Notice that the motion tween automatically applies to these new frames and keyframe.

10. Now extend the Sky layer so that it is visible through Frame 30. Click in Frame 30 of the Sky layer and insert a frame through the **Insert, Frame** menu command. This extends the blue background representing the sky to display throughout the gate page animation.

11. Play your movie again to see the animation of the airplane and the cloud.

14

Figure 14.14

Notice in the Timeline that the motion tween is automatically applied to Frames 16–30 on the Cloud layer.

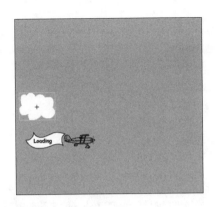

Creating the Conditional Loop

As you know from Chapter 12, "Attaching Actions and Sounds to the Buttons and Frames," you can apply actions to both buttons and frames. Next you will create a conditional loop that checks to see if the site has been loaded or streamed down before it enables the end-user to move to the next scene—the Home Page scene. You will apply actions and labels to certain frames in your movie to make this happen.

Creating Labels

First you want to create labels for certain frames. This allows you to call them in the ActionScripting that you set for the conditional loop. To label frames, follow these steps:

1. On the Preload scene, create a new layer above the Plane layer. Name the layer `Actions and Labels`.

 Tip

It is a good idea to create a layer that is dedicated to all actions and labels in a movie. This allows for easy identification of all actions and labels in a movie, and it is much easier to troubleshoot the programming in a movie if you have one location to look for all actions and labels.

2. Click Frame 30 and insert a keyframe. Then choose **Window**, **Panels**, **Frame** to open the Frame Properties dialog box.

3. Type `Start` in the Label box (see Figure 14.15). Press Enter to apply the label to the keyframe.

Figure 14.15

A small red flag appears in the keyframe, designating that a label has been applied to that frame.

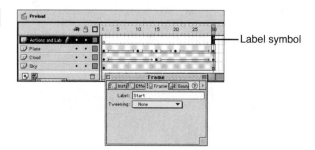

Label symbol

Tip

Hover your mouse over the keyframe with the label applied and notice the mouse changes to a hand symbol. A ScreenTip displays the label name.

4. Next, create another label for the designating the gate frame. Click Frame 28 and insert a keyframe. With the Frame dialog box still displayed, make sure Keyframe 28 is the action keyframe, and type Gate in the Label box (see Figure 14.16). Press Enter to apply the label to the keyframe.

Figure 14.16

Another red flag appears in Frame 28 designating that a label has been applied to that frame.

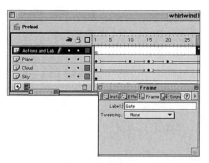

5. Now apply a label to the very last frame of the movie. You need to go to the Contact Us scene and then click Frame 1 of the Actions and Labels layer that you previously created. Notice that you have already applied the Stop action to this keyframe.

→ For more information on navigating between scenes, **see** Chapter 11, "Creating the Movie's Scenes and Buttons," **p. 241**.

6. With the Frame dialog box still displayed, type End in the Label box (see Figure 14.17). Press the Enter key to apply the label to the keyframe.

Action symbol

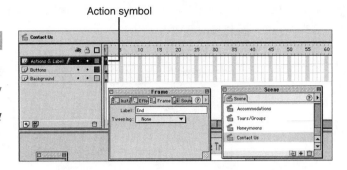

Figure 14.17

If you have an action already applied to a keyframe and then apply a label to the keyframe, you will not get the label symbol represented by red flag displayed in the frame. Notice that Frame 1 of the Actions and Labels layer contains a small a, *which designates an action in this frame.*

7. Close the Frame panel and return to the Preload scene.

Creating the Conditional Loop

After you have created your labels, you can apply the ActionScripting for the conditional loop:

1. In the Actions and Labels layer, click Frame 28 to select it.

2. Choose **Window, Actions** to display the Frame Actions tab of the Movie Explorer.

3. Click the **Basic Actions** command in the Toolbox list (see Figure 14.18).

Delete a Statement   Actions menu

Figure 14.18

*Click the **Basic Actions** menu command to display a list of all the basic ActionScript commands of Flash 5.*

Add a Statement ——
Basic Actions menu ——

Toolbox list ——

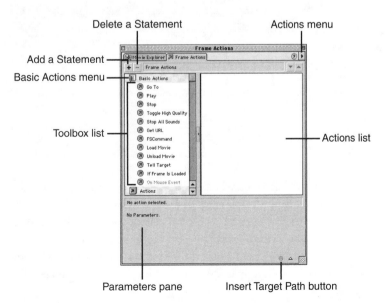

—— Actions list

Parameters pane   Insert Target Path button

4. Locate the `IfFrameLoaded` action from the Basic Actions list and drag it to the right Actions list (see Figure 14.19).

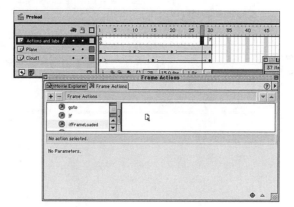

5. You now have access to the parameters for the `IfFrameLoaded` command. In the Parameters pane, click the **Scene** menu down arrow and select **Contact Us** from the list. Click the **Type** menu down arrow and select **Frame Label** from the list. Finally, click the **Frame** menu down arrow and select **End** from the list (see Figure 14.20).

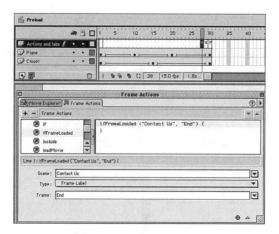

6. Now that you have the condition set for the `IfFrameLoaded` command, you need to tell Flash what to do when the condition is met. So you need to add another command to the `IfFrameLoaded` command. With the first line of the code still highlighted, locate the basic command, `Goto`, from the Toolbox list. Click and drag it under the first line of code in the Code window. Make sure you are directly under the first line of code. You are placing this command in

between the empty brackets, { } that appear after the IfFrameLoaded (Contact Us, End) command (seen previously in Figure 14.18).

7. After you set the Goto command in the code, you have access to the parameters for the code. In the Parameters pane, click the **Scene** menu down arrow and select **Preload** from the list. Click the **Type** menu down arrow and select **Frame Label** from the list. Finally click the **Frame** menu down arrow and select **Start** from the list (see Figure 14.21).

14

Figure 14.21

Now you set the action for what Flash is to do if the condition is met. You are telling it to go to the frame labeled Start in the Preload scene, which is the last frame in the Preload scene.

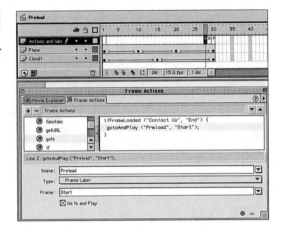

You have set your Gate condition and action to occur if the condition is met in Frame 28. The condition is that all frames must be streamed down and loaded for the entire movie, including last frame of the last scene. If the condition is met, you have told Flash to then go to the last frame of the Preload scene—the frame labeled Start. Next you need to set up the code that occurs if the condition is not met. Without this, Flash will automatically progress to the next frame in the Timeline if the condition is not met (meaning all the frames in the movie have not yet been loaded). Therefore, you need to set up a command that tells Flash to repeat the airplane animation of the Preload scene until the condition is met. To set that command, follow these steps:

1. Click Frame 29 and insert a keyframe.

2. If you closed your Frame Actions dialog box, open it again by choosing **Window, Actions**.

3. Click the **Basic Actions** command in the Toolbox list of the Actions dialog box to expand the list of basic actions and locate the Goto action from the list. Drag this action to the Actions list.

4. You now have access to the parameters for the Goto action in the Parameters pane. From the **Scene** drop-down menu, select **Preload** from the list of scenes. From the **Type** drop-down menu, select **Frame Number** from the list. In the Frame box, type 1 (see Figure 14.22).

Figure 14.22

By creating the Goto command in Frame 29 that redirects Flash to go to Frame 1 of the Preload scene, you are setting up a loop. Flash will repeat the airplane flying animation as the rest of the movie continues to load.

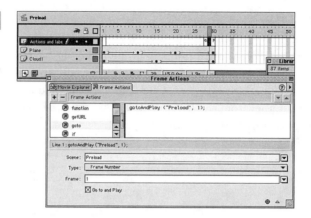

Flash automatically moves to Frame 29 if the condition in Frame 28 is not met. Frame 29 tells Flash to repeat the airplane animation that occurs in Frames 1–28. When it hits Frame 28 again, Flash again checks to see if the entire movie has been loaded in and if it has at this time, Flash is directed to go to Frame 30 and if it hasn't the loop occurs again. You have created a gate and conditional loop for your movie to progress to the home page.

Testing Your Gate Page

You can test your gate page to see the conditional loop at work by testing your movie. If you turn on the Bandwidth Profiler, you will see the streaming of the movie as it is downloaded and compare that to the animation on the Stage:

1. Test your movie by clicking the **Control, Test Movie** menu command (do not choose **Control, Test Scene** as we need to test the entire movie to see the conditional loop work). This launches the Flash Player and your movie is displayed and begins to run.

2. Stop the movie by clicking the **Control, Stop** menu command.

3. Now turn on the Bandwidth Profiler. Choose **View, Bandwidth Profiler** and then turn on Streaming by choosing **View, Show Streaming** (see Figure 14.23).

4. To test the gate page and view the streaming of the movie, choose **Control, Play**.

Notice that the streaming bar shows the process of the download or streaming of the movie, while the playhead shows the progression of the movie's Timeline. The streaming bar slows at Frame 30 because of the amount of action occurring on the Stage. The playhead will return to Frame 1 to replay the airplane animation, while the streaming progresses past Frame 30 and moves to the end of the movie. After the streaming bar reaches the last frame of the movie, you will see your playhead advanced to Frame 30. Because Flash will play all scenes in a movie, the movie progresses automatically to Frame 31 after reading Frame 30. The animation on the Stage changes to the home page. The gate page is working!

14

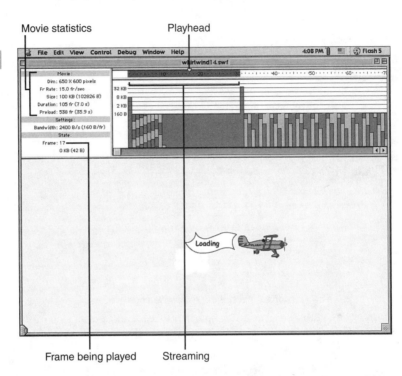

Movie statistics   Playhead

Frame being played   Streaming

Figure 14.23

*You might want to change your view of the movie to **Show All** menu command so you can see the entire Stage. Click the **View**, **Magnification**, **Show All** command to see the entire movie.*

Tip

The Bandwidth Profiler can also be adjusted to show the streaming of a movie at different connection speeds. Click the **Debugger** menu and select the connection speed setting that you want to see. Make sure you have the Show Streaming feature active by choosing **View**, **Show Streaming**. Then rewind and play your movie (see Figure 14.24).

Figure 14.24

*You can set a custom connection setting by selecting the **Customize** menu choice and then inputting the connection speed.*

Debug Window Help
List Objects   ⌘L
List Variables   ⌥⌘V
14.4 (1.2 KB/s)
✓ 28.8 (2.3 KB/s)
56K (4.7 KB/s)
User Setting 4 (2.3 KB/s)
User Setting 5 (2.3 KB/s)
User Setting 6 (2.3 KB/s)
Customize...

Tip

The Bandwidth Profiler also shows any frames that will cause a delay in play-back. These are the frames that appear above the red line. The position of the red line is determined by the connection setting you select.

EXCURSION

Testing Your Own User Settings for the Bandwidth Profiler

In the previous instruction, you tested your movie for streaming at a 14.4 or 28.8 connection speed in the Bandwidth Profiler. You can set any connection speed that you want by choosing **Debug, Customize**. This displays the Custom Modem Settings dialog box (see Figure 14.25).

Figure 14.25

You are limited to six menu choices for testing your movie.

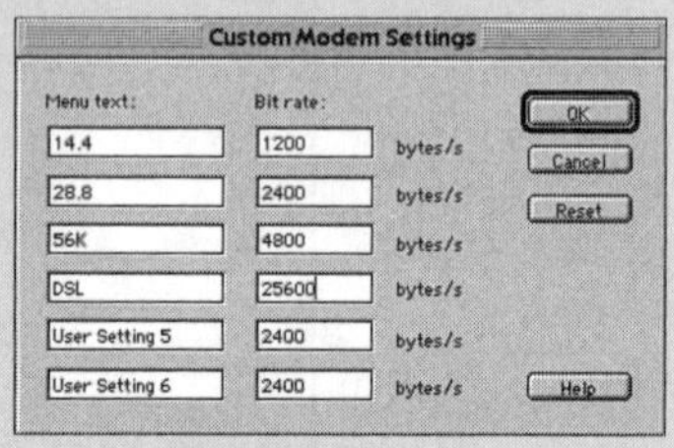

You can customize the last three User Settings:

1. Click in the "User Setting 4" Menu text box and change the text to **DSL**.

2. Then click in the Bit rate box next to this Menu text box and type 25600. Click OK to close the box.

3. Choose the **Debug, DSL** menu choice.

 4. Rewind your movie, set your movie to Show Streaming, and play the movie.

Working with Masks

A neat feature that can produce some very interesting results is applying a mask to a movie. A mask allows for certain Stage objects to be viewed while others are hidden. If you apply animation to the mask, you can cause Stage elements to appear based on the flow of the mask's animation.

In this procedure you will add more animation to the Preload scene, but you will use a mask with the animation so that it only displays certain Stage objects as the animation plays. The Stage object to be masked is the company logo and you will have it display as a cloud floats by above the flying airplane animation. To do this, follow these steps:

14

1. Click the Plane layer and insert a new layer. Name this layer Company Name.

2. Click the Rectangle tool and set your option settings to a white line and a white fill. Create a rectangle that is slightly larger than the entire Stage area.

3. Open your Library and drag an instance of the Logo symbol onto the Stage. Position the Logo instance centered at the top of the Stage (see Figure 14.26).

Figure 14.26

Use your Align command to align the company logo to the Stage.

4. Add another new layer above the Company Name layer and name it Mask.

5. (Control-click) [Right-click] the layer and select **Mask** from the shortcut menu. Your Mask and Company Name layer display a new symbol distinguishing that these two layers are part of the masking process (see Figure 14.27).

Figure 14.27

Any shape or animation that you create on the Mask layer will be the Masking object that is applied to the Company Name layer.

Masking layer ——

Layer in which mask is applied

6. Hide the Company Name layer.

7. Click the Mask layer to make it active. Unlock the layer and click Frame 1. From the Library, drag an instance of the Cloud1 symbol onto the Stage and position it in the top-left corner. Resize the Cloud1 instance so that it is about 5 inches long and 2 inches wide (see Figure 14.28). Position it so that it is half on and half off the Stage.

8. Click Frame 15 of the Mask layer and insert a keyframe.

9. Move the cloud to the far right of the Stage, so that it is half on and half off the Stage.

Figure 14.28

By hiding the Company Name layer, you can see the background of the Stage, which makes it easier to resize your Cloud1 symbol.

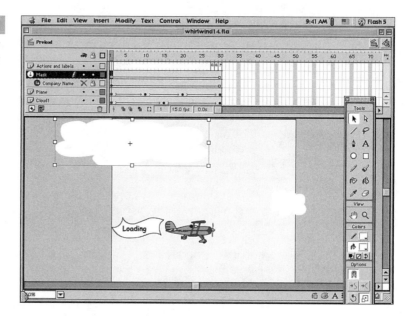

10. Select all the frames between 1 and 15 on the Mask layer by Shift-clicking the two keyframes, and apply a motion tween.

11. Click Frame 30 of the Mask layer and insert a keyframe. Delete the Cloud1 instance that is automatically created for Frame 30. Notice that the motion tween is automatically applied to Frames 16–30.

12. Click Frame 1 and copy the Cloud1 instance. Click Frame 30 and use the **Paste in Place** command to paste the copied Cloud1 instance.

13. (Control-click) [Right-click] the Mask layer and choose **Show Masking** from the shortcut menu. Unhide the Company Logo layer.

14. Play your movie in the Flash development mode to see the masking effect.

 Tip

When you turned on the **Show Masking** command for the shortcut menu, you locked both the Mask and the Company Name layers. You can just lock both the Mask and any layer being masked in the Layers list instead of choosing the **Show Masking** command to see your masking effect applied to a movie.

You will see the animated Cloud1 instance move over the Logo instance that you placed on the Company Name layer, showing just what is masked by the Cloud1 instance on the Mask layer (see Figure 14.29).

Figure 14.29

Because you made the white rectangle on the Company Name layer, the area displayed through the mask is white in color.

 Note

You can create all sorts of interesting effects with a mask. Experiment with this process to fully understand the special effects you can create.

EXCURSION

Masking More Than One Layer

You can mask more than one layer by selecting the layer positioned below the Mask layer, (Control-clicking) [right-clicking], and selecting **Properties** from the shortcut menu. This displays the Layer Properties dialog box. Select the Masked option from the Type section (see Figure 14.30). Click OK to close the dialog box. This will create a new Masked layer.

Figure 14.30

If you want to change a Mask layer or a Masked layer back to a normal layer, select the Normal option under Type from the Layer Properties dialog box.

Creating and Using Transitions

When you test your movie, you see the gate page work as the entire movie streams in, but the transition between the gate page and the home page is a little rough. It would be nice to create a short transition between the two…so let's do it. We will create a short transition that welcomes the user to the site and then fades away before the movie progresses to the home page. To create the transition, follow these steps:

1. From the Preload scene, add a new layer above the Mask layer. Name this layer Company Name2. Click in Frame 30 and insert a keyframe.

2. Click the Company Name layer to make it active; unhide and unlock it if necessary. Then click Frame 1 and copy both the white rectangle and the logo instance.

3. Click the Company Name2 layer and click the keyframe in Frame 30. Use the **Paste in Place** command to paste the copy you made of the Company Name layer contents. This will copy the white rectangle and the company name onto the new layer but place it exactly in the same position as the Company Name layer's contents.

4. Click Frame 45 of the Company Name2 layer and insert a Frame by pressing F5. By extending the Company Name2 contents to Frame 45, all other animation of the airplane and the yellow background seem to disappear and only the white rectangle and the logo instance are visible.

5. Click the Company Name2 layer and insert a new layer. Call this layer Welcome.

6. On the Welcome layer, click Frame 31 and insert a keyframe. Using your Text tool, create a text block and type Welcomes You!. Set your options to Comic Sans MS, 10 point, Bold, Black text, Centered. Use a paragraph return between the Welcomes and You so the two words are on their own lines. Position the text block below the company name but slightly to the left of the middle of the Stage (see Figure 14.31).

Figure 14.31

Use your Character panel to set the option attributes for the new symbol.

14

7. In the Welcome layer select Frame 40 and insert another keyframe. This copies the text block from Frame 31 to this keyframe. Select the text block and change the option settings so that the text is 128 points in size.

8. Select your Arrow tool and then reposition and resize the text block so that it again displays on two lines and is positioned centered on the Stage but still under the Logo instance.

9. Click the text block to make it active and break the text block apart to make it a graphic by choosing **Modify, Break Apart**.

10. Click Frame 31 and select the smaller text block. Again, break the text block apart so that it is no longer text but a graphic element.

11. Now apply a shape tween between Frame 31 and 40 of the Welcome layer. Select all frames between Frames 31 and 40 and open your Frame panel by choosing the **Window, Panels, Frame** menu command. Select **Shape** from the **Tweening** menu (see Figure 14.32).

Figure 14.32

The two text blocks must be converted to a graphic before you can apply the shape tween.

12. Add a new layer above the Welcome layer. Name this layer Transition.

13. In the Transition layer, click Frame 40 and insert a keyframe.

14. Click the Welcome layer and click Frame 40. Copy the graphic text block.

15. Make the Transition layer active and click Frame 40. Using the **Paste in Place** command, paste the copied graphic text block.

16. Now convert graphic text block to a Graphic symbol. Name it Welcome.

17. From the Transition layer, click Frame 45 and insert another keyframe. This copies the Welcome instance from Frame 40.

18. With the Welcome instance active, click the **Window, Panels, Effect** menu command. This displays the Effect panel with the Effect tab active. Click the menu and click **Alpha** from the list. Change the Alpha setting to 0 by clicking the box to the right of the Alpha menu and typing 0 (see Figure 14.33). Press Enter to apply the setting.

Figure 14.33

The Welcome instance will fade away when the 0% Alpha is applied to the instance.

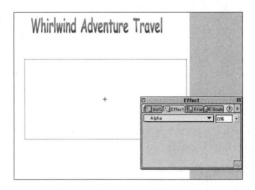

19. Select Keyframes 40 and 45 to select all the frames between the two keyframes. Apply a motion tween.

20. Rewind and play the scene. You will see the plane animate with the mask applied. Then the plane and blue background disappear and are replaced by a white Stage and the company logo. The words Welcomes You! appear and grow large and then fade away.

TryIt → Test your movie in the Flash Player. You will see your gate page work, looping around until the entire movie streams down. Then it progresses to the transition scene, which leads into the home page. Much nicer this time!

Save your Web site movie to save all the changes you have made. You will find an example of the Web site up to this point on the CD-ROM that accompanies this book. Open the `Chapter 14` folder and locate the file `whirlwind14.fla` if you need to see an example of the project Web site.

Where You've Been!

In this chapter, you created a gate page that will not advance the end-user to the home page until the entire movie has loaded (or streamed down) to the end-user's machine. You also added the special effects of a mask and a transition. You now have a nice introduction to your site that is pleasing to view as well as very functional.

What's Next?

The next chapter covers how to create the Contact Us form for the Web site. You will learn how to create form objects, apply variables, and troubleshoot your form.

Chapter 15

Creating the Contact Us Form for the Web Site

Features that greatly extend the power of Flash are forms and input text fields. This chapter focuses on these features and guides you through building a Contact Us form. You can create data entry fields in Flash movies to gather anything from passwords to user information to searches. This chapter focuses on building the front-end interface for gathering this information. Due to the various connectivity technologies that various ISPs (Internet service providers) use, this chapter covers only the front-end development.

Creating the Contact Us Form

To create the Contact Us form, you need to use two of the three types of text that Flash offers: static text and input text. You have been using *static text* throughout the Web site up to this point. It is text used for display purposes only. *Input text* is a text block that is created so that the end-user can input or type in text to communicate back to you. The third type of text, dynamic text, will be covered in Chapter 16, "Creating the Accommodations Page." *Dynamic text* is used to display dynamically updated text on a Web site, such as stock quotes or weather reports.

Using Text on a Form

In keeping with the planning of the Web site covered in Chapter 4, "Planning Your Travel Company Web Site," you want this simple form to be used for customer communication about travel plans and any needs or concerns about travel. First, you need to create the opening greeting and instructions for filling out the Contact Us form. To accomplish this, follow these steps:

1. Click the Text tool from the toolbox and open the Character panel by clicking the Character button from the Launcher Bar.

 Tip   You can also access the Character panel by choosing **Window**, **Panels**, **Character**.

2. In the Character panel, set the Font modifier option to Comic Sans MS by clicking the arrow next to the Font option box and selecting **Comic Sans MS** from the list. Then set the Font Size option to 14 points by clicking in the Font Size option box and replacing the existing setting with 14. Set the Text Fill Color option to black (see Figure 15.1).

Font Height option

Figure 15.1

The Character panel also has tabs for accessing additional text settings so that you can create static text.

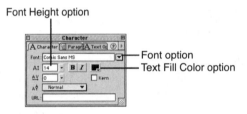

Font option
Text Fill Color option

3. Click the Paragraph tab to change to the Paragraph panel and set the Indentation option to 5 px. Keep the other option settings at their defaults (see Figure 15.2).

Figure 15.2

On the Paragraph panel, you can set a text block with paragraph settings.

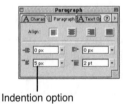

Indention option

4. Click the Text Options tab to access the Text Options panel and make sure the default setting of Static Text is selected. If not, select **Static Text** from the **Text Type** drop-down menu (see Figure 15.3).

5. Move your mouse cursor onto the Stage and click to set the text block. Type
`Use the form below to let us know your travel plans and travel desti-`
`nations. If you have any special concerns or travel needs please let`
`us know those too. A Whirlwind Travel Sales person will be back to`
`you to discuss these plans in detail. We want to hear from you!`

Text Type option

Figure 15.3

On the Text Options panel, you can select the type of text you will be creating.

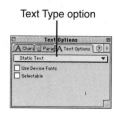

15

6. Position the text block by using the Arrow tool near the top of the white rectangular area.

7. Horizontally center the text block within the white rectangular area by selecting the area and the text block with the Arrow tool. Then open the Align panel by choosing **Window, Panels, Align** command. Click the Align horizontal center option (see Figure 15.4).

Figure 15.4

Make sure you select the text block and the entire white rectangular area, which includes both the line and the fill of the rectangular area.

Align horizontal center option

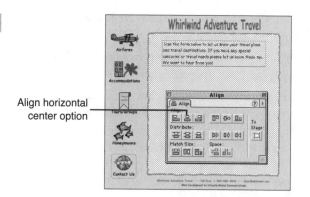

→ For a more detailed description of how to create static text blocks, **see** Chapter 7, "Using Text in Flash," **p. 153.**

You have created the instructions for using the form on the Contact Us page. Now you need to set up the labels and the input text fields to collect the end-users' information.

Creating Text Field Labels and Text Input Fields

With the opening form instructions set, you now can create the first text field label and text input field. You will be creating both static and input text blocks. Follow these instructions to create the Name text label and field for the Contact Us form:

1. Click the Text tool from the toolbox and open the Character panel if it is not already open by clicking the Character button on the Launcher Bar.

2. In the Character panel, set the Font option to Comic Sans MS by selecting **Comic Sans MS** from the **Font** drop-down list. Then set the Font Height option by replacing the existing setting with 12. Set the Text Fill Color option to forest green. Click the Bold option to set a bold format for the text (see Figure 15.5).

Figure 15.5

Your Character panel should match this figure.

3. Click the Paragraph tab to access the Paragraph panel and change the alignment to Left Justified.

4. Click the Text Options tab to access the Text Options panel and make sure the default setting of Static Text is selected. If not, click the arrow on the **Text Type** drop-down menu and select **Static Text**.

5. Move your mouse cursor onto the Stage and click to set a text block. Type Name to create your first text field label.

6. To create the input text field, click the Character tab again and set the Font option to _sans by selecting **_sans** from the **Font** list. Then set the Font Height option by replacing the existing setting with 12. Set the Text Fill Color option to black (see Figure 15.6).

Figure 15.6

The _sans font is a default system font. This means it will appear the same on any computer platform.

 Tip

The three default system fonts are _sans, _serif, and _typewriter. These fonts allow text to appear the same no matter what browser or computer platform an end-user might be using to access your form. These fonts take up less memory than if you designate a set font for text input fields.

Note

If you don't want to use a default system font for an input text block, you can choose any of the other fonts listed in the Font option drop-down menu of the Character panel. If you choose a non-system font, you must select one of the Embed Fonts options located at the bottom of the Text Options panel. If you select an embedded font outline option, the inputted text appears as if it were static text of the same font setting on your form. Using an embedded font outline option increases your file size significantly. Always have a good reason for using embedded fonts. Remember, in the world of Web development, 1K matters!

15

7. Set the attributes for the text field. Click the Text Options tab to switch to the Text Options panel. Click the arrow on the **Text Type** drop-down menu and select **Input Text**. New option settings then appear (see Figure 15.7).

Figure 15.7

You can use the Input Text options to customize the input fields on your form.

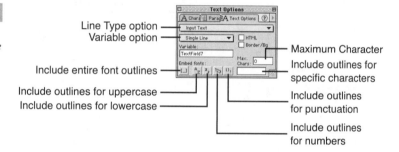

Line Type option — Variable option — Include entire font outlines — Include outlines for uppercase — Include outlines for lowercase — Maximum Character — Include outlines for specific characters — Include outlines for punctuation — Include outlines for numbers

8. Leave the Line Type option at the default setting of Single Line. Click the Border/Bg option to select it. Move your mouse cursor onto the Stage and click to set a text block. Return to the Text Options panel, click in the Variable option box, and replace the contents with Name (see Figure 15.8).

Tip

The Border/Bg option, if selected, creates a border or background color for the input text field. If you do not select this option, the Stage background is visible behind the input text field, and there is no border around the input text field.

Note

By typing Note into the Variable option box, you have assigned a variable and variable name to this text field. This variable must match a field in the back-end database that you link to. You can think of a variable as a container for storing the text so that it can be retrieved by the CGI script and posted to the correct data field or document on the Web server.

Figure 15.8

Setting a number in the Maximum Characters box limits the number of characters the end-user can type into that field.

9. Adjust the size of the Name input text block on the Stage by clicking the square handle in the lower-right corner of the block and dragging to create a text block about 2 inches wide (see Figure 15.9). Don't worry about aligning the field label with the input field; you'll do that later.

Figure 15.9

Notice that an input text block has a square handle in the lower-right corner, whereas a static text block has a circle or a square handle in the upper-right corner.

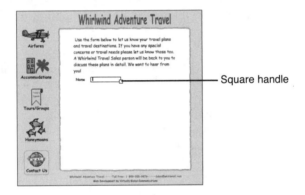

Square handle

 Tip

If you enter text into an input text block as you create it, this text can be used as additional instructions or an example of how data can be input into the text block. For example, you could have used "Enter Your Full Name Here" in the input text block that you just created. The end-users would need to click in the text field and delete the instruction text; however, they would know exactly what you want them to type into the field—their full name.

10. If rulers are not displayed, display them by choosing **View**, **Ruler**. Click and drag a horizontal Guide from the top ruler, position the Guide below the text label and the input field, and then click and drag a vertical Guide from the left ruler. Position it after the Name label. Then click and drag another vertical Guide from the left ruler. Position it before the input text block. You will use these guides to align all the labels and input fields for the form.

 Warning

Make sure that the **View**, **Guides**, **Show Guides** menu command is selected, or you will not see your Guides when you pull them out.

15

You also might need to turn off the **View**, **Snap to Objects** command and the **View**, **Grid**, **Snap to Grid** command. These features tend to interfere with aligning an object to a Guide.

11. Align these two text blocks so that they adhere or snap to the Guides (see Figure 15.10). You might need to turn on the **Snap to Guides** command by choosing **View**, **Guide**, **Snap to Guides**.

Figure 15.10

By using Guides, you are beginning to set up your form and align the fields for a more pleasing display.

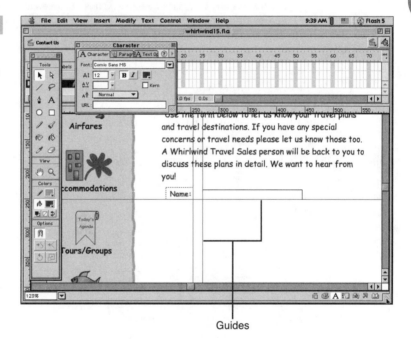

Guides

12. Using Table 15.1 and repeating steps 1 through 11, create the remaining fields for this form. Be sure to set up the input text blocks with the designated attributes as listed in the table. Set up additional horizontal Guides by pulling them from the top ruler. These Guides can be staggered 50 pixels between each text label and input field.

Table 15.1   Labels and Input Fields for the Contact Us Form

Label	Input Field Variable	Input Field Attributes
Address:	Address	Multiline, Border/Bg, Word wrap
City:	City	Single Line, Border/Bg
State:	State	Single Line, Border/Bg
Zip:	Zip	Single Line, Border/Bg

Table 15.1   continued

Label	Input Field Variable	Input Field Attributes
Travel Destination:	Destination	Single Line, Border/Bg
Travel Dates:	Dates	Multiline, Border/Bg, Word wrap
Special Travel Needs & Concerns:	Needs	Multiline, Border/Bg, Word wrap

Tip

Variable names are case sensitive. Make sure you are consistent in your use of uppercase and lowercase for these names. You need to make sure your database or text file uses the exact spelling and case for these variable names so that the fields match up.

13. As Table 15.1 shows, you need to create three input text blocks that are multiple lines. Adjust their size on the Stage so that they can hold three lines of text. Your final form should like similar to Figure 15.11.

Figure 15.11

Adjust the text blocks and input text fields to fit on your form page. Use your Guides to help space and align the labels and fields.

Tip

You might want to hide your Guides after you set up your form. The **View, Guides, Show Guides** menu command is a toggle switch. Selecting this menu command the first time turns the Guides on, selecting this menu command a second time turns the Guides off.

Tip

Another helpful hint is to turn off the Snap to Guides feature. It is a toggle switch, so you can choose **View, Guides, Snap to Guides** to deselect it.

Communicating with a Text File or Server-Side Script

Now that you have your input text fields set up with attributes and variable names, you need to create a button that will transmit the data to the server. This button will allow the user-entered data to be transmitted to the Web server, database, or text file that will store the result. You will use the Get URL action to send your variables— the user-entered data in the input text fields—to the Web server. By adding a button, you are allowing the end-users the option of transmitting the data when they are finished filling out the form.

1. Using the Rectangle tool from the toolbox, create a 1-inch by 1/2-inch rectangle with a forest green fill and a 1-point black line. Create the rectangle in the work area of your movie.

2. Click the Text tool from the toolbox and open the Character panel. Set your Character panel settings to a Text Color option of black and Font option of Comic Sans MS. Also, click the Bold option to apply Bold formatting.

3. Click the Text Options tab and set the Text Type option to **Static Text**. Leave the Paragraph panel settings at their defaults.

4. Move your mouse cursor into the work area close to the rectangle and click to create a text block. Type the word Submit.

5. Using the Arrow tool from the toolbox, position the text block on top of the green rectangle.

6. Align the text block and the rectangle so that the text block is centered in the rectangle. To do so, select both the rectangle and the text block. Then open the Align panel by choosing **Window, Panels, Align**. Click the Align horizontal center and Align vertical center options (see Figure 15.12).

Align vertical
center option

Figure 15.12

Align horizontal
center option

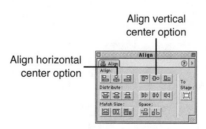

You can use the Align panel to center an object inside another object by selecting the Align horizontal center and Align vertical center options.

7. With both the text block and the rectangle selected and centered, create a symbol for this object by choosing **Insert, Convert to Symbol**. Name the symbol `Submit Button`. Set the Behavior to Button (see Figure 15.13).

Figure 15.13

Make sure you select the Button behavior for this symbol.

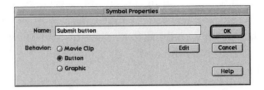

→ For a more detailed description of how to create buttons, **see** Chapter 12, "Attaching Actions and Sounds to the Buttons and Frames," **p. 265.**

8. Position the symbol on the Stage under the form data. Using the Align panel, center the button in the white rectangular area by selecting the area and the button and then clicking the Align vertical center option. Close the Align panel.

9. [Control-click] (Right-click) the Submit button and select **Actions** from the shortcut menu. Choosing this option displays the Object Actions dialog box.

10. Scroll down the Basic Actions list until you find the `Get URL` action. Click and drag it into the Scripting pane on the right side of the dialog box. This action displays the script for the Get URL action and the associated parameters in the lower portion of the dialog box for you to configure.

11. Click in the URL box and type `http://www.mywebserver.com`. (This fictitious URL is an example of what one would look like. You need to check with your ISP for instructions on submitting form data to its Web server.) Click the arrow on the **Variables** drop-down menu and select **Send using POST** from the list (see Figure 15.14).

Figure 15.14

If you click the arrow next to Window, you can set an optional argument specifying the window or HTML frame that the document should be loaded into.

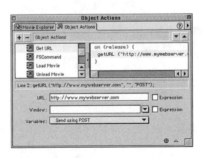

→ For a more detailed description of how to use the Object Actions dialog box, **see** Chapter 12, "Attaching Actions and Sounds to the Buttons and Frames," **p. 265.**

12. Close the Object Actions dialog box. At this point, you have set the method for transferring the form data to your Web server.

> The settings shown here for the Get URL script will not work. A Flash file must be published before the HTML link will work. Check with your ISP for more information on transmitting form data to its Web server.

15

→ For a more detailed description of attaching a form to a back-end database or text file, **see** Chapter 1, "Why Use Flash?," **p. 9**.

You have set up your form. Next, you should test it to be sure that it is transferring the variable data to the correct document and into the correct fields. Talk with your ISP for the correct process for transferring data and then test this process.

EXCURSION

Connecting Forms with a Web Server

Connectivity between the front-end Flash form and a back-end database is accomplished through a script, usually a CGI script written in the Perl programming language. This script sends instructions over the Internet from the Web page to the Web server. The data from each variable that you create on the form is transferred directly to the database, with information from each variable plugging into a database field coded with the same name. Text files are often used to store the data; therefore, this data is easily accessible to other applications so that you can massage the data into the various formats that you might need to use it!

Troubleshooting Forms

The transfer of data between a form and the Web server can work perfectly, but sometimes you need to troubleshoot your form to figure out why data is not being transferred correctly. The following list describes common errors that can occur when you're working with forms:

- Check that you have your input text blocks set up correctly. A common error is to have them set up as a static or dynamic text block.

- Check that your URL is set up correctly as per your ISP. A common error is to omit the `http://` from the URL.

- Check that you have variable names exactly matching the database fields or text file fields. A common error is not to have the spelling the same or the case of the letters match; uppercase and lowercase letters must match.

- Check that you have the correct method set for sending or receiving variables; for example, make sure you use the Post or Get method set based on the type of form that you are using.

 Tip

> You must specify how you want to load variables used in a form. Use the Get method for a small number of variables. This method appends the variables to the end of the URL. Use the Post method for long strings of variables. This method transfers the variables in a separate http header.

After you test your form and the data transfer and all is working, you have completed your Contact Us form! Save your Web site movie to save all the changes you have made. You will find an example of the Web site up to this point on the CD-ROM that accompanies this book. Open the Chapter 15 folder and locate the file whirlwind15.fla if you need to see an example of the project Web site.

Where You've Been!

This chapter covered how to create static and input text blocks for the creation of labels and input fields for a form. You created the general information that the Whirlwind Adventure Travel company needs to begin helping clients with their travel needs. You set up variables and created a button for transferring the variable data to the Web server.

What's Next?

The next chapter takes the form-creation process one step further and covers how to use drag and drop technology to determine variables. That chapter will instruct you on creating the Accommodations page of the Web site. You'll use many of the form skills and features that you learned in this chapter in the next chapter as well.

Chapter 16

In this chapter

- *Creating an Interactive Form*
- *Using Smart Clips*
- *Creating Drag-and-Drop Interactivity*
- *Troubleshooting Techniques*

Creating the Accommodations Page

In this chapter, you will create an interactive form using techniques similar to those used in Chapter 15, "Creating the Contact Us Form for the Web Site," where you created the simple Contact Us form. However, this time you will use some of the new features of Flash 5. One of these features is *smart clips*. Smart clips are very beneficial for advanced and beginning Flash users alike. Even with limited ActionScripting skills, beginning Flash users can add interactive components to their movies. You will use smart clips to add radio buttons and a pull-down menu to your Accommodations page. You will also add drag-and-drop interactivity to the form.

This chapter begins to introduce more advanced ActionScripting skills and techniques. Again, like Chapter 15, this chapter will cover only the front-end interface for the form. To make the form functional on the Internet, you will need to enlist the aid of a database programmer and your Internet service provider (ISP) to set up the back-end functionality. These skills are outside the scope of this book.

→ For a more detailed description of database interactivity, **see** Chapter 1, "Why Use Flash?," **p. 9**.

Building the Interactive Form

Per the planning document that you created in Chapter 4, "Planning Your Travel Company Web Site," you will create a form that allows the end-user more hands-on interactivity with accommodations choices for this form. Whirlwind Adventure Travel has accommodations in the following land areas—North America, South

America, Greenland, Asia/Russia, Europe, Australia, and Japan/Indonesia. The end-user will choose a land area that she is interested in visiting and find accommodations there. As stated in Chapter 4, these are broad land areas used in this project for the sake of simplicity. If you were to really use this form, you would want to narrow down choices to specific countries and even providences and states.

Once a user selects a land areas of interest, she will designate a price range as well as the number of bedrooms she will need for her vacation. This form allows the end-user to choose a location for accommodations and then specify some criteria to narrow down the search for accommodations in that location. You'll use drag-and-drop programming and smart clips when creating this form. The form will be very simplistic in its criteria and focus only on land areas. The skills and concepts you learn in this chapter can be easily transferred to your own work and projects.

→ For a more detailed description of smart clips, **see** Chapter 2, "What's New with Flash 5," **p. 25**.

Smart Clips Basics

Smart clips are a new feature of Flash 5. In fact, Macromedia has included a Library of sample smart clips with the Flash 5 software. You can find them by choosing **Window**, **Common Libraries** and then choosing the library from the list. Aside from the other common libraries listed here, two of these listed libraries contain smart clips: the **Learning Interactions** and **Smart Clips** menu choices. For this chapter, you will use the **Smart Clips** menu choice, so choose **Window**, **Common Libraries**, **Smart Clips**. Choosing this menu command opens the Smart Clips Library (see Figure 16.1). Position this Library in the work area so that you can use it a little later to create your accommodations criteria features.

Figure 16.1

Notice that the smart clips have a different Library icon representing them than other Library items you've used before.

Smart Clip icon ——

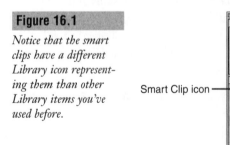

In previous versions of Flash, you needed to be very familiar with ActionScripting to create drop-down menus, radio buttons, or check boxes for a form. Now, with smart clips, even novice Flash developers can use these objects in their movies.

Tip

The Learning Interactions Library contains smart clips for use in developing interactive learning modules or tutorials (see Figure 16.2).

Figure 16.2

Through the Learning Interactions Library, you can create online tutorials with testing features that ensure the end-user is learning.

16

Setting Up Page Structure

Before you can begin to add the interactive elements to your Accommodations page, you need to set up the static text blocks and add the world map graphic. Follow these steps to set up your page structure:

1. Create a new layer called World Map. Then, using the **File**, **Import** command, import the world.gif file from the Chapter 16 folder on the CD-ROM that accompanies this book and place it on this layer.

2. Break this image apart by choosing **Modify**, **Break Apart**. Then, using the Lasso tool and its Magic Wand options and features, select and delete the white background so that all you have is the land areas. Set the Magic Wand settings to **Pixels** and a Threshold of 30. You need to delete the white color for all lakes and inlets for many of the land areas too.

→ For more detailed instructions on importing and optimizing an image, **see** Chapter 6, "Importing Graphics for the Travel Company Web Site," **p. 127**.

3. For now, group the land areas and position them at the top of the white rectangular area. I'll call this grouped graphic the "world map" for future references. Center the world map by using the Arrow tool (see Figure 16.3).

Figure 16.3

You can also use the Align panel to horizontally center the world map graphic in the white rectangular area.

4. Click the Background layer to make it the active layer. Click the Text tool and open your Character panel. Set your options to **Comic Sans MS** font, black color, bold, and 12 points.

5. Click the Text Options tab of the Character panel and set the Text Type option to **Static Text**. Then create the following text blocks on your page:

   - Click and drag the above land area that you are looking for accommodation into the destination box below.

   - How many bedrooms are you looking for in your accommodation?

   - What is your price range for accommodations?

6. Position these three text blocks below the world map.

7. Click the Rectangle tool and, below the world map, create a rectangle with a blue, 1-point, solid line and no fill. Make the rectangle 100px in height and 200px in width.

8. Position the text blocks and the rectangle as shown in Figure 16.4.

Figure 16.4

The end-user can drag his or her choice of land area into this rectangle.

The page is now set up with the background information and the graphics that you will need for the form.

Creating a Radio Button

With the background text blocks created, you are now ready to add your smart clips. The first ones to add are the radio buttons for setting the number of bedrooms the end-user can choose from. Follow these steps to add and configure a radio button for the bedroom options:

1. Create a new layer above the Background layer and name it `Criteria`. Make it the active layer.

2. Make the Smart Clip Library active by clicking it. Locate the RadioButton smart clip and drag it onto your Stage. Position it below the text block that refers to selecting the number of bedrooms (see Figure 16.5).

Figure 16.5

Position the RadioButton smart clip to the far left of the white rectangular area.

RadioButton smart clip —

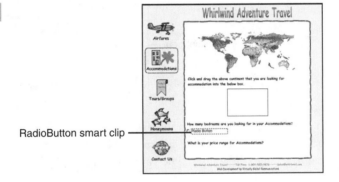

3. Configure the smart clip to customize the parameters associated with it so that it works with your movie. (Control-click)[Right-click] the RadioButton smart clip and choose **Panels**, **Clip Parameters** to open the Clip Parameters dialog box (see Figure 16.6).

Tip
A clip parameter is really a value of a variable. You can customize the value to fit your movie.

Note
You can also increase or decrease the Clip Parameters section by positioning your cursor on the border between the Clip Parameters and Description sections. When you do, the cursor turns into a double-arrow tool that allows you to click and drag this border either up to decrease the Clip Parameters area or down to increase the area.

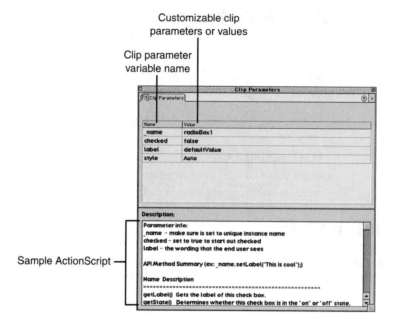

Figure 16.6

The Clip Parameters dialog box can be resized. Click in the lower-right corner and drag the window to the size you need.

4. In the Clip Parameters or values section of the dialog box, double-click radioBox1 under the Value column. This action highlights radioBox1, allowing you to change the name. Type 1bed (see Figure 16.7).

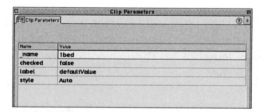

Figure 16.7

RadioBox1 is the variable _name parameter or value.

5. Leave the variable "checked" value at false. Double-clicking false opens a drop-down menu that allows you to change the value to true. If you keep this setting to false, the radio button does not appear checked.

6. Double-click variable "label" value of defaultValue to highlight it and type 1 Bedroom. This will be the label for the radio button.

7. Leave the variable "style" set to the value of Auto. Double-clicking the Auto value opens a drop-down menu that allows you to make the radio button appear to be either a Macintosh-style or Windows-style radio button. Your Clip Parameters settings should look like Figure 16.8.

Figure 16.8

If you leave the variable "style" set to the value of Auto, the radio button appears in either the Macintosh or Windows style, based on the browser the site is being viewed in.

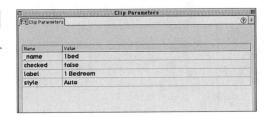

8. Close the Clip Parameters dialog box. Notice that your radio button does not change to reflect your new settings. Because a smart clip is actually a movie clip that has its own Timeline different from the main movies, you will not see the settings until you test the scene (or movie) by choosing **Control, Test Scene** (or **Control, Test Movie**).

→ For a more detailed description of movie clips, **see** Chapter 14, "Advanced Animation Techniques," **p. 305**.

Because smart clips are a Flash 5 feature, you must have your Publish settings set to a version setting of Flash 5 for them to function correctly in the Flash Player. See Chapter 13, "Publishing the Movie for the Travel Company Web Site," on setting your version setting to Flash 5.

→ For a more detailed description of publish settings, **see** Chapter 13, "Publishing the Movie for the Travel Company Web Site," **p. 287**.

9. Repeating steps 2 through 8, create two more radio buttons and customize their Clip Parameter settings for a 2 Bedroom radio button with a variable "_name" value of 2bed and a variable "label" value of 2 Bedroom, and a 3 Bedroom radio button with a variable "_name" value of 3bed and a variable "label" value of 3 Bedroom. Make sure you position these radio buttons on the Criteria layer. Your movie should now look like Figure 16.9.

Testing the Smart Clip

Because you cannot view your customized smart clip in Flash development mode, you need to be able to test its functionality. To do so, you must test your movie or the scene that holds the smart clip. Choose **Control, Test Scene** to test just the Accommodations scene of your movie. There, you can see your customized radio buttons (see Figure 16.10).

Figure 16.9

You can also use a Guide to position your radio buttons horizontally under the static text block.

Figure 16.10

Click one button and then click another. Only one of the three radio buttons you've created can be selected at a time.

 Tip

If your radio buttons are not displayed correctly, you can resize them in Flash development mode. If you are in Flash Player mode, close this window to return to Flash development mode. Select the smart clip to be resized on your Stage. Click the Scale option of the Arrow tool on the toolbox and adjust the size of the button by dragging one of the resize handles.

Creating a Drop-Down Menu

With your radio buttons up and functioning, you now can create a drop-down menu listing the different price ranges for accommodations. In previous releases of Flash, creating drop-down menus required a strong knowledge of ActionScripting, but with smart clips, you'll see that creating them is a breeze! To create the drop-down menu for this project, follow these steps:

1. Make the Criteria layer the active layer if it is not already active. Open your Smart Clip Library by choosing **Window**, **Common Libraries**, **Smart Clips**.

2. Locate the Menu smart clip in the Smart Clips Library. Drag an instance of this symbol onto your Stage and position it after the static text block referring to pricing for accommodations (see Figure 16.11).

Figure 16.11

This smart clip will be customized to show price ranges for accommodations.

3. (Control-click) [Right-click] the Menu smart clip instance on the Stage to access the shortcut menu. Select the **Clip Parameters** menu command to open the Clip Parameters dialog box (see Figure 16.12).

Parameters for the Menu smart clip

Figure 16.12

This smart clip has two parameter variables that can be customized— items and style.

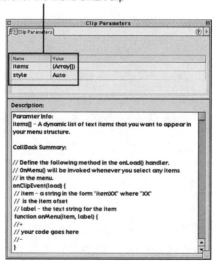

4. Double-click the variable "Items" value of (Array[]) to open the Values dialog box (see Figure 16.13).

16

Figure 16.13

In the Values dialog box, you can customize the value for the drop down menu you are creating.

Add or delete a value

Move a value up or down the list

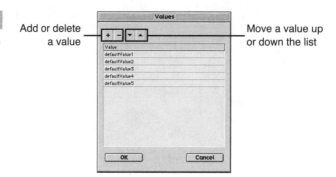

5. Double-click the defaultValue1 choice in the list to select it and then type `$100-$149 per night` (see Figure 16.14).

Up and down buttons

Figure 16.14

You can select any default value and change it to the menu choice you want. You then can use the Up or Down buttons to move the choice to the correct location in the list.

6. Repeat step 5 and add the following menu choices to the list:

   • `$150-$199 per night`

   • `$200-$249 per night`

   • `$250-$299 per night`

   • `$300+ per night`

7. Your Values dialog box should look like Figure 16.15. Click OK to close the dialog box. Then click the close button in the title bar of the Clip Parameters dialog box to close it.

8. Test your scene by choosing **Control, Test Scene** to see the new menu and menu choices (see Figure 16.16).

Figure 16.15

You can add as many menu choices as you need in the Values dialog box. Just click the Add button and change the Value name.

Figure 16.16

You can select any of the menu choices by dragging through the list and clicking the one you want.

You have now added a drop-down menu to your Accommodations form with very little scripting.

EXCURSION

Creating Your Own Smart Clip

Now that you know how to use existing smart clips, you can also create your own for use with your movies or to share with others. To create a smart clip, you must first start with a movie clip symbol. To assign clip parameters to a movie clip, (Control-click) [right-click] the movie clip symbol in the Library and select **Define Clip Parameters** from the shortcut menu. Choosing this command displays the Define Clip Parameter dialog box in which you can set up the variables and values that can be customized by the end-user. You can also create your own unique interface for the smart clip.

Assigning Variables to the Radio Buttons

Now that you have created your criteria, you need to assign variables so that you can link this form into a back-end database and transmit the data to the Web server. Just like you created variable names for your input text blocks, you need to create variables names for the instances of each of the smart clips on your Stage. To do so, follow these steps:

1. On your Stage, click the first radio button for the 1 Bedroom criterion to select it. Then open the Instance panel by choosing **Window**, **Panels**, **Instance**.

2. Click the Name box and type 1bedroom (see Figure 16.17).

Figure 16.17

*You can change the behavior of the instance in the Instance panel by clicking the **Behavior** drop-down menu and choosing a new behavior.*

Variable Name box

3. Repeat step 2 for the other two radio buttons and create the variable names 2bedroom and 3bedroom based on the labels of the radio buttons.

4. Click the Menu instance and click the Instance panel to make it active (if it is not already).

5. Click in the Name box and type Pricing (see Figure 16.18).

Figure 16.18

The Menu variable will be named Pricing and will be assigned the end-user's menu choice when he or she makes a selection.

6. Close the Instance panel by clicking the close button in the title bar. You have now added variable names for the criteria created thus far in your form.

You will find that as more and more people use smart clips, more and more third-party vendors and Web sites will distribute them. Refer to the Macromedia Dashboard (by choosing **Help**, **Macromedia Dashboard**) for more information on third-party smart clips currently available.

Using Drag-and-Drop Interactivity

With the addition of smart clips, you now have started to build your interactive form. Next, you will add a really neat feature of Flash that further allows the end-user browsing your site control over environment and form choices. This feature is referred to as *drag-and-drop* functionality.

The key to the drag-and-drop feature is to use buttons and then convert them into their own movie clip. As a movie clip, they have their own Timeline, independent of the main movie. Therefore, the end-user can drag and drop them.

Dragging Movie Clip Actions

The following example uses a world map. For this example, you'll create land areas to set your criteria. This broad example is used for the sake of simplicity. If you were really creating this criterion for a form, you would want to break down the locations in more detail. This book keeps the example broad in scope, but you can easily apply the coding behind each land area to more defined examples of location—for example, states in the United States. First, you need to set up your world map graphic to get it ready for the ActionScripting of the drag-and-drop functionality by following these steps:

1. Click the World Map layer to make it active and then click the world map graphic that you grouped earlier in this chapter. Lock all other layers by (Option-clicking) [Alt+clicking] the World Map layer dot in the Lock/Unlock All Layers column.

2. Earlier in the chapter, you grouped the world map graphic; now you need to ungroup it by choosing **Modify**, **Ungroup**.

3. To group each land area that you want to use as a criterion for locating an accommodation, use the Arrow tool and create this grouping. The Whirlwind Adventure Travel company has accommodations on these land areas: Asia-Russia, Australia, Europe, Greenland, Japan-Indonesia, North America, and South America.

4. Convert each of these land areas into a button symbol named with this convention: b_North America, b_South America, and so on. By using a b_ in front of the land area name, you are distinguishing it as a button. For the rest of this instruction, I'll use North America as the example.

 Warning Make sure you name the symbol b__North America; otherwise, the rest of the ActionScript code won't match the symbol name and won't function correctly.

➔ For a more detailed description of creating symbols, **see** Chapter 8, "Using Symbols, Libraries, and Instances to Recycle and Organize Graphic Elements," **p. 177**.

Tip

You also might want to set your Hit area for each of the land area buttons in the symbol-editing mode. In particular, the Japan/Indonesia button might be difficult for the end-user to grab without setting a defined Hit area.

➜ For a more detailed description of creating buttons and defining a Hit area, **see** Chapter 12, "Attaching Actions and Sounds to the Buttons and Frames," **p. 265**.

5. Click the North America land area grouping and open the Actions panel by choosing **Window, Actions**.

6. Click the Add button (+) in the upper-left corner and choose the **Basic Actions, OnMouseEvent** ActionScript command. The OnMouseEvent code then appears in the Actions list. Select the Press option in the Parameters panel and then reselect the Release option to turn off that option (see Figure 16.19).

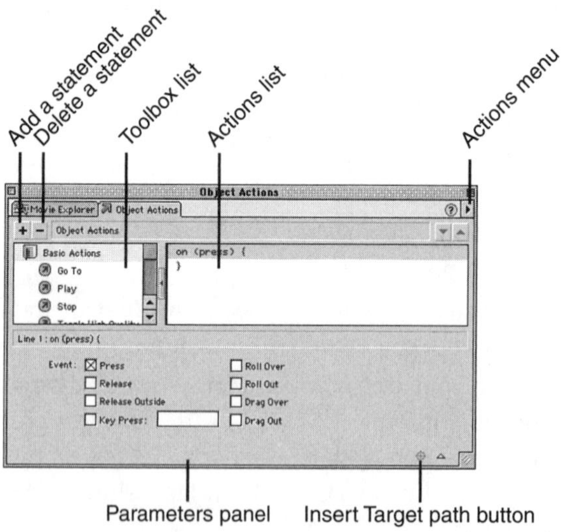

Figure 16.19

You should select the Press mouse event because it initiates the "drag" process for the drag and drop functionality.

Add a statement   Delete a statement   Toolbox list   Actions list   Actions menu

Parameters panel   Insert Target path button

Note

You might have noticed that the ActionScript commands in the Toolbox list of the Object Actions panel include some color-coding. Some actions have a green highlight, and some have a yellow highlight. Color-coding is a new feature of Flash 5. The commands with a green highlight are still supported by the version of Flash that you set in your Publish Settings, but a better command or scripting is available to achieve the same results. The yellow highlight indicates that these commands are supported only in the Flash version you have selected in your Publish Settings. This highlighting changes based on the version of Flash that you have set in your Publish Settings for the movie.

→ For a more detailed description of setting your Publish Settings, **see** Chapter 13, "Publishing the Movie for the Travel Comapny Web Site," **p. 287**.

7. With the first line of code highlighted in the Actions list, click the Add button (+) again and choose the **Actions, startDrag** ActionScript command. New code is added below the on (press){ code (see Figure 16.20). You have just set the coding for the "drag" action of the drag-and-drop functionality.

Figure 16.20

Flash always adds a new action and its code below the highlighted code in the Actions list.

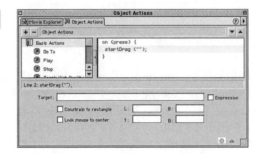

The on (press) code is an event handler. This means that an action or event must occur before this code is initiated. In this case, the end-user needs to press the mouse button to initiate the startDrag function.

8. You're ready to create the "drop" code for the drag-and-drop functionality. In the Actions list, select the } located in the third line of code (see Figure 16.21).

Figure 16.21

By selecting the closing bracket symbol in the ActionScript code, you are designating that a new function or action will be added and the previous code or action is complete.

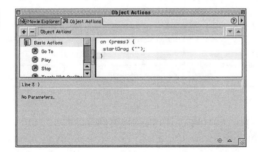

9. Click the Add button (+) in the Actions panel and choose the **Actions, stopDrag** ActionScript command (see Figure 16.22).

10. Now you need to convert this button symbol into a movie clip. Click the North America button symbol to make it active and convert it to a movie clip symbol. Name this movie clip symbol M_North America.

New mouse event or handler

Figure 16.22

Notice that a new mouse event or handler is added with the stopDrag *code. The* stopDrag *function is initiated through a mouse event on the end-user's part.*

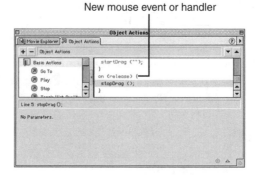

11. Test your Accommodations scene by choosing **Control**, **Test Scene**. Choosing this menu command launches the Flash Player. Click the North American land area and drag it to a new location in the movie (see Figure 16.23).

Figure 16.23

You can move the North American land area anywhere on your screen.

12. Repeating steps 5 through 10, configure the other land area buttons with the drag-and-drop functionality. Then convert them to movie clips. Name them appropriately so that they are similar to your land area button names. This time, use an M_ in place of the b_ to designate the symbol as a movie clip, such as M_North America, M_South America, and so on.

 13. Test your scene by choosing **Control**, **Test Scene** to make sure that all your land area instances drag and drop correctly.

Naming Your Land Area Instances

Now that you have created your buttons and movie clip symbols, you need to name the movie clip instance of each land area on the Stage. This way, you can designate one land area movie clip instance from another when it is called in the code that you will create next. To do so, follow these steps:

1. Click the North America movie clip instance on your Stage and open the Instance panel.

2. In the Name box, type North America (see Figure 16.24).

Figure 16.24

Naming each land area instance not only helps your ActionScript code work but also sets up variable names for the form criteria.

3. Click the South America movie clip on your Stage to make it active. In the Instance panel, type South America in the Name box.

4. Repeat Step 3 with the other land area movie clips, naming them appropriately.

To set up the functionality that snaps the land area into the destination box of the form, you need to have variable names applied to each land area. Because you have named your land areas, you can now proceed to the next section for setting your drop target.

Setting the Drop Target

Now that you have created your drag-and-drop functionality and named your land area instances, you can refine and add to the ActionScript so that you restrict where the end-user drops the land area. In the Whirlwind Adventure Travel Web site, this would be the destination box area. This area needs to have some additional functionality, code, and a variable name assigned to it in order for the process to work. Follow these steps to configure the destination box:

1. Click the destination box to make it active. Using your Paint Bucket tool, fill the destination box with the same blue color that you used for the outline of the white rectangular area. You need to sample this line first with the Dropper tool if you do not know what blue color chip you used before.

Tip

You must fill this shape because it needs to have something there when the end-user drags a land area over it. If the shape doesn't have a fill, it will not detect the object being dragged over it. You could also use a white fill or a fill with a 0% alpha setting.

2. Convert the destination box into a movie clip and name it `mbox`. You will add code to the box movie clip to make it "smart" (smart in the way that it knows when an object is located within its area).

3. Edit the box movie clip in symbol-editing mode by (Control-clicking) [right-clicking] the land area and choosing **Edit** from the shortcut menu. Next, you need to add a dynamic text block below the destination box (see Figure 16.25). Set the text block options as follows:

   - **Character tab**—Font of **Comic Sans MS**, Text (fill) color of blue, 12 point Font Size.
   - **Paragraph tab**—Alignment of Center.
   - **Text Options tab**—Text type of **Dynamic Text**, Line type of **Single Line**, Variable name of `selection`, the entire font outline option for the Embed fonts. Make sure the Selectable option is not checked.

Figure 16.25

Your text block setting should match this figure's setting for each of the panels.

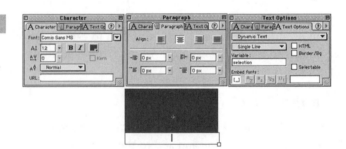

4. Return to the Accommodations scene. Click the mbox movie clip instance on your Stage to make it active and open the Instance panel. Type `box` in the Name box on the Instance panel (see Figure 16.26).

Figure 16.26

By naming the instance on the Stage, you are also setting your variable name for the form.

Your movie should look similar to Figure 16.27.

Figure 16.27

The dynamic text block shows the instance name of the land area when it is dropped into the destination box area.

Snapping the Movie Clip

With the destination box set and a text block created to identify the land area that is dropped into the destination box, you are now ready to create the code that will cause the land areas to drop into the destination box. Or, if the end-user misses the destination box, the land area will return to its location in the world map. To create this code, follow these steps:

1. Create the code for the land areas that records their original location. Edit the North America movie clip instance on your Stage in symbol-editing mode.

2. Click in frame 1 of Layer 1 and open your Actions panel.

3. Click the Add button (+) and choose the **Actions**, **set variable** ActionScript command. In the Parameters panel, click the Variable box and type x. Then click the Value box and type _x. Click the Expression option next to the Value box to turn on this option (see Figure 16.28).

Tip

Expressions are any part of the code that creates or produces a value. In the preceding code, x = _x is an expression.

Figure 16.28

The ActionScript code of
x = _x appears in the
Actions list of the
Actions panel.

Warning

If you forget to click the Expression option, your code is passed as a *string*. A string is any character enclosed in quotation marks. Strings can be connected together to create a new string but cannot produce a numerical value.

4. With the first line of code highlighted, click the Add button (+) again and choose the **Actions**, **set variable** ActionScript command again. In the Parameters panel, click the Variable box and type y. Then click the Value box and type _y. Click the Expression option next to the Value box to turn it on (see Figure 16.29).

Figure 16.29

You have instructed
Flash to record the x, y
coordinate location of
this movie clip on the
Stage by entering this
code.

Tip

Any code that begins with an underscore character (_) refers to a movie clip property or a global property.

Note

Variables are identifiers that contain values for any data type. You can update, change, and create variables. The data values that are stored can be retrieved and used by any script that calls for variables.

5. Click the North America image on the symbol-editing Stage. This action changes the Frame Actions panel to the Object Actions panel.

6. Click in the lower-right corner of the dialog box and drag it so that it is longer. Changing the size of the dialog box increases the size of the Actions list so that you can add more script to this movie clip and see all of it at once.

7. In the Actions list, click the stopDrag () line of code so that it is highlighted. You will add additional code below to create the snap functionality.

8. Click the Add button (+) and choose the **Actions**, **If** ActionScript command (see Figure 16.30).

Figure 16.30

You will apply logic to the North America movie clip through the If/Else ActionScript to determine whether the land area is over the destination box.

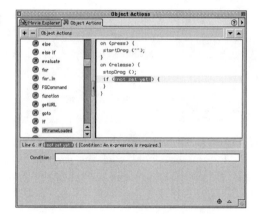

9. Click the Add button (+) again and choose the **Properties**, **_droptarget** ActionScript command. In the Condition box set your cursor after the _droptarget command and insert a space. Then type eq " /box" (see Figure 16.31).

Figure 16.31

The _droptarget property is set to equal the box instance on the Stage through this code.

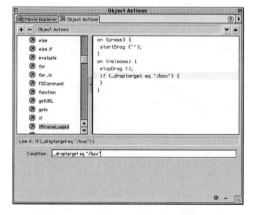

10. Click the Add button (+) and choose the **Actions, set variable** ActionScript command. In the Parameters panel, click the Variable box and type _x. Then click the Value box and type _root.box._x. Click the Expression option next to the Value box (see Figure 16.32).

Figure 16.32

This code snaps the land area to the box's x coordinate.

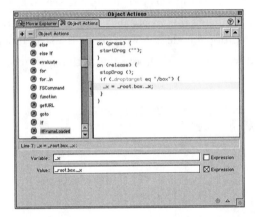

11. Click the Add button (+) and choose the **Actions, set variable** ActionScript command. In the Parameters panel, click the Variable box and type _y. Then click the Value box and type _root.box._y. Click the Expression option next to the Value box (see Figure 16.33).

Figure 16.33

This code snaps the land area to the box's y coordinate.

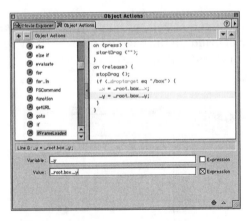

12. Click the Add button (+) and choose the **Actions, set variable** ActionScript command. In the Parameters panel, click the Variable box and type _root.box.selection. Then click the Value box and type _name. Click the Expression option next to the Value box (see Figure 16.34). You have set your code for snapping the land area into the box and having the text block display the land area name.

Figure 16.34

This code causes the dynamic text block that you named selection *to reflect the name of the land area instance being dropped.*

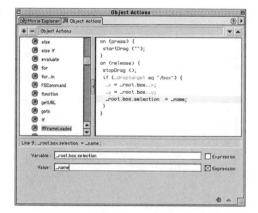

13. Test your scene by choosing **Control, Test Scene**. You should be able to move your land areas into the destination box. They will snap into the center of this box.

14. Repeat Steps 1 through 13 for all your land area movie clips. Test each one to make sure you have the code correct.

 Tip

You can copy and paste any ActionScript for both frames and objects by highlighting the code in the Actions list of the Actions panel and using the keyboard equivalent commands for **Copy** and **Paste**: (Cmd-C) [Ctrl+C] and (Cmd-V) [Ctrl+V]. Not having to re-create code for similar functionality of buttons and frames can save you a great deal of time.

 **Warning**

When you're copying and pasting code in the Actions panel, the menu commands **Copy** and **Paste** do not always work. For consistent functionality, you must use the keyboard equivalent keys.

Adding Logic for the Movie Clip to Return to Its Position in the World Map

Now you need to set up the logic for what happens if the end-user misses the destination box. You want the land area to go back to its original location in the world map:

1. Click the Add (+) button and choose the **Actions, else** ActionScript command (see Figure 16.35).

Figure 16.35

The else code appears in the Actions list. No parameters are associated with this command.

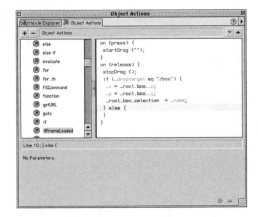

2. Click the Add button (+) and choose the **Actions, set variable** ActionScript command. In the Parameters panel, click the Variable box and type _x. Then click the Value box and type x. Click the Expression option next to the Value box (see Figure 16.36).

Figure 16.36

This code snaps the land area back to the original x coordinate of its location in the world map.

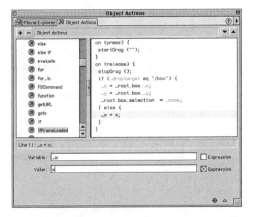

3. Click the Add button (+) and choose the **Actions, set variable** ActionScript command. In the Parameters panel, click the Variable box and type _y. Then click the Value box and type y. Click the Expression option next to the Value box (see Figure 16.37).

4. Close the Actions panel and exit the symbol-editing mode to return to the Accommodations scene.

Figure 16.37

This code snaps the land area back to the original y coordinate of the land area location in the world map.

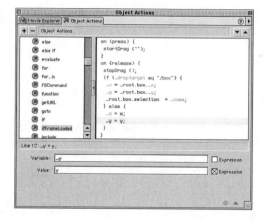

 5. Test your scene by choosing **Control**, **Test Scene**. While you're in the Flash Player, drag the North America land area into the destination box. You should see it snap into the center of the box, as well as display the name of the land area in the dynamic text block (see Figure 16.38). Then drag it out of the box and drop it in another location on the Stage. You should see it snap back to its original location in the world map.

Figure 16.38

The drag-and-drop function now snaps the land area into the destination box.

6. To make this page fully functional, repeat steps 1 through 5 to re-create this code for all the land areas you have created.

Tip   You can print a copy of the Actions panel by clicking the Actions menu in the upper-right corner and selecting **Print** from the list.

Adding the Submit Button to the Form

To complete the form, you need to add the Submit button that you created in Chapter 15. You will find this symbol in your Library. Open your Library and use the following steps to add this button to your form:

1. Locate the Submit button in your Library and drag it to your Stage.

2. Position the Submit button under the Accommodations form data (see Figure 16.39).

Figure 16.39

Your Accommodations form should look like this Figure.

3. Using the Align panel, center the button in the white rectangular area by selecting the area and the button using the Shift-click technique, and then clicking the Align Vertical Center option in the Align panel. Close the Align panel.

4. [Control-click] (Right-click) the Submit button and select **Actions** from the shortcut menu to open the Object Actions dialog box.

5. Click the Add (+) button and choose **Actions, Get URL**. Click and drag it into the Scripting pane on the right side of the dialog box. This action displays the script for the Get URL action and the associated parameters in the lower portion of the dialog box for you to configure.

6. Click in the URL box and type `http://www.mywebserver.com`. (This fictitious URL is an example of what one would look like. You need to check with your ISP for instructions on submitting form data to its Web server.) Click the arrow on the **Variables** menu and select **Send Using POST** from the list.

→ For a more detailed description of database interactivity, **see** Chapter 1, " Why Use Flash?,"
p. 9.

Troubleshooting Actions

Flash 5 has several features that check for ActionScript errors in the Flash development and Flash Player modes. These different features allow you to check or troubleshoot your code for errors.

Color-Coding of Syntax in the Actions Panel

Flash 5 color-codes the *syntax* in the ActionScript. (Syntax refers to the rules of grammar or punctuation for code.) You might have noticed that certain commands are color-coded differently than other commands in the Actions list of the Actions panel. This color-coding can help you identify errors in your code. The following list describes the color-coding of ActionScript:

- Keywords and predefined identifiers, such as play and stop, are blue.
- Properties are green.
- Comments are magenta.
- Strings surrounded by quotation marks are gray.

If you make an error in the syntax of the code as you are creating it in the Actions panel, the error is highlighted in red if you are in the Normal mode (see Figure 16.40).

Red highlight

Figure 16.40

The if (_droptarget eq "/box") *has an extra* } *in the code. It should not be there.*

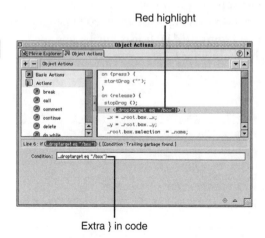

Extra } in code

Color-coding makes it easy to identify your errors as you are creating the code. If you move your mouse pointer over the error, you see a ToolTip explaining the problem. When you select the code in the Actions list, the error message is displayed in the title of the Parameters panel.

Checking Your Syntax

You should always check your code for syntax errors prior to exporting or publishing a movie. Therefore, do the following:

1. Select the object or frame with the ActionScript that you want to check for errors.
2. Open your Actions panel and click the **Actions** menu in the upper-right corner. Choose the **Check Syntax** command from the list.
3. Flash checks your code for errors in syntax. If it finds any errors, it highlights them in red.

Warning

You can test a movie that contains errors in the ActionScript, but all errors are reported in the Output window. Flash does not include any of the code that has errors in the exported movie. See the next section for more information on the Output window.

Using the Output Window

The Output window appears when you test a movie and you have errors in your ActionScript. This window also appears when you open a Flash 4.0 or earlier version movie in Flash 5 (see Figure 16.41). It lists line by line the code that is wrong. This feature helps troubleshoot your code.

Options menu

Figure 16.41

This Output window appears when you open a Flash 4.0 or earlier version movie in Flash 5.

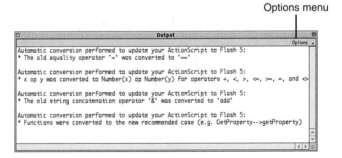

 **Warning**   You can open the Output window at any time in Flash Player mode by choosing **Window, Output**.

You can work with the contents of the Output window through one of the following commands:

- **Options, Copy** enables you to copy the code listed in the Output window to the Clipboard for pasting into another application.
- **Options, Clear** clears the Output window's contents.
- **Options, Save to File** saves the code in the Output window to a text file.
- **Options, Print** prints a hard copy of the Output window's contents.

Using Trace

Flash 5 now offers a feature that allows you to send information or comments to the Output window: the trace action command. You can add this code to your Actions list in the Actions panel by clicking the Add (+) button and choosing the **Actions, trace** ActionScript command (see Figure 16.42).

Trace command

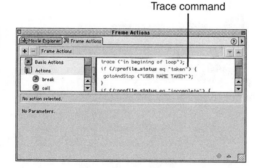

Figure 16.42

Here, you can see an example of a trace command. If an error appears in the following code listed in the Actions list, the Output window begins the associated error message with the text that appears in the parentheses that follow the trace command—in this instance, in beginning of loop.

Debugging Code

Another nice feature of Flash 5 is the Debugger (see Figure 16.43). This feature works only while you are in the Flash Player mode. The Debugger allows you to find errors in the ActionScript code of a movie. It displays a list of movie clips and loaded movies. You can then change the values of variables and properties to determine correct values, all while the movie is running. This way, you can test your new variables and properties to determine the correct code. Then you can go back to your movie in Flash development mode and correct the code.

Figure 16.43

The Debugger window in the active state.

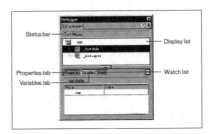

To activate your Debugger, you must turn it on in the Publish Settings dialog box (see Figure 16.44).

You can password protect your Debugger

Figure 16.44

Click the Debugging Permitted option to turn on this feature.

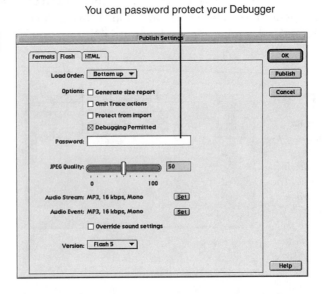

 Note

To use the Debugger, you must have the Flash Debug Player, which is a special version of the Flash Player. The Flash Debug Player is installed automatically when you install the Flash 5 authoring application.

 **Tip**

An alternative to using the Debugger with forms is to set up your editable text fields on a guide layer. This way, you can track your variable values directly in the form.

Good Troubleshooting Practices

As you become more proficient with using Flash and creating movies, you will want to develop good coding practices. In the areas of troubleshooting and authoring practices, these rules of thumb will make your job much easier:

- Be consistent in your naming conventions for instances, symbols, and movie clips that are called out in code. You might want to avoid using spaces in words. This chapter used variable and function names that began with a lowercase letter and used a capital letter for each new word. You can use whatever convention for your code that makes sense to you, but the key is to be consistent.

- Always try to use variable names that make sense within the context of the movie. The name should reflect the content of the variable.

- Get in the habit of using the `trace` action for your complex ActionScript code. The trace actions command sends comments to the Output window, so you can easily focus on what code is working and what is not.

- If you use the Movie Explorer in Flash Player mode, you can view display lists and all actions in a movie.

- You should use the `comment` action to display comments and instruction notes in the Actions panel.

You have now completed your Accommodations page and have learned some new ActionScript commands. Save your Web site movie to save all the changes you have made. You will find an example of the Web site up to this point on the CD-ROM that accompanies this book. Open the `Chapter 16` folder and locate the file `whirlwind16.fla` if you need to see an example of the project Web site.

Where You've Been!

This chapter introduced you to smart clips and how to use them in your movie. You created radio boxes and a pull-down menu. You also used the drag-and-drop functionality to create the criteria for narrowing down the location for accommodations. Just as in Chapter 15, this chapter focused on the front-end of a form, instructing you on the form setup for transferring data to the Web server. You also learned some new troubleshooting features and techniques for future development of Flash movies.

What's Next?

The next chapter is the final chapter of this book. You will learn some additional Flash development techniques that can be applied to your work. You will learn how to create a panoramic 360° movie so that the end-user can scroll through the image. And you will learn how to create a screen saver from a Flash movie.

Next Steps with Flash

The preceding chapters covered many of the fundamental skills required for using Flash. You have learned how to create, import, and optimize images, as well as create buttons and symbols. You've also learned about animation techniques and scripting. You've created a gate page, as well as used a mask in your animation. You have come a long way in your Flash skills and you now have the basics to begin to design in Flash. So, what's next? Flash is versatile and can be used to communicate many ideas and concepts for all your designing needs. You are truly limited only by your imagination for what you can create in Flash. This chapter shows a creative use of Flash to build a panoramic 360° movie that allows the end-user to interact with it. You'll also learn how to create a screen saver from a Flash file.

Creating a 360° Movie

You have probably seen a 360° movie on a Web site in the form of a "virtual tour" on a real estate or similar type of site. You can create such a movie in Flash that allows the end-user to explore whatever you choose for your content. For learning purposes in this book, you will create a 360° movie of a mountain scene for the Tours/Groups page of the Whirlwind Adventure Travel Web site.

Creating and Positioning the Images

You can use a few different techniques to create a panoramic 360° movie. This chapter presents a simplified technique that makes use of buttons for scrolling through a 360° view. As you progress in your ActionScripting ability, you might want to add additional code to this technique to refine it. To create your panoramic 360° movie, follow these steps:

1. On the Tours/Groups page, click the Background layer to make it active.

2. Open the Character panel by clicking the Show Character button on the Launcher bar and create a static text box with the following options: **Comic Sans MS** font, 12 point font size, black color, 5px indentation, and **Static Text** for the Text Type. Type the following text: Tour the Swiss Alps on your next vacation. We offer an excellent package including accommodations, five days skiing, visit the house used in the Sound of Music, and shopping! You'll be exercised, wined and dined, as well as entertained.

   Click the buttons below to explore the panoramic view you will have from your master bedroom of your accommodations!

3. Position the text block below the title Listing of Advertised Tours in the white rectangular area. Close the Character panel.

4. Using the Align panel, horizontally center the text block within the white rectangular area. You have just created the introduction to your panoramic 360° movie.

With your text block created, you can begin to develop the panoramic movie. For the project in this book a panoramic image has been supplied. If you use this process for one of your own projects, you will need to create your own panoramic image. You can do this many ways; one way is to use a camera and take a photo of an area every 15° until you have completed a circle. Then, by using a photo imaging program, you can piece all the 15° images together to create one picture that shows the view of the area in a full 360° view. The following steps guide you through the process of creating the movie clip symbols required to begin the creation of the interactive panoramic 360° movie.

1. To begin creating the panoramic movie, you first need to create a movie clip. To do so, choose **Insert, New Symbol**. In the New Symbol dialog box, name the movie clip MC_Mountains and set its Behavior to Movie Clip. By doing so, you launch the symbol-editing mode.

2. Import the JPEG image mountains.jpg from the Chapter 17 folder included on the CD-ROM that accompanies this book (see Figure 17.1).

3. Open the Info panel by choosing **Window, Panels, Info**. Select the imported JPEG file and set the x coordinate to 0 and the y coordinate to 280. Then set the positioning from the upper-left corner (see Figure 17.2). Click anywhere on the Stage to set your coordinates for the mountain picture. Close the Info panel.

Figure 17.1

Because this is a panoramic view picture, it is very wide, and the left and right ends of the picture, when joined seamlessly, advance from the end to the beginning of the 360° view.

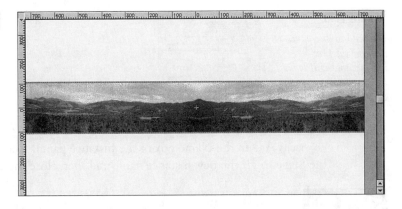

Upper-left corner   x and y coordinates   Center point of movie position

Figure 17.2

By setting the y coordinate to 280, you are setting the location of the panoramic movie to appear in the lower portion of the white rectangular area.

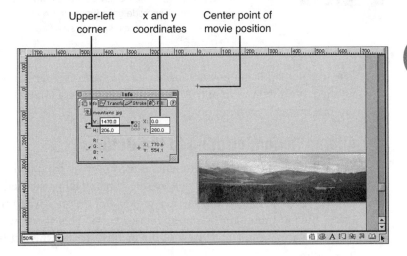

4. Return to your movie by clicking the Tours/Groups tab in the upper-left corner of your symbol-editing mode window. Create a new layer above the Buttons layer and name it `Movie`.

5. Open your Library if it is not already open and drag two instances of the MC_Mountains movie clip symbol onto your Stage for the Movie layer. Do not worry about where you position them on the Stage.

6. Open the Instance panel by choosing **Window, Panels, Instance**. Click one of the MC_Mountains movie clips instances on the Stage to make it active. Type `mc_mountain1` in the Name box of the Instance panel (see Figure 17.3). Name the instance as indicated in the Figure 17.3 using the exact case for all letters as shown. This will enable the following code to call these instances.

Figure 17.3

Use the Instance panel to name the first instance that will make up the panoramic 360° view.

7. Click the other MC_Mountains movie clip to make it active and type mc_mountain2 in the Name box of the Instance panel. Click anywhere on the Stage to set the new instance name and then close the Instance panel.

 Tip   Be sure to name the instances exactly as steps 6 and 7 indicate. Do not capitalize the instance name. The code called for in the rest of the chapter requires that the exact names be used for these instances.

The initial images and positioning set up for creating your panoramic 360° view are finished. Next, you will apply ActionScripting to the Timeline and buttons to make this panoramic view function.

Adding ActionScripting to the Buttons

You will make the panoramic mountain picture work by applying ActionScripting that positions the two figures side by side. Then, taking the ActionScripting one step further, you will make it call the mc_mountain2 instance when the viewer reaches the end of the mc_mountain1 instance, or vice versa. This action will create the illusion of moving around in a 360° view of the picture. To add the ActionScript, follow these steps:

1. In your new Movie, create a new layer above the Movie layer and name it Navigation.

2. Open the Buttons Library by choosing **Window**, **Common Libraries**, **Buttons**. From the Buttons Library, open the Arrow Buttons folder and drag an instance of the 1 Left Arrow symbol onto your Stage (see Figure 17.4).

Figure 17.4

You can use any of the buttons in the Buttons Library.

3. Drag an instance of the 1 Right Arrow symbol onto the Stage. Position both buttons using the Arrow tool so that they are horizontally centered on the Stage. Position both buttons at the bottom of the white rectangular area (see Figure 17.5).

Figure 17.5

Just eyeball to center the two arrow buttons horizontally in the white rectangular area.

4. Using the Scale option of the Arrow tool, resize the buttons so that they are not so large. Re-center them if necessary.

5. Click the left button to make it active and open the Object Actions panel by choosing **Window, Actions**.

6. In the Object Actions panel, click the Add button (+) and select the **Basic Actions, OnMouse Event** ActionScript command. The code for this command then appears in the Actions list (see Figure 17.6). Leave the parameters set to a release event.

Figure 17.6

*The parameters for the **OnMouse Event** command appear in the Parameters pane of the Actions panel.*

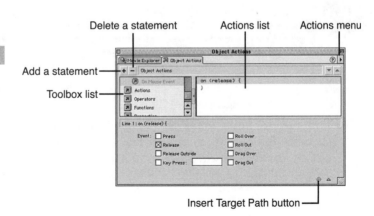

7. With the on (release){ ActionScripting line highlighted, click the Add button (+) again and select the **Actions, set variable** ActionScript command. The set variable ActionScripting appears in the Actions list and the Parameter settings appear in the Parameters pane.

Tip

Flash always adds additional code below the highlighted line of code.

8. In the Parameters pane of the Object Actions panel, click the Variable box and type x. Click the Value box and type x-20. Click the Expression option next to the Value box (see Figure 17.7).

Figure 17.7

You are setting the button to move the movie 20 pixels to the left by setting Value to x-20.

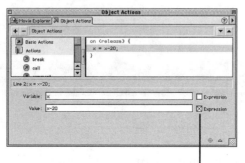

Set the Value to an Expression

9. Next, you will call a function that doesn't exist yet, but you will create it shortly. To do so, you need to switch to the Expert Mode in the Object Actions dialog box. Click the **Actions** menu in the upper-right corner of the Object Actions dialog box and select **Expert Mode** from the list. Your Toolbox list changes, showing a full screen for the Actions list.

 Tip

You can change your preference for having either the Expert Mode or the Normal Mode displayed as a default setting in the Object/Frame Actions panel by choosing **Edit**, **Preferences**. Click the General tab and change the mode in the Actions Panel section of this dialog box.

10. Position your cursor in the code of the Actions list after x=x-20 and press (Return) [Enter] to create a blank line under the x=x-20 line. Press the Tab key to align your cursor with the x=x-20 line of code and then type setPosition (x); (see Figure 17.8).

Figure 17.8

You can type any code directly into the Actions list of the Object Actions panel when you switch to the Expert Mode.

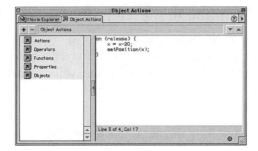

11. Highlight all ActionScript commands in the Actions list and copy them using the keyboard shortcut (Cmd-C) [Ctrl+C].

12. Click the right arrow button to make it active. In the Actions panel, you will see a blank Actions list. Click to set your cursor in this list and paste the copied script using the (Cmd-P) [Ctrl+P] keyboard shortcut. Notice that the right arrow button is set to the Normal Mode in the Object Actions panel.

 Note

When you are in the Object/Frame Actions panel and change to Expert Mode, you change mode only for that particular object or frame. If you access another object or frame, Flash remembers what mode was set for it, not the one you're switching from.

13. Click the second line of code in the Actions list, x=x-20, to access the Parameters for this code. Under the Parameters pane of the dialog box, change the minus sign to a plus sign in the Value box so that your code reads x=x+20 (see Figure 17.9).

Figure 17.9

If you click the Actions menu, you will see that you are in the Normal Mode for the right arrow button.

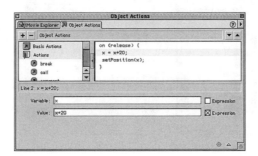

This code moves the picture 20 pixels to the right each time the button is clicked. Now you can save your movie.

Adding ActionScripting to the Timeline

Now you need to create the nonexistent function you referred to in the left and right arrow button ActionScripting that you created. You will create this function as ActionScript code for the Timeline. This function will designate where to position the two movie clip instances of the mountain picture on the Stage. To add this function, follow these steps:

1. Click on the Movie layer, Frame 1. Open your Frame Actions panel if it is not already open.

2. Switch to Expert Mode by clicking the **Actions** menu in the upper-right corner of the Frame Actions dialog box and selecting **Expert Mode** from the list.

3. Click to set your cursor in the Actions list of the Actions panel. Then type in the following code for the function:

```
function setPosition (x) {
    x = x%mc_mountain1._width;
    mc_mountain1._x = x;
    if(x>0){
    mc_mountain2._x = x-mc_mountain1._width;
    } else {
    mc_mountain2._x = x + mc_mountain1._width;
    }
    mc_mountain1._y = 0;
    mc_mountain2._y = 0;
}

setPosition(0);
```

4. Your Actions list should exactly match Figure 17.10. Make sure you typed the code in exactly as listed.

Figure 17.10

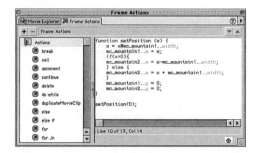

Because you switched to the Expert Mode for this frame's actions, Flash will remember that you are in this mode the next time you access the Actions for this frame.

5. Save your movie and then test it by choosing **Control**, **Test Scene**. You should see the mountain picture positioned below the static text paragraphs and the navigation buttons below. When you click the buttons, you scroll 20 pixels in the direction that the button indicates.

EXCURSION

Understanding the Panoramic Function Code

To understand the Panoramic function code, let's look at specific parts of the code. The first line of code declares that it is a function and sets the function name. All the commands embedded in the {} are statements that are executed any time the function is called. Remember, your left and right arrow buttons call this function, so any time someone clicks a button, this function is executed.

The second line of code, `x = x%mc_mountain1._width`, looks confusing but the `%` symbol is a *modulus operator*. A modulus operator can be equated to the mathematical symbols `*` (multiplication), `/` (division), `+` (addition), and `-` (subtraction). To understand a modulus, let's compare it to regular division. If you take 10/3, you get the result 3 because 3 goes into 10 three times. The remainder or modulus of 10/3 is 1 because 3*3=9 and 10-9=1. Therefore, 10%3=1. This description might be confusing at first, but whenever you use a%b, you always know that the result is between 0 and b. In the case of the panoramic view, this operation works great. The code causes you to get a new x coordinate that you know is going to be between 0 and the width of your new image movie clip.

These lines of code

```
x = x%mc_mountain1._width
mc_mountain1._x = x;
    if(x>0){
    mc_mountain2._x = x-mc_mountain1._width;
    } else {
    mc_mountain2._x = x + mc_mountain1._width;
```

use logic of the IF/ELSE statement to set the x coordinate of the mc_mountains1 or mc_mountains2 movie clips to a new x coordinate as set by the modulus line of code and cause the movies to be butted up against each other—hence, the effect of a panoramic view.

If your buttons are too low in the Flash Player window when you test your movie, you might want to go back to Flash development mode and move them up. Return to the movie and reposition your buttons. Then test your movie again to see the changes.

If your MC_Mountains movie clip is not positioned correctly below your static text blocks when you test your movie, you need to adjust the y coordinate of the MC_Mountain movie clip in symbol-editing mode. Return to the movie and open the MC_Mountains movie clip in symbol-editing mode. Using the Info panel, adjust the y coordinate. Then test your movie again to see the changes.

Applying a Mask

Your panoramic 360° view is working, but it appears across the entire movie. You want to have it appear only in the white rectangular area. You can apply a mask to the Movie layer to limit the amount of area that the MC_Mountains movie clip displays at one time. To do so, follow these steps:

1. Click the Movie layer to make it active and then create a new layer named Mask.

2. (Control-click) [Right-click] the Mask layer and select **Mask** from the shortcut menu.

3. Unlock the Mask layer so that you can edit it. Then click the Rectangle tool from the toolbox. Click the Stroke Color option and choose the No Fill color chip. Select any color for the Fill Color option.

→ For a more detailed description of creating and using masks, **see** Chapter 14, "Advanced Animation Techniques," **p. 305**.

4. Move your mouse cursor onto the Stage and create a rectangle. Select the rectangle with the Arrow tool to make it active and then open your Info panel by choosing **Window, Panels, Info**. Set the rectangle size to 400px width and 200px height. Set the y coordinate to 280 (see Figure 17.11).

Mask layer

Figure 17.11

Don't worry about setting the x coordinate in the Info panel; you'll use the Align panel next to exactly center the rectangle horizontally in the white rectangle area.

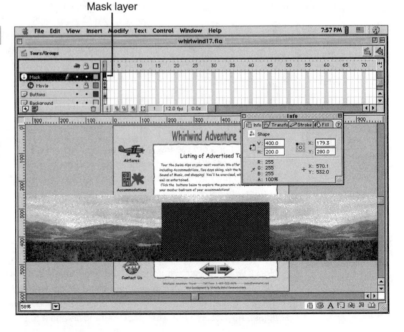

5. Select both the white rectangular area and the mask rectangle. Open the Align panel by choosing **Window, Panels, Align** and horizontally center the two objects.

6. Test your scene by choosing **Control, Test Scene** (see Figure 17.12).

Figure 17.12

Click the buttons to scroll through your panoramic movie.

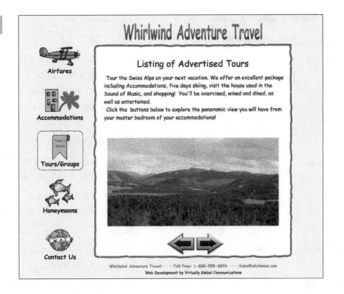

Creating a Flashed Screen Saver

After you create a Flash movie, you have another option to take the movie one step further: You can create a screen saver from it. This screen saver can have all the functionality of other screen savers; you can password-protect entry into your system through it or cause it to activate or not activate based on the location of the mouse cursor on the screen. Many screen saver conversion software packages are available on the market today.

 Note   Macromedia recommends a few screen saver conversion software packages on its site at www.macromedia.com. Type Screen Saver in the Search feature on the Macromedia site to access the current list.

Preparing a Flash File for Conversion to a Screen Saver

Different Flash file formats can be converted into screen savers by the third-party screen saver software packages. Most of these software packages require that you export or publish your Flash movie to a Projector file for either Macintosh or

Windows. But some work with .FLA files directly or with .SWF files. Table 17.1 lists these screen saver software programs and compares their various features.

→ For a more detailed description of exporting or publishing a Flash movie, **see** Chapter 13, "Publishing the Movie for the Travel Company Web Site," **p. 287**.

Table 17.1   Screen Saver Conversion Software Applications

Program	Platform	Features
Screentime	Macintosh/Windows	Creates screen savers from projector Flash files. Screen savers can be interactive. You can quit or shut down your screen saver with a keystroke or a mouse action. Screen savers also can be set to time out. Flash drag-and-drop functionality is supported in the screen saver.
		Supports Flash 4 and earlier files and features.
FlashJester's Creator	Windows	Creates screen savers from Windows projector files. Screen savers can be interactive; end-users can type text into the screen savers.
		Supports Flash 5 and earlier files and features.
The Living Screen's Screensavertool	Macintosh/Windows	Creates screen savers from Projector files. Supports Flash layer technology. No unauthorized access to the end-user's machine. Software has a direct integration of the Load Movie function of Flash.
		Supports Flash 4 and earlier files and features.
YAFS	Windows	Creates a screen saver from Flash .SWF files. You do not need to include the FS (Full Screen) commands in the Flash .FLA files.
		Supports Flash 4 and earlier files and features.
FlashForge	Windows	Creates a screen saver from a Flash file or from a Flash Projector file. You can also automatically include the screen saver installer as part of the screen saver download. Creates interactive screen savers. The screen saver works independently of any other browser plug-ins or explorers.
		Supports Flash 4 and earlier files and features.

All the screen saver software programs in Table 17.1 allow you to download a demo version from their Internet sites. The CD-ROM that accompanies this book provides a demo version of The Living Screen's Screensavertool.

To convert a Flash movie to a screen saver, follow these steps:

1. Download the screen saver software you want to use.

2. Convert your Flash movie into the Flash version supported by the screen saver software application through the Publish Settings dialog box.

3. Set the publish settings for the file format. Export or publish the movie.

4. Open the Flash file in the screen saver application and follow the instructions for creating the screen saver provided by the screen saver's vendor.

Publishing Your Completed Web Site

Your site is complete! Now you can publish your site and check its functionality in a browser. To do so, just follow these steps:

1. Choose **File**, **Publish Settings** to open the Publish Settings dialog box. Change any of the settings that you set in Chapter 13, "Publishing the Movie for the Travel Company Web Site," to include the features and functionality that you now want. Publish your movie by clicking the Publish button.

2. Open a browser and load the HTML file that you created when you published into the browser.

3. Test your Web site thoroughly. You should find that it functions the same as it did in the Flash Player mode. It might appear different in the browser based on the HMTL settings you set in your Publish Settings dialog box. If you do not like the appearance, reset your Publish Settings and publish it again. Test the movie again in the browser.

Congratulations!

You have completed an entire interactive Web site! Good job! Save your Flash movie to save the changes you have made. You will find an example of the completed Web site on the CD-ROM that accompanies this book. Open the `Chapter 17` folder and locate the file `whirlwind17.fla` if you want to see an example of the completed project Web site.

Where You've Been!

This chapter covered how to create a panoramic 360° movie in your Web site. You learned how to add interactive buttons so that the end-user could navigate around the 360° view. You also learned about taking your Flash movies one step further and converting them into screen savers. You can use the screen saver on your own machine or distribute it throughout your company or to others. Be aware that copyright laws apply to distribution of your screen saver to others for profit. This means any graphics, sounds, or content need to be original if you are distributing your movie for profit.

Throughout this book, you have learned many new skills, techniques, and features of Flash. The following list summarizes the various areas of Flash that you have covered:

- You started from scratch with planning your site and then began to learn the skills required to create and import artwork into your movie.
- You learned how to use all the Flash tools on the toolbox as well as many of the options associated with the tools.
- You created symbols and used instances of the symbols on your Stage.
- You learned how to customize your instances so that they were slightly different than from the original symbol.
- You created layers and animation from your artwork and instances on your Stage.
- You learned how to use your Timeline, create keyframes, create regular frames, and delete frames.
- You created both motion and shape tweening animation.
- You created a guide and mask layer for your animations.
- You created a gate page that does not allow the end-user to access your site's contents until the entire site has streamed down.
- You learned how to publish your movie in many different formats.
- You created movie clips and then used them in your movie.
- You created scenes and then created transitions between them.
- You created a couple of forms, one for collecting data and another with more advanced end-user interactivity built in.
- You learned about smart clips and integrated existing smart clips into your movie.
- You learned how to add ActionScripting commands to buttons and frames.
- You created drag-and-drop functionality on one of your form pages.
- You created a panoramic 360° movie within your Web site and added button functionality for navigating around the movie.
- You learned how to convert your Flash movie into a screen saver.

What's Next?

You are now ready to begin your own development of Flash movies and Web sites. You have many of the skills needed to begin working in this area. I hope you have enjoyed the book and found it beneficial. I wish you well in your Flash development endeavors. Keep in mind that you are limited only by your own creativity as to what you can accomplish in Flash. So, keep on Flashing!

17

Index